Jewish Religious Law

Progressive Judaism Today
General Editor: David J. Goldberg, Rabbi of the Liberal Jewish
Synagogue, St John's Wood, London

JEWISH RELIGIOUS LAW

A Progressive Perspective

❖ ❖ ❖

John D. Rayner

Berghahn Books
NEW YORK · OXFORD

Published in 1998 by

Berghahn Books

© 1998 John D. Rayner
All rights reserved.
No part of this publication may be reproduced
in any form or by any means without the
written permission of Berghahn Books.

Library of Congress Cataloging-in-Publication Data

Rayner, John D.
    Jewish religious law : a progressive perspective / John D. Rayner.
        p.   cm. -- (Progressive Judaism today)
    Includes bibliographical references.
    ISBN 1-57181-975-4 (hb. : alk. paper). -- ISBN 1-57181-976-2 (pbk. :
    alk. paper)
    1. Jewish law--Reform Judaism.   I. Title.   II. Series.
BM197.R339   1998
296.1'8--dc21   98-10685
                                                                    CIP

British Library Cataloguing in Publication Data

A catalogue record for this book is available from
the British Library.

Printed in the United States on acid-free paper.

To Ben, with all my love

❖   ❖   ❖

CONTENTS

❖   ❖   ❖

PREFACE

❖   ❖   ❖

'And now, Israel, what does the Eternal One your God require of you?'
(Deut. 10:12). From a Jewish religious point of view that is the most important of all questions. For how, from such a point of view, can there be anything more desirable than to know how God wishes us to live, and therefore
how to make the best possible use of our abilities and opportunities?

The great achievement of the Pharisees and their successors, the Rabbis,
was that they addressed themselves to that question with unremitting dedication, generation after generation, and so produced a prescription for Jewish living of the most amazing comprehensiveness and detailedness.

However, they did so on the basis of assumptions, such as the inerrancy
of Scripture, which, for those who accept modern liberal values, have lost
their credibility and which, in any case, made it inevitable that the system
would become increasingly rigid in the course of the centuries, so that today
it is in many ways antiquated.

To this system, called Halachah, there have been among Progressive Jews
two opposite attitudes. Some, without questioning the system, have simply
gone along with it when it suited them and ignored it when it did not. Others have explicitly or implicitly rejected it as something that belongs to
Orthodoxy but has no place in Progressive Judaism.

When I became active in Britain's Liberal Jewish movement, it was predominantly rejectionist. Words like Halachah and Mitzvah were rarely
heard; all talk was about 'beliefs' and 'observances', with much emphasis on
the former and little on the latter. To redress the imbalance, I wrote a little
book, *The Practices of Liberal Judaism*, which was first published in 1958.

Then, in the 1960s, I spent two years as a Graduate Fellow at the Hebrew Union College, Jewish Institute of Religion in Cincinnati, where I
steeped myself in Rabbinic literature and began to understand the great
merits – but also the serious defects – of the Halachah; and when I returned
to Britain I found myself teaching the subject at Leo Baeck College for the
next thirty years.

Gradually it became clear to me that what Progressive Judaism needs to
do is neither to accept nor to reject the Rabbinic Halachah but to recon-
struct it consistently with its own principles. That conviction became a

recurring theme in my speaking and writing, and this volume is a collection of what I hope have been my more successful attempts to articulate it both in general terms and in its application to particular topics which I have had occasion to deal with.

Needless to say, the particular topics are no more than a small miscellany (sequentially arranged according to the four parts of the Shulchan Aruch) intended to illustrate some of the practical implications of the theory expounded in the earlier chapters.

In both respects – theory and illustrations – I hope that this book may serve as a contribution to the formulation of an unequivocally liberal Halachah, and stimulate others to carry on the task.

For its shortcomings I have to accept responsibility; for any merits it may have I am indebted, among many others, to the late Professor Alexander Guttmann, who taught me how to read the relevant literature, and the late Rabbi Dr Solomon B. Freehof, whom I was also privileged to know and whose writings have opened up many of its highways and byways for me; זכרונם לבדכה, may both, through their abiding influence, continue to be a source of blessing.

John D. Rayner
London, 1998

List of Abbreviations

❖   ❖   ❖

AZ	Avodah Zarah ('Idolatry', Mishnah/Talmud Tractate)
BB	Bava Batra ('Last Gate' , Mishnah/Talmud Tractate)
Ber.	Berachot ('Benedictions', Mishnah/Talmud Tractate)
BK	Bava Kamma ('First Gate', Mishnah/Talmud Tractate)
BM	Bava Metzi'a ('Middle Gate', Mishnah/Talmud Tractate)
Cant.R.	Canticles Rabbah ('Great' Midrash on the Song of Songs)
CCAR	Central Conference of American Rabbis
Chag.	Chagigah ('Festival Offering', Mishnah/Talmud Tractate)
Ch.M.	Choshen Mishpat ('Breastplate of Judgement', Part 4 of Tur/Shulchan Aruch)
Chron.	Chronicles
Chul.	Chullin ('Profane Things', Mishnah/Talmud Tractate)
Deut.	Deuteronomy
Eccles.	Ecclesiastes
EH	Even ha-Ezer ('Stone of Help', Part 3 of Tur/Shulchan Aruch)
Exod.	Exodus
Ezek.	Ezekiel
Gen.	Genesis
Git.	Gittin ('Divorce Bills', Mishnah/Talmud Tractate)
Hor.	Horayot ('Decisions', Mishnah/Talmud Tractate)
Hos.	Hosea
Isa.	Isaiah
Jer.	Jeremiah
Jud.	Judges
Ket.	Ketubbot ('Marriage Contracts', Mishnah/Talmud Tractate)
Kid.	Kiddushin ('Betrothals', Mishnah/Talmud Tractate)
Lev.	Leviticus
Mak.	Makkot ('Stripes', Mishnah/Talmud Tractate)
Mal.	Malachi
Matt.	Matthew
Meg.	Megillah ('Scroll', Mishnah/Talmud Tractate)
Men.	Menachot ('Meal-Offerings', Mishnah/Talmud Tractate)

Ned.	Nedarim ('Vows', Mishnah/Talmud Tractate)
Neh.	Nehemiah
Nid.	Niddah ('Menstruation', Mishnah/Talmud Tractate)
Num.	Numbers
Num.R.	Numbers Rabbah ('Great' Midrash on Numbers)
O.Ch.	Orach Chayyim ('Path of Life', Part 1 of Tur/Shulchan Aruch)
Pes.	Pesachim ('Passovers', Mishnah/Talmud Tractate)
Ps.	Psalm or Psalms
Rambam	Rabbi Moses ben Maimon (Maimonides)
Ramban	Rabbi Moses ben Nachman (Nachmanides)
RH	Rosh Hashanah ('New Year', Mishnah/Talmud Tractate)
RSGB	Reform Synagogues of Great Britain
Sam.	Samuel
San.	Sanhedrin ('High Court', Mishnah/Talmud Tractate)
Shab.	Shabbat ('Sabbath', Mishnah/Talmud Tractate)
Sh.Ar.	Shulchan Aruch ('Prepared Table', Code by Joseph Caro)
Shek.	Shekalim ('Shekels', Mishnah/Talmud Tractate)
Sot.	Sotah ('Suspected Adulteress', Mishnah/Talmud Tractate)
Suk.	Sukkah ('Booth', Mishnah/Talmud Tractate)
Ta'an.	Ta'anit ('Fast', Mishnah/Talmud Tractate)
Tanch.	Tanchuma (Midrash, named after a Palestinian Amora)
Tos.	Tosefta ('Addition', compendium of laws similar to Mishnah); also Tosafot ('Additions', supercommentaries on Rashi's commentary on the Talmud)
UAHC	Union of American Hebrew Congregations
ULPS	Union of Liberal and Progressive Synagogues
Yad.	Yadayim ('Hands', Mishnah/Talmud Tractate)
YD	Yoreh De'ah ('Teacher of Knowledge', Part 2 of the Tur/Shulchan Aruch)
Yev.	Yevamot ('Sisters-in-law', Mishnah/Talmud Tractate)
Zech.	Zechariah

GLOSSARY

❖   ❖   ❖

Acharonim	Later halachic authorities (sixteenth century onwards)
Aggadah	'Narrative' (non-legal rabbinic literature)
Agunah	'Tied woman' (unable to remarry because not divorced or because her husband is not known to be dead)
Aleinu	'It is our duty' (concluding prayer)
Aliyah	'Going up' (to the Bimah, or to Eretz Yisrael)
Amidah	'Standing' (daily prayer = Shemoneh Esreh)
Amora, pl. Amora'im	'Speakers' (Palestinian and Babylonian Rabbis 200–500 CE)
Aruch ha-Schulchan	'Prepared is the Table' (law-code by Yechiel Michael Epstein, Russia, 1829–1908)
Avinu Malkenu	'Our Father, our King' (penitential prayer)
Avot	'Fathers' (Mishnah Tractate)
Baraita	'External' (Tannaitic teaching not in Mishnah)
Beit Din (pl. Batei Din)	(also Beth Din) 'Law court'
Bimah	Platform (in synagogue)
Birkat ha-Mazon	'Blessing for Food' (grace after meals)
Chacham, Chachamim	'Sages' (lay scholars, Pharisees)
Chalitzah	'Taking off the shoe' (ritual of release from levirate marriage)
Chanukkah	'Dedication' (festival commemorating rededication of Temple)
Chasid, Chasidim	'Pious Ones' (members of pietistic movement founded by Israel Ba'al Shem Tov in the eighteenth century)
Consistoire	United Jewish community in France, etc.
Einheitsgemeinde	United Jewish community in Germany, etc.

Eretz Yisrael	Land of Israel
Eruvin	'Combinations' (Mishnah/Talmud Tractate)
Gaon, Geonim	'Excellency' (heads of Babylonian rabbinic academies in the post-Talmudic period)
Gemara	'Teaching' (Aramaic) or 'Completion' (Hebrew), elaboration of Mishnah = Talmud
Get	'Bill' (of divorce)
Haftarah	'Dismissal' (public reading from the Prophets)
Haggadah	'Narration' (a) = Aggadah; (b) Passover Eve liturgy
Hak-hel	'Assemble' (public reading of Torah as ordained in Deut. 31:10–13)
Halachah	'Law' (Rabbinic Law; legal content of Rabbinic literature)
Ha Lachma Anya	'This is the bread of affliction' (passage of Passover Haggadah)
Hasmoneans	Maccabeans (dynasty descended from Mattathias)
Havdalah	'Separation' (ceremony at conclusion of Sabbath)
Hiph'il	Causative conjugation of Hebrew verbs
Iggun	The condition of being an Agunah
Kaddish	'Holy' (Aramaic concluding and mourner's prayer)
Karaites, Karaism	'Scripturalists' (anti-Rabbinic sect founded by Anan ben David in Babylonia, eighth century)
Kasher (kosher)	'Fit' (especially fit to be eaten)
Kavvanah	Intention, attention, fervour
Kedushah	'Holiness' (also a doxology so called)
Kiddush	'Sanctification' (ceremony inaugurating Sabbath or Festival)
Kohen, Kohanim	Priests or putative descendants of the ancient priests
Kol Nidre	'All the vows' (Aramaic annulment of unfulfillable vows)
Lashon ha-ra	'Evil tongue' (malicious speech, slander, gossip)
Lulav	Palm branch (ceremonially used during Sukkot)
Mamzer	'Bastard' (offspring of incestuous or adulterous union)
Mechilta	'Measures', 'hermeneutic rules' (Tannaitic Midrash on Exodus)

Mezuzah	'Doorpost' (cylinder containing miniature scroll inscribed with Scripture passages, fastened to doorpost)
Midrash	'Exposition' (Rabbinic Bible interpretation)
Milchemet Mitzvah	'Obligatory war'
Minhag	'Custom'
Minyan	'Number' (quorum)
Mishnah	'Teaching' (compendium of Oral Torah, c. 200 CE)
Mishneh Torah	'Recapitulation of the Torah' (comprehensive codification of Jewish law by Moses Maimonides, 1177, Egypt)
Mitzvah, Mitzvot	'Commandment'; sometimes 'praiseworthy action' (law, religious observance, good deed)
Niph'al	Passive conjugation of Hebrew verbs
Pe'ah	'Corner' (Mishnah/Yerushalmi Tractate)
Pesach	Passover
Pharisees	Democratising Jewish sect (second century BCE – first century CE)
Pi'el	'Intensive' conjugation of Hebrew verbs
Rabbi	'My master' (accredited exponent of Torah)
Reconstructionism	Naturalistic religious movement founded by Mordecai Kaplan (1881–1983) in the United States
Rishonim	'Earlier' halachic authorities, c. 1000–1500 CE
Rosh Hashanah	New Year
Sadducees	Aristocratic and priestly sect, opponents of the Pharisees (second century BCE – first century CE)
Seder	'Order' (division of the Mishnah; domestic celebration of Passover Eve)
Sefer Torah, Sifrei Torah	Scrolls of the Law (containing handwritten text of Pentateuch)
Semachot	pl. of Simchah, 'joy', used euphemistically for 'sad occasions' ('Minor Tractate' about rules of mourning)
Shavuot	'(Seven) Weeks' (Pentecost)
Sheliach Tzibbur	'Messenger of the Congregation' (precentor)
Shema	'Hear' (Deut. 6:4–9, 11:13–21, Num. 15:37–41, liturgically recited)
Shemoneh Esreh	'Eighteen (Benedictions)' (daily prayer = Amidah)
Shevuot	'Oaths' (Mishnah/Talmud Tractate)

Shofar	'Ram's horn' (ceremonially blown on Rosh Hashanah)
Shulchan Aruch	'Prepared Table' (law-code in four parts by Joseph Caro, Palestine, 1565, modelled on the Arba'ah Turim)
Shulchan Aruch ha-Rav	'Prepared Table of the Master' (law-code by Shneur Zalman of Lyady, founder of Lubavitcher movement, Eastern Europe, 1747–1813)
Sifra	'Book' (Tannaitic Midrash on Leviticus)
Sifrei	'Books' (Tannaitic Midrashim on Numbers and Deuteronomy)
Sukkah	'Booth' (as used on Sukkot)
Sukkot	Festival of Booths or Tabernacles (harvest festival)
Tachanun	'Supplication' (penitential prayers)
Talmud	'Teaching' (huge elaboration of Mishnah, unless otherwise stated, the Babylonian one, c. 500 CE)
Tanna, Tanna'im	'Teacher' (Palestinian Rabbis 70–200 CE)
Targum	'Translation' (especially Aramaic one of the Bible)
Techinnot	'Supplications' (private prayers, especially in Yiddish)
Tefillah	'Prayer' (especially the principal daily prayer = Amidah = Shemoneh Esreh)
Torah	'Teaching' (especially Pentateuch)
Torah min ha-Shamayim	'Torah from Heaven' (affirmation of divine authority of Pentateuch)
Tosefta	'Supplement' (Collection of Baraitot arranged as Mishnah)
Treif	Yiddish from Hebrew Taref ('torn') (non-kosher)
Tur	Short for Arba'ah Turim, 'Four Rows' (law-code in four parts by Jacob ben Asher, Germany and Spain, c. 1270–1340)
Yad	Short for Yad Chazakah, 'Mighty Hand' (popular name of Maimonides' fourteen-part Mishneh Torah, the numerical value of Yad being fourteen)
Yerushalmi	'Jerusalemite' (Palestinian Talmud, early fifth century)
Yibbum	Levirate marriage
Yoma	'The Day (of Atonement)' (Mishnah/Talmud Tractate)
Yom Kippur	Day of Atonement

Chapter 1

❖   ❖   ❖

PROGRESSIVE JUDAISM

When the World Union for Progressive Judaism was founded at an international conference in London in 1926, the adjective 'Progressive' was chosen, after much debate, as the one most likely to prove acceptable to most delegates, coming as they did from broadly like-minded synagogal groupings in the represented countries, some of which used other designations, such as 'Liberal' and 'Reform', to describe themselves.

Since then 'Progressive' has become a generally accepted umbrella term to designate those religious movements in recent Jewish history which have taken the view that the modern world requires a more or less thoroughgoing revision or reconstruction of pre-modern Judaism.

It is in that broad sense that the term 'Progressive Judaism' is used in this volume, yet also with a certain bias which needs to be acknowledged at the outset: namely that the true significance of Progressive Judaism is best understood from the vantage-point of the more radical tendency within it, as exemplified in its past history by men such as Abraham Geiger and Samuel Holdheim in Germany, David Einhorn and Kaufmann Kohler in the United States, and Claude Montefiore and Israel Mattuck in Britain.

That tendency has sometimes gone to extremes which its contemporary heirs would disown, and has undergone much revision in the light of more recent developments in life and thought; but its exponents did bring to their task a refreshing honesty, unblinkered by mere traditionalism or populism, which is still needed to grasp what Progressive Judaism is essentially all about.

To anticipate the answer to that question which will be proposed in this introductory chapter and assumed in the rest of this volume: the key to a correct understanding of Progressive Judaism is to recognise that it is an attempt to evolve a post-Rabbinic Judaism. But to

make that statement fully meaningful we need to go back a long way
into the past.

Continuity and Change

Our starting point is the fact, obvious to any student of the history of
Judaism, that it exhibits both continuity and change. But while that
is true of every period, the pace of change has varied. Sometimes it
has been imperceptibly slow, sometimes more rapid. But in retrospect two episodes stand out as times of such major crisis that they
necessitated change on a massive scale. One of these reached its cli-
max with the destruction of the Temple in 70 CE; the other was the
Emancipation, epitomised by Napoleon's Sanhedrin of 1807.

Both of them shook Judaism to its foundations, but did not dis-
lodge the foundations themselves. Briefly summarised, these foundations, which may be regarded as the permanent elements and
abiding characteristics of Judaism, are as follows.

The universe is a single whole which owes its existence to a single
Creator who is, however, fundamentally different from the Creation
and therefore not to be identified with any constituent element of it:
mineral, vegetable, animal, or human. This transcendent God is nevertheless also immanent: concerned with, and active in, the universe,
and especially the history of the human species on earth. Here God's
moral attributes, of justice and compassion, come into play. Because
of them, it is God's wish that humanity shall establish a just and compassionate society, and to this end God has communicated a knowledge of the Divine Will to chosen individuals, such as the Patriarchs
and the Prophets, and collectively, through Moses, to the Israelites
assembled at Mount Sinai, so that they might serve as an advance
guard in the journey of humanity towards its divinely appointed goal.
In order to fulfil that role, they are to observe a discipline of worship
and observance, including a sacred calendar of sabbaths and festivals,
and transmit their tradition from generation to generation.

These are the fundamentals, and they remained just as valid after
70 CE as they had been before. The only serious challenge to them
came from Christianity, which, by deifying Jesus, diminished God's
transcendence; by teaching the Trinity, obscured God's unity; and
by speaking of a 'New Covenant', called into question the continuing mission of the Jewish people and the obligatory character of the
discipline that it entailed. By these deviations, Christianity, even
while retaining much of its Jewish roots, nevertheless placed itself
outside Judaism.

Biblical Judaism

During the Biblical period of its history, these primary elements of Judaism, which proved permanent, combined with secondary ones, which did not. Chief among these was the Temple, where the One God of the Jewish people and of humanity was worshipped twice daily, at dawn and dusk. This involved an elaborate sacrificial cult, and a hereditary class of priests who performed it. Another feature of Biblical Judaism was the geographical concentration of the people in one land on the eastern seaboard of the Mediterranean, and the sovereignty they exercised over it for several centuries.

Yet another was the monarchy. That is more surprising, for in the ancient world kings were commonly regarded as divine, and exercised absolute power, so that the very concept of monarchy signalled a potential challenge to monotheism. And indeed there is in the Bible a strongly anti-monarchic strand. When the crown is offered to Gideon he refuses, saying: 'I will not rule over you, neither shall my son rule over you; God shall rule over you' (Jud. 8:23). When Samuel is persuaded by popular pressure to anoint Saul, he does so reluctantly, and only after extracting from the people a confession that they have done a wicked thing in asking for a king (I Sam. 12:12, 19).

In the end, though, a compromise was reached. A monarchy was established, but on the clear understanding that it was to be vested exclusively in the Davidic dynasty, and that its incumbents were to reign only by divine consent and in God's name; if they failed to act accordingly, prophets would reprimand them, and if they still failed, dire consequences would follow for the entire nation.

Prophecy was indeed another secondary feature of Biblical Judaism which did not endure. For since, unlike priesthood and monarchy, it was not hereditary but depended entirely on charisma, it was essentially unpredictable. As a matter of historical fact, at least as perceived by subsequent Jewish tradition, it came to an end soon after the Babylonian Exile.

Thus all these secondary features of Biblical Judaism proved impermanent. The Jerusalem Temple was destroyed. The sacrificial cult ceased because ever since King Josiah it had been strictly forbidden anywhere else. The priesthood lost its principal role, since there were no sacrifices to offer. The monarchy was destroyed by a series of conquests, Assyrian, Babylonian, Persian, Greek and Roman. The people were dispersed from the Land. And the fountain of prophecy dried up. So the dependence of Biblical Judaism on these things – Temple, Sacrifice, Priesthood, Monarchy, Land and Prophecy – proved its undoing.

Pharisaic and Rabbinic Judaism

That Judaism survived such a series of body blows is due to two facts. First, that the foundations, which we have already identified, stood firm. Secondly, that by the year 70 a new kind of Judaism – independent of Temple, Sacrifice, Priesthood, Monarchy, Land and Prophecy – had already taken shape.

How long, can be debated. The Tradition greatly exaggerates its antiquity. It speaks of a twofold Torah, Written and Oral, going back all the way to Moses on Mount Sinai. It assigns a key role to Ezra the Scribe, and to an institution called כנסת הגדולה, the 'Great Assembly', composed of 120 men including the last of the Prophets.

There is no historically solid support for any of this. That there was a body of traditions of various kinds going back to remote antiquity, may indeed be assumed. But there is no evidence that the Written Torah, let alone the Oral Torah, in the later meaning of those terms, existed before the Babylonian Exile. When the pre-Exilic Prophets use the word Torah they refer to divine messages they have themselves received, never to the Pentateuch. Only the book of Deuteronomy is alluded to before – and that only shortly before – the Exile (II Kings 22:14–20). In other words, Biblical Judaism was not a book religion, or did not become one until after the Exile, for the simple reason that the book in question was still being written.

Similarly, the Talmudic descriptions of the 'Great Assembly' are chronologically impossible. Even the assertion, constantly repeated in the textbooks, that the Synagogue goes back to the Babylonian Exile, lacks any substantial foundation. If it were so, it would be very hard to explain why synagogues are nowhere mentioned in the Bible, even though much of it was written in the post-Exilic period, or even in books like Ben Sira, which gives a detailed description of Judean society as late as 200 BCE. If synagogues nevertheless did exist in Palestine during the intervening three-and-a-half centuries (as apparently they existed in Egypt in the reign of King Ptolemy III), one would have to say that they played no great role in Jewish life, presumably because they were suppressed by the High Priest, who, during just that period, exercised autocratic rule and would not have tolerated the emergence of a new institution, rivalling the Temple, with its own leadership, rivalling the priesthood.

The very word Synagogue suggests that it dates from the Greek, not the Persian period, and, more generally, all the evidence points to the second century BCE as the time in which the new kind of Judaism most probably emerged. Furthermore, it was from its inception closely associated with the *Pharisees*, and we are therefore on fairly safe ground if we regard them as its pioneers.

To the Pharisees, then, belongs the credit of having evolved a new kind of Judaism – independent of Temple, Sacrifice, Priesthood, Monarchy, Land or Prophecy – which enabled Judaism to survive when, just over two hundred years later, the last vestiges of these things were swept away.

How did they do it? Partly by perpetuating the permanent elements of Judaism, which remained valid; and partly by evolving a new set of secondary ones to replace those which had proved impermanent.

It should be said here that the Pharisees did not actually *repudiate* the secondary features of Biblical Judaism. True, the Temple was destroyed, but one day, they taught, it would be rebuilt. The sacrificial cult had ceased, but one day it would be reinstated, and meanwhile it was meritorious to study the rules and regulations that governed it. The priests had been made redundant, but one day they would resume their ancient office, and meanwhile they must preserve the purity of their pedigree. The people were dispersed, but one day they would return to their homeland, and meanwhile the festivals were to be celebrated according to the rhythm of its agricultural seasons. The monarchy had come to an end, but one day a descendant of the royal line, called משיח (Messiah, Anointed One), would again sit on David's throne.

So the memory of these institutions, and the hope for their eventual restoration, played a part in Pharisaic Judaism, but by way of nostalgia rather than everyday reality. Alongside the one-and-only Temple in Jerusalem, the Pharisees established synagogues wherever Jewish communities came to exist. Instead of the sacrificial cult, they created a revolutionary new form of worship, involving congregational study and prayer, with its own liturgy. Instead of priests or kings or prophets, they instituted a new form of leadership, requiring neither pedigree nor charisma, but only learning.

What kind of learning? Here we come to the main feature of Pharisaic Judaism. Unlike Biblical, or at least pre-Exilic, Judaism, it was *a book religion*. For the Pharisees canonised – or completed the canonisation of – Scripture. They decided which of the surviving books of ancient Hebrew literature were to be regarded as having been written under the guidance of רוח הקדש, the Holy Spirit, and therefore included in the Bible. Within the canon, they gave pre-eminence to the first five books comprising the Torah in the narrower sense of the word, which not only tells the early history of the Jewish people but contains practically all that has survived of ancient Hebrew law. For the Pharisees were essentially *lawyers*, and their chief concern, to which they devoted the greater part of their intellectual energy, was to construct a code of conduct governing every aspect of a Jew's life, which they called the *Halachah* (the Hebrew equivalent of an Aramaic word for 'law'). More precisely, the Pharisees evolved the concept of a twofold Torah: the Written Torah, which is the Pentateuch and especially its legislation, comprising 613 commandments, and the Oral Torah, by which they meant an ancient but still growing body of traditions interpreting, amplifying and supplementing the Written Torah. The Oral Torah was at first intended to remain oral, but was eventually committed to writing in the Mishnah, the Talmud and the subsequent Rabbinic literature.

At this point we need to ask whether the Pharisaic teachers and the Rabbis, as their successors were called after 70 CE, were fundamentalists. If we disregard the unpleasant associations which the term fundamentalism has acquired in recent times – of naïveté, intolerance and militancy – and use it strictly in the sense of a belief in the inerrancy of Scripture, we must say that they were.

There are only two reasons why that has ever been questioned. One is that the Pharisees and Rabbis were not literalists. But that only means that in their view the Bible does not always mean what at first sight it *appears* to mean. What it does mean has to be understood in the light of the Oral Tradition. But what it does mean, so understood, is true. How can it be otherwise, since the Holy Spirit is not in the habit of making mistakes?

The only other source of doubt is a handful of passages in Rabbinic literature which seem to show an almost modern awareness of the process of historical development, for instance the well-known story of how Moses found himself unable to understand what Rabbi Akiva, 1,500 years later, was teaching in his name (Men. 29b). But these passages are few and far between, and they only show that the Rabbis could sometimes laugh at themselves and step momentarily outside their habitual universe of discourse.

Anybody who knows Rabbinic literature, as distinct from picking convenient quotations from the anthologies, knows that the Pharisees and Rabbis were fundamentalists, and that the entire superstructure of Rabbinic Judaism, especially on its halachic side, rests on the fundamentalist premise of תורה מן השמים, that 'the Torah is from Heaven' (San. 10:1). As Maimonides wrote in the eighth of his Thirteen Principles, 'The whole of the Torah now in our possession is identical with the Torah that was given to Moses, and is all of divine origin ... Moses, like a scribe writing from dictation, wrote all of it, its chronologies, narratives and precepts ... There is no difference in that respect between verses like "And the sons of Ham were Cush and Mizraim, Phut and Canaan" (Gen. 10:6) ... and verses like ... "Hear, O Israel" (Deut. 6:4)' (*Perush ha-Rambam* to San. 10:1).

In addition to the doctrine of the twofold Torah, the Pharisees evolved many other new ideas and institutions. These included a whole system of religious education, a whole liturgy, and a whole regimen of domestic observances, such as the kindling of Sabbath and Festivals lights, *Kiddush*, *Havdalah* and *Birkat ha-Mazon*. For Pharisaism was essentially a *democratising* movement which sought to make Judaism a people's religion. That meant bringing its observance out of the Temple both into the Synagogue and into the home, and required the raising of a religiously knowledgeable laity.

Even though the Pharisees were democratisers, they nevertheless did not see – or at any rate they did not carry through consistently – all the implications of democracy. For instance, as we have seen, they did not object to the idea of a hereditary priesthood. On the contrary, they perpetuated a whole caste system, for the Mishnah lists no less than ten family stocks – priests, levites, Israelites, *mamzerim*, proselytes etc. – who 'came up from Babylon' (Kid. 4:1). And as we have likewise seen, they went along with the idea of a hereditary monarchy vested in the house of David. Indeed, they regarded the Hasmonean rulers as usurpers because they were not so descended. Nor did it occur to the Pharisees that the democratic principle entailed equal rights for men and women. For though they alleviated the position of women in some respects, they also perpetuated, and hardened into legislation, some of their disabilities.

Finally, the Pharisees developed a whole new theology, including a fairly well-defined eschatology, which involved, among other things, the Coming of the Messiah and the Resurrection of the Dead. Neither of these were Biblical doctrines, though there are incipient traces of them in the Bible. For instance, nowhere in the Bible does the word משיח occur in its later, eschatological sense. That was essentially a creation of the Apocalyptists – charlatan prophets who pretended to know things beyond human knowledge. The Pharisees and Rabbis, with varying degrees of enthusiasm, went along with these apocalyptic notions and wrote them into their Bible commentaries and other non-legal, or aggadic, writings.

The Emancipation and its Consequences

The system which the Pharisees devised and the Rabbis perfected worked extraordinarily well for many centuries. It made possible, and succeeded in ensuring, the continuity of Jewish life in all sorts of circumstances, including dispersion and persecution. Admittedly, it was occasionally challenged by other systems, such as Karaism, and did not avoid internal divisions, for instance between Chasidim and Mitnagg'dim. But overwhelmingly it dominated the life of Jewish communities in all the lands of Jewish settlement, from India to Spain, and from Egypt to Britain. It is, from any point of view, a remarkable success story.

Then came the Emancipation which within a generation or two produced a massive defection from Rabbinic Judaism. Some Jews converted to Christianity. Some gave up their Jewish identity and merged by assimilation into the non-Jewish environment. Some identified themselves with new ideologies such as Marxism. Some experimented with new forms of Judaism, and to them we shall presently return. Some remained within the orbit of Rabbinic Judaism but neglected in varying degree to observe its requirements as codified in the Shulchan Aruch. Only a minority actually defended and re-asserted *in toto* the traditional, Rabbinic system, often with an intransigence uncharacteristic of previous ages, and they became known as the Orthodox party.

Today Orthodox Judaism, for various reasons, is experiencing a remarkable revival. Nevertheless, it is unlikely to capture more than a small minority, and it *may* prove to be a passing phenomenon. The overwhelming majority of Jews seem unwilling to pay the price, in terms of the self-exclusion from non-Jewish society, as well as the self-discipline, which Orthodoxy requires.

The great question is why this massive contraction of Rabbinic Judaism's influence has occurred. There are a number of reasons which we may broadly call *external*. For one thing, as Jews became citizens of the countries in which they lived, so the rabbinic courts lost the powers of law enforcement they had enjoyed in the self-contained, self-governing communities of former times. For another, the social pressure to conform, which had previously worked in favour of compliance with Jewish tradition, now worked, on the contrary, in favour of assimilation to the lifestyle of the non-Jewish environment. Then there was the sheer attraction of European culture with its music, art and literature, its philosophy, science and technology. In addition, the schools and universities through which the new generations of Jews passed not only provided a mode of entry into that culture, but competed with, and largely displaced, the Jewish educational system, so that emancipated Jews tended to become ignorant of their own heritage, including its languages, Hebrew as well as Yiddish, and to that extent began to feel like strangers in the old-style synagogues, which made no concessions to their situation.

All these external factors were, and continue to be, powerful centrifugal forces, and they go a long way towards explaining the wholesale abandonment of Rabbinic Judaism that has occurred. But not *all* the way. There is also – and more fundamentally – the *internal* factor, as we may call it, that for most emancipated Jews Rabbinic Judaism *lost its credibility*.

For to enter the modern world was to absorb its critical spirit. Precisely that is what distinguishes it from the medieval world. In the Middle Ages, the dominant thought-form was *scholasticism*: the belief that the Scriptures – Jewish, Christian or Muslim, as the case might be – contained the truth, the whole truth and nothing but the truth; that theology is therefore the queen of the sciences, to which all other sciences are subservient; that whatever contradicts it must *ipso facto* be rejected as false; and that to deny its teachings is a heresy for which you may be burnt at the stake, or excommunicated.

That whole *Weltanschauung* was gradually eroded: first by the Renaissance; then, with Descartes, by philosophy's declaration of independence from theology; then by the Enlightenment; then by the rise of modern science and historical scholarship. By the nineteenth century it was generally taken for granted that people had the right to question everything, including their religious tradition, and even religion as such.

In that situation many Jews turned away, not only from Judaism, but from religion altogether: they became atheists or agnostics. But many more, who retained a more or less positive attitude towards religion in general and Judaism in particular, nevertheless lost faith in the Rabbinic form of it. First and foremost because of its fundamentalism, which, as we have been using the term, is only another word for scholasticism and therefore the exact antithesis of the modern spirit.

More specifically, the application of critical-historical scholarship to the Bible demolished the traditional view of the manner of its composition, most obviously by demonstrating that the Pentateuch is a compilation from several sources, all of them centuries later than Moses.

But that is not the worst of it, for it is always open to defenders of the traditional view to adopt the ploy of retorting that it does not matter how or when the Bible was written, that its authority is independent of such considerations. More important, therefore, than the *historical* criticism of the Bible is the *religious* criticism of the Bible. For even more unmistakably than the Bible reveals different chronological strata, does it reveal different religious strata – different conceptions of God, and of right and wrong.

The higher ones are fine. They appeal, as always, with an immediate and irresistible persuasiveness. But much in the Bible, and even in the subsequent, Rabbinic interpretation of the Bible, is not compatible with these. Once you have freed yourself from any dogmatic presupposition, nothing in the world will ever persuade you again that the God of justice and mercy, so splendidly revealed in many parts of the Bible, ordered the genocide of the Amalekites; or the penalisation of the innocent children of forbidden unions for the sins of their parents; or the prohibition of intermarriage with Ammonites and Moabites even if they convert to Judaism; or the death penalty for a wide variety of offences; or the disabilities of women in communal worship and matrimonial law. And these are only a few of many examples that could be given.

It is immensely to the credit of the bolder Progressive Jewish thinkers, from Abraham Geiger to Claude Montefiore, that they faced these questions squarely, and refused to be fobbed off with specious harmonisations. It took much courage in their times. Today what they said is more or less commonplace among non-fundamentalists. Even Conservative thinkers like Rabbi Dr Louis Jacobs have said: 'It can no longer be denied that there is a human element in the Bible' and that 'it contains error as well as eternal truth' (Jacobs, 1984, p. 242).

What is now absolutely clear to many of us is that the Bible was written by human beings, who were often but not always inspired; who, even when inspired, were still limited by their human fallibility as well as by the socio-cultural milieu in which they lived; who strove valiantly, but not always successfully, to understand and interpret the mind of God. We revere the Bible for its greatness but we do not therefore accept uncritically all that it has to say. And similar remarks apply to the literature of the Oral Torah.

I am not suggesting that all this became immediately apparent to all emancipated Jews. But I do think that many of them, without necessarily being able to articulate it, *sensed* it. They sensed that the doctrine of תורה מן השמים, of a divine Torah, which is the rock-foundation of Rabbinic Judaism, is no longer tenable. It always was a myth, and some individuals, like Spinoza, had begun to suspect this even in earlier times. The Emancipation finally demolished it, and thereby knocked the bottom out of Rabbinic Judaism. That, above all, explains the widespread defection from it.

Of course it is not *only* a matter of fundamentalism. There are other aspects of Rabbinic Judaism which, once submitted to critical scrutiny, also give rise to incredulity. If, for instance, we believe in justice and compassion, equality and democracy, how can we subscribe to the caste system of the Mishnah? How can we accept a hereditary priesthood? How can we go along with the discrimination against women which pervades the system? These and many other secondary features of Rabbinic Judaism, including the belief in the Resurrection of the Dead, become unsustainable. But as it was primarily its dependence on the Temple that proved the fatal flaw of Biblical Judaism, so it was primarily its commitment to the myth of the divinity of the Torah that proved the fatal flaw of Rabbinic Judaism.

As for the timeless foundations of Judaism, they remain valid. And not only they, but many of the secondary features of Rabbinic Judaism also retain their validity. The Synagogue, for instance, looks set to endure long into the next phase of Judaism, if not for ever. Many of the Pharisaic prayers can still be recited with sincerity. The kindling of Sabbath lights remains a beautiful custom, and so do many of the other details of the sacred calendar and the devotional discipline which the Rabbis constructed on biblical foundations. The Rabbinic doctrine of the good and evil inclinations remains a helpful way of understanding human nature, and their teachings about repentance and atonement need little improvement. And so one could continue for a long time ...

Progressive Judaism

Now it is hardly necessary for me to spell out what my thesis is. It has been implicit in what I have been saying all along. It is that the Emancipation produced a crisis of such magnitude that it has no parallel in the history of Judaism other than the destruction of the Temple in 70 CE. Once again Judaism was shaken to its foundations. Once again, the foundations stood firm. But once again the superstructure needed to be substantially modified. The time had come once more for a *paradigm shift*. The post-Emancipation age requires a new kind of Judaism, as different from Rabbinic Judaism as Rabbinic Judaism was from Biblical Judaism, yet retaining the permanent values of both.

What is Progressive Judaism? It is an attempt to construct such a post-Rabbinic Judaism.

But that is not how it is perceived by all, even within its own ranks. In particular, there is a tendency to regard it as a continuation, with only relatively minor modifications, of Rabbinic Judaism. It is a tendency to be found chiefly on the conservative fringe of Progressive Judaism and beyond it, in Conservative or Masorti Judaism, and which I will call the conservative tendency.

According to this view, Rabbinic Judaism has within it all the flexibility that is necessary to make it work satisfactorily in the modern world. The trouble is merely that it has become too rigid in the course of the centuries, and Orthodoxy is the culmination of that process. All we need to do, therefore, is to re-open the wells, to revive the greater dynamism of an earlier Rabbinic Judaism, and then all the problems of modern Jewish life and thought will solve themselves. Orthodoxy, for all its immense learning, misunderstands the Tradition which it claims to know so well. Conservative Jews know better. They are the true heirs of the Pharisees.

In particular, great emphasis is laid in this tendency on Halachah. Not that all its exponents are assiduous students of it, but the word is a word to conjure with. And it is always the *Rabbinic* Halachah that is meant. The possibility that there might be some other Halachah is not contemplated or conceded. In all essentials, so goes the argument, the Rabbinic Halachah is sound and valid and authoritative for us. There are admittedly a few problems, but with a little courage and ingenuity they can be solved.

I find that stance quite unconvincing. For one thing, it ignores the fact that the whole Rabbinic system rests on a fundamentalist *premise* and pretends either that that premise is still tenable or that it does not matter whether it is tenable or not. It ignores the fact that the *methods* of the Rabbinic Halachah involve misinterpretations and circumventions of the plain meaning of texts such as non-fundamentalists cannot employ with intellectual integrity. And it ignores the fact that whole vast *areas* of Rabbinic Judaism, which are integral to it, have lost their validity for non-Orthodox Jews.

For instance, of the six parts of the Talmud one (קדשים, 'Holy Things') is devoted entirely to the sacrificial cult. How can you reject that and say you are a Rabbinic Jew? Another part (טהרות, 'Cleannesses') is devoted entirely to the laws of ritual purity and impurity. If you consider that obsolete, how can you say that you stand in the mainstream of Rabbinic Judaism? Another part (נזיקין, 'Damages') deals with civil and criminal law, which is mostly antiquated, though some of the ethical principles on which it is based remain valid. If you do not intend to revive that system, and if you reject some of its major provisions, including capital punishment and corporal punishment, how can you say that you subscribe to Rabbinic Law? Still another part (זרעים, 'Seeds') deals mainly with the laws of agriculture, and I am not aware that Progressive Jews, however conservative, have been advocating their reinstatement. Yet another part (נשים, 'Women') deals with matrimonial law. It is predicated throughout on the inequality of men and women and on the permissibility, in principle, of male polygamy – for the medieval decree against this only prohibited but did not abolish it. It also forbids *kohanim* to marry divorcees or proselytes, and *mamzerim* to marry fellow Jews not so tainted. If you reject these pervasive features of the system, how can you say that you uphold it?

The whole position of the conservatives becomes increasingly difficult to accept, the more one scrutinises it. Much of it turns out, on inspection, to be either a case of pietistic self-deception or political posturing. Furthermore, it is my impression that this is beginning to be recognised within conservative circles. What, in particular, has brought the matter to a head is the granting of equal rights, including the right to be ordained as rabbis, to women. The change in attitude to homosexuality has been another factor. These are things one cannot do without stepping outside the parameters of Rabbinic Judaism.

In this connection it is noteworthy that the Reconstructionist movement, which began within the Conservative movement, has joined the World Union for Progressive Judaism; also that it has followed the example of the American Reform movement in accepting patrilineality as a way of establishing Jewish status on a par with matrilineality; and that the more conservative branches of the Progressive movement have in recent years, like the more radical ones, created liturgies that combine tradition with innovation.

The question Progressive Jews need to ask themselves is whether they are renovators of Rabbinic Judaism or pioneers of a new, post-Rabbinic Judaism. My answer is clear, and it only remains to ask one final question: מאי נפקא מינה, what practical difference does it make?

If we adopt the view I have been advocating, there will still be various tendencies, more traditionalist and more radical, within Progressive Judaism; but at least they will be speaking the same language. Nor am I necessarily arguing for a particularly radical kind of Progressive Judaism. On the contrary, once we know what we are doing, we shall be freer than ever to furnish our house as traditionally as we like. Indeed, we have a positive duty to preserve or reinstate anything and everything, both of the Biblical and of the Rabbinic phases of our heritage, that is still valid and serviceable.

Nevertheless it will be clear that we are not in the business of patching up pre-Emancipation Judaism but of constructing a new, post-Emancipation Judaism. And therefore, too, we shall not need to look over our shoulders, or waste our time seeking approval from those who remain committed to pre-Emancipation Judaism. As a matter of fact, we shall not be in competition with them at all, or claim that we can do their job better than they can, for we shall be doing a different job.

We shall co-exist with them, it is to be hoped, in mutual courtesy, respect and understanding – and co-operation, too, as far as possible. But we shall do our own thing, and not allow ourselves to be distracted from doing it.

And if that sounds sectarian, let us remind ourselves of two points. First, that we shall not do it for ourselves alone, but for all those who in the generations to come will seek a form of Judaism that preserves all that remains valid of the various past phases of our heritage but without dragging along the baggage of discredited beliefs and antiquated practices. Secondly, that our *ultimate* aim is the aim of *every* kind of Judaism, namely to preserve and transmit the timeless essentials of our faith: One God, one world, one humanity, one covenant people, one goal, which is the establishment of justice, compassion and peace on earth. By that criterion all our efforts will ultimately be judged, and the contemplation of that thought offers no scope for complacency.

Chapter 2

❖   ❖   ❖

PROGRESSIVE JUDAISM FIFTY YEARS AFTER THE HOLOCAUST

The Aftermath of the Holocaust

The commemorations of the fiftieth anniversary of the defeat of Hitler marked the end of a chapter of Jewish as well as world history. Not that we may henceforth put the Holocaust out of our minds. Heaven forbid! Surely we have all vowed, with Abraham Shlonsky, לזכור ודבר לא לשכוח, 'to remember and never to forget'. We owe it to the victims, we owe it to the survivors, we owe it to posterity.

Besides, the consequences of the Holocaust are still with us: in broken hearts and broken lives, and in the syndromes that affect the second and third generations. The persistence of anti-Semitism, the widespread violation of human rights, and the emergence of new forms of ethnic cleansing and genocide: all these furnish daily evidence that the poison is still active and the lessons have yet to be learnt.

However, during the last fifty years the Holocaust has dominated our agenda in a way that must now begin to recede. We have rightly given priority to the practical tasks which its aftermath demanded of us: to rehabilitate the survivors, to build new institutions, to train a new leadership, and above all to contribute to the upbuilding of *Eretz Yisrael,* which has done as much as all our other communities put together for the postwar reconstruction of Jewish life.

As these tasks have made heavy demands on our resources, we have tended to neglect what would in normal circumstances have been our primary task: to develop the distinctive philosophy and practice of Progressive Judaism.

In saying that, I do not mean to suggest that we have stood still. On the contrary, there has been a massive shift in all our communities:

towards greater traditionalism. The combined effect of the Holocaust and the establishment of the State of Israel has been to induce in all of us an intensified desire to identify ourselves with our people: to go back to our roots and to close our ranks. However, this return to tradition has been pragmatic rather than principled: a concession to popular sentiment or political pressure rather than the result of conscientious deliberation.

Again, I do not mean to suggest that the last fifty years have produced no new theology. But it has been mostly 'Holocaust Theology', and much of that has been based on what seems to me the mistaken premise that the Holocaust raises fundamentally new questions about the nature of God. We have always known that God does not revoke our free-will, however monstrously we misuse it. God's activity in human history is that of a Teacher, who shows us the way, and gives us strength when we choose to walk in it, but does not coerce us. As the Talmud says, 'If we wish to do evil, the door is open; if we wish to do good, God helps us' (Resh Lakish, Yoma 38b).

To say that is not to diminish the enormity of the Holocaust, which remains for ever beyond comprehension, comparison or consolation. It is to say that the new questions it raises are not about God – except that it has compelled us finally to abandon, as we should have done long ago, the belief in an interventionist God – but about humanity. It has shown that the human capacity for evil is far more horrendous and enduring than, in more optimistic times, we used to imagine.

At any rate, the theological writing of the last half-century has done little to advance the task of formulating a distinctively Progressive Judaism. There have indeed been noteworthy exceptions, such as the writings of Eugene Borowitz, and attempts at re-definition, such as the 1976 *Centenary Perspective* of the Central Conference of American Rabbis, but they lack the incisiveness of earlier platforms.

Lack of Clarity

Only in two areas has there been substantial creativity. One is Halachah, principally thanks to the writings of Solomon Freehof, Walter Jacob and Moshe Zemer. The other is liturgy, with the creation of a whole new generation of prayerbooks. Nevertheless, in both these areas I see considerable confusion as to where exactly Progressive Judaism stands on the key issues. Do we or do we not affirm the authority of Bible and Talmud? Do we or do we not go along with the traditional eschatology with its personal Messiah, total ingathering of the exiles, and restoration of the Temple with its sacrificial cult? To

these and similar questions the literature to which I have been referring often fails to furnish clear answers.

Sometimes this lack of clarity is defended as a virtue. On the one
hand, it is argued that in matters of belief Judaism is traditionally
imprecise and undogmatic. On the other, it is maintained that in
matters of practice, where Judaism has traditionally demanded precision and conformity, Progressive Judaism, with its emphasis on
individual autonomy, must allow unlimited diversity. But these are
only excuses. What is called for is not a minutely defined system but
merely a consistent set of beliefs and practices: one that allows ample
room for local variations and individual preferences but nevertheless
constitutes a coherent whole. It is this task of shaping and reshaping
the inner content of our Movement, largely neglected in the last fifty
years under the pressure of more urgent preoccupations, which, I
submit, we need now to resume.

It is not our only task. Much and even most of our work is uncon-
troversial: we simply strive to live Jewish lives and to build Jewish
communities. However, unless we can say with some degree of clarity, as well as conviction and passion, what it is that we distinctively
stand for, our Movement will have neither cohesion nor thrust and,
especially in the newly re-opened areas of Central and Eastern
Europe, it will stand little chance against the unrelenting propaganda
of a resurgent, triumphalist Orthodoxy brimming with self-confi-
dence and self-righteousness.

Modernity

What then is Progressive Judaism? The short answer is supplied by
the title of Michael Meyer's excellent history (Meyer, 1988): it is a
response to modernity.

'Modernity' is a convenient umbrella term for a whole series of
intellectual, social and political movements – including the Renaissance and the Reformation, the rise of modern philosophy and science, the French Revolution and the Industrial Revolution – which
have, by gradual stages, transformed the medieval world into the
world as we know it. This transformation brought to the fore a
whole cluster of interrelated values which we may lump together
under the heading of 'Enlightenment'. They are: a spirit of free
inquiry in all branches of human knowledge; the priority of reason
over dogma in the pursuit of truth; the right of individuals to obey
their consciences, and of minorities to preserve their traditions; the
toleration, and even celebration, of diversity; the equal entitlement

of all to the privileges and responsibilities of citizenship; democracy; and the hope of progress towards a future in which good will prevail over evil.

These values evolved gradually. Some of them, like the full implications of sex equality and of cultural pluralism, have only recently come to be perceived. However the general thrust of the Enlightenment was already clear when, through the Emancipation, we Jews first became exposed to it. It was then that a major rift appeared between the Reformers, who embraced the Enlightenment, and their Orthodox opponents, who were hostile or ambivalent towards it.

'Yes' to Enlightenment

The first point to be made about Progressive Judaism, therefore, is that it affirms the Enlightenment. Not, indeed, uncritically. We are aware of the errors to which excessive rationalism, individualism and optimism can lead. So there are important qualifications to be made. However, subject to these, we do affirm the liberal values of intellectual and political freedom, of reason and conscience, of tolerance and diversity, of equality and democracy, and of hope, in spite of everything, for the ultimate future of humanity.

It is especially important to make this point because there is a tendency in some quarters to speak disparagingly of the Enlightenment, as if it were somehow responsible for the Holocaust. That, of course, is a terrible mistake. It is a mistake because to the Enlightenment we owe our Emancipation. It is a mistake, more fundamentally, because the values of the Enlightenment are themselves Hebraic, in the sense that they are applications and implications of principles, such as freedom and justice, which are deeply embedded in Jewish tradition. It is a mistake, most tragically, because it involves a view of the causation of the Holocaust which is the exact opposite of the truth.

The Holocaust did not happen because there was too much liberalism: it happened because there was too little liberalism! Because the liberal values of reason, conscience, justice, tolerance and democracy were too faintly cherished and too feebly defended against the onslaught of a neo-paganism that mocked and, with its jackboots, trampled on every one of them.

Far from disparaging the Enlightenment, we should reaffirm it. Far from distancing ourselves from Western civilisation, we should embrace it. Far from sneering at the forces of liberalism, we should give them every support. For from them hangs, as by a thin thread, the prevention of another Holocaust and the survival of humanity.

'No' to Fundamentalism

That it affirms the values of the Enlightenment is, I submit, the first
of four main points to be made about Progressive Judaism fifty years
after the Holocaust, and the second follows from it. For what is the
chief characteristic that distinguishes modernity from medievalism?
It is the spirit of free inquiry to which I have already referred.

The dominant medieval world view, known as scholasticism, produced many noble achievements but rested on a premise which set
a clear limit to intellectual freedom, namely the belief that Scripture
– Jewish, Christian or Muslim, as the case might be – contained the
truth, the whole truth and nothing but the truth, so that to it and its
authoritative interpretation all human thought must be subservient.
In a broader sense, that belief in the divinely guaranteed inerrancy
of a body of sacred writings is known as fundamentalism; and in that
broader sense it is the basis of traditional Judaism.

It goes back to the period after the Babylonian Exile, when the
canonisation of the Hebrew Scriptures began, and it was adopted in
a particularly rigid form by the Sadducees. However the Pharisees,
too, embraced it. For though they evolved the doctrine of an Oral
Torah, clarifying and amplifying the Written Torah, and though they
brought much latitude, imagination and dynamism to the interpretation of both, they nevertheless stood on the principle of תורה מן השמים
(San. 10:1), that the twofold Torah is of divine origin and therefore
authoritative in every particular. On this foundation the whole vast
structure of Rabbinic Judaism was reared.

Rabbinic Judaism dominated Jewish life for many centuries, and
flourished especially in the Middle Ages. However, with the Emancipation it experienced a precipitous decline which, in spite of the
recent resurgence of Orthodoxy, is still continuing. Today Rabbinic
Judaism effectively governs the lives of only ten to fifteen percent of
the Jewish people. For this decline there are many reasons, but the
basic one is surely this: that the Enlightenment, with its spirit of free
inquiry, swept away the whole scholastic world view. Once the critical study of sacred texts became admissible, the fundamentalist
reading of Scripture could no longer be sustained. Just as its dependence on the Temple proved the undoing of Biblical Judaism, so the
Pharisaic doctrine of the divinity of the Torah was the fatal flaw of
Rabbinic Judaism.

This perception is not new; it has been around for a long time; but
we have been slow to grasp it and its implications. I believe the time
has come to be frank and say: we reject fundamentalism unequivocally. We may still affirm *torah min ha-shamyim* in the general sense

that Scripture as a whole bears the imprint of divine revelation, but we can no longer pretend that it is divine in every particular. To hold God responsible for the command to exterminate the Amalekites (to take only one of many examples) is not pious: it is blasphemous. There is no such thing as a divine book in the fundamentalist sense. All literature is human, and all human attempts to understand the Mind of the Creator are necessarily imperfect. In religion, as in everything else, certainty is not attainable. That realisation is the defining characteristic which distinguishes modernity from medievalism, and Progressive Judaism is that form of Judaism which seeks to come to terms with it. That is my second point.

Post-Rabbinic Judaism

However, if we reject fundamentalism outright, then we can no longer pretend to stand within the Rabbinic system that is predicated on it. I know that this view is not shared by all. The conservatively inclined among us have long tended to invoke an earlier, more dynamic phase of Rabbinic Judaism, which they claim to represent and seek to renew, and to look upon Orthodoxy as a regrettable aberration from it. I think that was always a delusion and is increasingly coming to be recognised as such.

The gulf that separates us from Rabbinic Judaism, with its fundamentalist reading of Scripture; with its resort to legal fictions to get round difficulties; with its belief in the sacrificial cult, and in the laws of ritual purity and impurity; with the place it gives to capital punishment and corporal punishment in its criminal law; and with its subordination of women, which runs all through its matrimonial law – that gulf is much too vast for the claim that the Rabbinic universe of discourse is our universe of discourse to carry any credibility.

The issue of women's rights in particular has forced that recognition upon us, and is beginning to force it on Conservative Judaism as well. There is no way in which women can be given complete equality with men in Rabbinic Judaism. Already for generations Orthodox rabbis have struggled to bring about significant improvements in that respect. They have failed, not because they are ignorant or stupid or lacking in good-will, but because it cannot be done.

Our task as Progressives is not to patch up Rabbinic Judaism but to evolve a new form of Judaism, as different from Rabbinic Judaism as that was from Biblical Judaism, yet preserving all that was good and remains valid in both. To a large extent that is indeed what we have been doing all along; but we have been less than clear about it.

The time has come to say it out loud. It is a long overdue clarification, and though it may sound revolutionary, it does not necessarily entail a shift to the left, for we shall be as free as ever to furnish our Progressive Jewish mansion as traditionally as we wish. Nor will it harm our relations with the Orthodox; on the contrary, it may improve them. For we shall no longer be saying that ours is a correct version, and theirs an incorrect version, of one and the same kind of Judaism, for it will be a different kind of Judaism, or that we can do their job better than they can, for we shall be doing a different job.

To the Jewish world at large, comprising untold numbers of unaffiliated and misaffiliated, we shall present a clear choice. We shall be saying to them: 'The Orthodox would have you believe that there is only one way of being Jewish, which is to carry on unchanged the Rabbinic Judaism of pre-modern times, as if the Emancipation and the Enlightenment had never happened: that it is either that or nothing. But we tell you that there is an alternative. The alternative is Progressive Judaism, which is not Rabbinic Judaism liberally interpreted, but post-Rabbinic Judaism, a form of Judaism appropriate to the modern world. If that is what you are seeking, then please join us'. That is my third point.

Particularism and Universalism

My fourth and last point relates to one aspect of this post-Rabbinic Judaism which seems to me to require special attention. I refer to the old question of particularism and universalism. It is a commonplace to say that in Judaism there has always been a tension between the two. But tension is not equilibrium. In Rabbinic Judaism, though both were present, particularism was a great deal more pronounced than universalism. In 'Classical Reform' there was a tendency to go to the opposite extreme. That is no longer true of Progressive Judaism. In the fifty years since the Holocaust we have veered considerably towards particularism. Surely nobody can any longer doubt our commitment to the Jewish People and the State of Israel. What needs now to be re-emphasised is the universalism, and that in three areas.

The first is liturgy. The liturgy of Rabbinic Judaism abounds with pleas for God's favour on behalf of the Jewish people, but contains hardly a single expression of concern for the well-being of the rest of humanity, except in an eschatological context. Historically, that is very understandable. But now that we live in a global village, and have begun to understand and respect other religions, it is no longer acceptable. We may no longer show such unconcern

for the other 99.7 percent of the world's population who are as
much God's children as we are. Surely, therefore, we may no
longer praise God as רופא חולי עמו ישראל, Healer of the sick of the
Jewish people, or as המברך את־עמו ישראל בשלום, the One who blesses
the Jewish people with peace, without explicitly including the rest
of humanity; for healing is universal, and peace is indivisible.
Surely there is a need for new prayers on behalf of the human family as a whole. Some of the new liturgies address that need; others,
regrettably, do not.

The second area in which we need to express our universalism
more strongly is 'outreach', which I take to mean that we have a positive duty to show friendship to non-Jews, especially those who marry
into our community, as well as their children, and those who visit our
synagogues, and to make it very clear that if any of them wish to join
us in our community of faith, a warm welcome awaits them.

The third and most important area in which to express our universalism is social action: that is, to work with all who share our
ideals for the betterment of human society, both in the State of Israel
and throughout the world. It is, in other words, תקון עולם, the 'repair-
ing of the world'.

Remarkably, this universalistic note was already sounded nearly
fifty years ago, and by a man who knew more about the Holocaust
than any of us. For it was Leo Baeck who, at the Fifth International
Conference of the World Union for Progressive Judaism, held in
London in 1946, said: 'We have too much little Judaism ... The
greater Judaism is our special strength ... Judaism must not stand
aside when the great problems of humanity [are at stake] ... We are
Jews also for the sake of humanity'.

Leo Baeck's challenge received little response at the time. Now,
fifty years after the Holocaust, it demands, with renewed urgency, our
attention. On our response to it the future of Progressive Judaism –
and perhaps much more than Progressive Judaism – may well depend.

Chapter 3

❖   ❖   ❖

HALACHAH AND AGGADAH
Law and Lore in Judaism

Midrash and Mishnah

Everything that exists is either green or not green. That self-evident truth is generalised in symbolic logic into the proposition that A and non-A exhaust the universe. Likewise, we are told, whatever is not Halachah is Aggadah. If so, Halachah and Aggadah exhaust the universe! But of course the use of these terms is limited by their context, which is the literature of Judaism and, more specifically, of Rabbinic Judaism.

To explore that limited but still vast universe of discourse, let us begin in the second century BCE: the century which saw the Maccabean Rebellion, the emergence of new sects such as the Pharisees and Sadducees, the completion of the Hebrew Bible, and the beginnings of a new, miscellaneous literature including the Apocrypha and the Dead Sea Scrolls.

It also saw the inception, or perhaps resumption and intensification, of another activity which did not produce any literary results until much later. This activity, in which the Pharisaic teachers specialised, concerned what they called תורה שבעל־פה, the 'Oral Torah', that is, a large and growing body of traditions, both interpreting and supplementing תורה שבכתב, the 'Written Torah' of the Pentateuch, which was handed down by word of mouth.

More precisely, it was a twofold activity. On the one hand, it was the interpretation of Scripture. That was called *Midrash*, which means 'seeking out', and would normally proceed chapter by chapter, verse by verse, or, in the case of homiletical Midrash, according to the nature of the occasion and the design of the preacher. On the other hand, it involved the gathering, sifting, clarifying, harmonising and elaborating of 'preceptive' or 'regulative' traditions. That was called *Mishnah*, which means 'Teaching', and would normally proceed topic by topic.

Which came first, Midrash or Mishnah, has been much debated. According to one theory (see 'Midrash and Mishnah' in Lauterbach, 1951), Midrash is the older method; it was employed already by the Soferim (Scribes), only their activity ceased with the death of Simon the Just in 270 CE, to be resumed in 190 BCE by a new legislative body comprising priestly and lay elements, soon in conflict with one another. In particular, they disputed over the new practices which had sprung up during the eighty years' interregnum. These were generally favoured by the lay people, who became the Pharisaic party, but opposed by the priests, who became the Sadducees. To justify the newer practices, the Pharisees would normally resort to Scripture interpretation, but because in many instances it was no longer possible to do that in a convincing manner, they adopted the Mishnah method as well, simply asserting that the laws in question were part of the sacred oral tradition.

A different theory was put forward by Professor Ellis Rivkin (see 'Ben Sira and the Non-Existence of the Synagogue' in *In the Time of Harvest, Essays in Honor of Abba Hillel Silver*, ed. D.J. Silver, 1963). According to this, the Soferim were not expounders of Scripture but writers of a literature, especially Wisdom Literature, independent of Scripture, while the concept of an Oral Torah, coeval with the Written Torah, was a creation of the Pharisees which served their purpose of asserting the rights of the laity. (It is significant that the 'chain of tradition' enunciated in the opening statement of the Mishnah tractate *Avot* is not a priestly one, running through Aaron and his descendants, but a lay line, proceeding from Moses to Joshua, the Elders, the Prophets and the Men of the Great Assembly.) On this theory, Midrash and Mishnah alike were Pharisaic innovations dating from the second century BCE.

However that may be, the twofold activity continued after the destruction of the Temple in 70 CE, when Pharisaism became normative and its teachers, previously known as Chachamim (sages, lay scholars), came to be called Rabbis. In the narrower sense, therefore, this is the starting point of Rabbinic Judaism.

Tannaitic Literature

Chronologically, its classical period divides into two, of which the first extends from 70 until about 200 CE and is known as the Tannaitic period because the five generations of Rabbis who flourished in Palestine during that time are referred to as Tannaim, from an Aramaic word corresponding to the Hebrew word underlying the term Mishnah. The Tannaim were therefore Mishnah teachers. But, as has already been indicated, they also employed the Midrash method, especially in the synagogues.

Towards the end of the Tannaitic period this twofold activity, conducted orally since the days of the Pharisees, ceased to be purely oral. The tradition had become too vast to be memorised, and so the process of committing it to writing began. Thus the Midrash method produced collections of Bible interpretations on the books of Exodus (the Mechilta), Leviticus (the Sifra), Numbers and Deuteronomy (the Sifrei), while the Mishnah method produced a topically arranged compendium of laws, consisting of sixty (later, by subdivision, sixty-three) tractates grouped into six orders, which was edited by Rabbi Judah ha-Nasi and became known as 'our Mishnah' to distinguish it from a similar but more discursive and less authoritative collection called Tosefta ('Supplement').

It is in this Tannaitic literature that the terms Halachah and Aggadah first appear. The word Halachah is the Hebrew form of an Aramaic word, הִלְכְתָא, which occurs frequently in Targum Onkelos (the Aramaic Version of the Bible) as a translation of such words as משפט (judgment, ordinance) and is perhaps related to the Aramaic word הֲלָךְ, to be found in the book of Ezra (4:13), where it seems to refer to some kind of a land tax. At any rate, the derivation of the word from the verb הלך, 'to walk', has no direct bearing on its meaning.

In Tannaitic sources the word Halachah refers, first, to an individual law, particularly as taught by the Mishnah method, without reference to a Scriptural proof-text, and therefore also to an individual paragraph of Judah ha-Nasi's Mishnah, for which the terms Mishnah and Halachah are used interchangeably. But it is also used, secondly, as a collective noun, for the whole body of individual Halachot which came to be accepted as authoritative.

The word Aggadah (also, especially in Babylonia, Haggadah) comes from a Biblical Hebrew verb meaning 'to tell' and may therefore be translated 'narrative', but derives more specifically from the phrase מגיד הכתוב ('The Scriptural text tells ...') which was used by the school of Ishmael as a technical term in its Bible exegesis. (Bacher, 1899/1965, Part I, pp. 30–37). As with Halachah, so the noun Aggadah can be used either individually or collectively, i.e., either for a single Bible interpretation or for the whole genre.

What transpires, therefore, is that the terms Halachah and Aggadah correspond rather closely to the terms Mishnah and Midrash respectively. The chief distinction to be borne in mind is that a Midrash may be a legal or a non-legal Scripture interpretation, depending on the nature of the text being interpreted, whereas Aggadah is characteristically non-legal.

Amoraic Literature

Amora'im, meaning 'sayers', is the name given to the Palestinian and Babylonian Rabbis of the period of approximately 200–500 CE. They continued the twofold activity of their predecessors. But, unlike them, they already had before them written (or at least well memorised) texts of much of the Oral Torah, particularly the Mishnah, which served them as a text-book for their studies and discussions; and in the course of time these produced an elaboration of the Mishnah many times bulkier than the Mishnah itself. Eventually this elaboration was in its turn committed to writing in the form of the Talmud, another word for 'Teaching', in two recensions: the Palestinian or 'Jerusalem' Talmud, redacted in the fifth century, and the larger and more authoritative Babylonian Talmud, completed in the sixth century.

Because the Talmud incorporates the Mishnah, which it quotes instalment by instalment, a term was needed by which to refer to the Talmud proper, and for that purpose the word *Gemara*, from a verb which in Hebrew means 'to complete' and in Aramaic 'to learn', came into use.

The Amoraim also engaged in Bible interpretation, especially in Palestine, where the challenge of Christianity made Jewish preaching especially important. The result was an enormous Midrashic literature, drawing extensively on the Bible interpretations of the Palestinian Amoraim, edited both during and after the Amoraic period. Some of these Midrashim follow the books of the Bible chapter by chapter and verse by verse; these are called exegetical. Others are essentially collections of sermons, arranged according to the sabbaths and festivals of the year; they are called homiletical.

But the Gemara is the context *par excellence* in which the terms Halachah and Aggadah are commonly used, particularly in a collective sense, to refer to two different types of material. Anything that appertains to law is Halachah, but 'law' in a very broad sense which includes anything that is or can be expressed in the imperative; anything that is regulative of life in any of its aspects, regardless of whether or not it is capable of law enforcement by human agency; anything that is relevant to the answering of the question, 'And now,

O Israel, what does the Eternal One your God require of you?' (Deut. 10:12). It therefore includes not only civil and criminal law, but also ritual and moral law, and much else besides.

The word Aggadah describes anything in the Gemara that is not halachic, i.e., that is unrelated, or only remotely related, to the process of fixing the law. It includes Bible interpretations; legendary and other embellishments of Biblical narratives; anecdotes about post-Biblical characters including the Rabbis themselves; speculations about God and God's relation to the world, humanity and Israel; and a great deal else. In the words of the *Encyclopaedia Judaica*, 'Parables and allegories, metaphors and terse maxims; lyrics, dirges, and prayers, biting satire and fierce polemic, idyllic tales and tense dramatic dialogues, hyperboles and plays on words, permutations of letters, calculations of their arithmetical values (*gematria*) or their employment as initials of other words (*notarikon*) – all are found in the *aggadah*' (Vol. 2, p. 356).

Halachah, then, tells us what should be done, Aggadah tells us what is; Halachah is prescriptive, Aggadah is descriptive; Halachah deals in precepts, Aggadah deals in concepts; Halachah is about action, Aggadah is about belief; Halachah is practical, Aggadah is theoretical; Halachah is law, Aggadah is lore.

Naturally, the lines of demarcation between them are not hard and fast. They overlap, they flow and merge into one another. If, for instance, as often happens, the question is debated, what is the Scriptural source of a particular law, or what is the reason for a particular commandment, or what is the state of mind in which it should be performed, or if an anecdote is told to illustrate a legal point, or to indicate which opinion a particular Rabbi held, are we then in the realm of Halachah or Aggadah? Often the matter can be argued either way with equal plausibility.

Halachah and Aggadah

In *general* terms the distinction is nevertheless clear, and it is a distinction which can be extrapolated from the Gemara, which is its primary context, to Rabbinic literature, and indeed to Jewish literature, as a whole.

In the Bible, for instance, only the legislation of the Pentateuch is strictly halachic, all the rest is mainly aggadic. In Rabbinic literature, as we have seen, Halachah is to be found chiefly in the Mishnah, Tosefta, Mechilta, Sifra, Sifrei, and the halachic portions of the Gemara; Aggadah is to be found in the aggadic portions of the Tannaitic Midrashim and of the Gemara, and in the Amoraic Midrashim.

In the post-Talmudic period, Halachah is represented by the Responsa, the Codes, and the Commentaries on the Codes; Aggadah is represented by works of Bible commentary, philosophy, theology, mysticism, poetry, history, fiction, etc.

All of Jewish literature can therefore be classified under these two headings. Halachah and Aggadah represent two modes, or modalities, in which Judaism has historically expressed itself.

Halachah is concerned to answer the question, how we must conduct ourselves in order to comply with God's will. That has always been the chief preoccupation of Judaism, and surely rightly so. For how can there be a more important question, or a nobler enterprise than the attempt to answer it? Hence halachic matters are always treated with special seriousness in Jewish tradition. In particular, there is a strong drive towards clarity, precision and uniformity. The assumption is that to every halachic question there is one and only one right answer; that, given enough learning, it is always possible to find that answer; and that it is vitally important that the answers, once ascertained, should be obediently accepted by all Jews everywhere.

The underlying assumption, therefore, is that God's will is knowable, and knowable with certainty. That is the fundamental premise of Pharisaic-Rabbinic Judaism, based on a particular concept of Revelation and hence of the authority both of the Written and of the Oral Torah. It is precisely at this point that Progressive Judaism parts company with the traditional view, with consequences to be explored more fully in the following chapters.

But even within the traditional system, Halachah, although invested with immense importance, does not receive exclusive emphasis. For the Rabbis were well aware that it is not enough to know what God requires. Equally important is the will, and the motivation, to do it; and that is where Aggadah comes in. 'Do you wish to know the One by whose command the world was created? Then learn Haggadah, for that is how you may get to know the Creator and come to cleave to God's will' (Sifrei Deut. §49 to Deut. 11:22).

The function of Aggadah is to inspire, to edify, to enthuse, even to entertain. It was in reference to aggadic preaching that it was said: 'Whoever speaks words of Torah in public, if his words are not as pleasant to his hearers as honey and milk mixed together, it would have been better if he had not spoken at all' (Cant.R. 4, 11, 1).

The whole approach of the Rabbis to Aggadah is quite different from their approach to Halachah: freer, more relaxed, more prepared to accept diversity of opinion, to 'live and let live'. In Halachah, as we have seen, the aim is to establish the law unambiguously and definitively. As long as the discussion is in progress, divergent views are indeed freely expressed and respectfully heard. Concerning the Schools of Hillel and Shammai, who disagreed on many points of law, a *Bat Kol* (Heavenly Voice) said: אלו ואלו דברי אלהים חיים, 'Both alike are the words of the living God'; nevertheless it was added: והלכה כבית הלל, 'But the law is in accordance with the School of Hillel' (Eruvin 13b).

In the end, as far as possible, every halachic issue is to be decided one way or the other. There are some, but not many, 'loose ends' in the Halachah. Even discussions that end תיקו ('Let it stand') are not unconcluded arguments about real issues but, as Rabbi Dr Louis Jacobs has demonstrated, artificially constructed intellectual problems that are in principle incapable of solution by the accepted rules (see Jacobs, 1981). By contrast, when it comes to Aggadah, any number of divergent and even contradictory opinions are allowed to stand side by side, usually without any attempt either to harmonise them or to decide between them. Aggadic Midrashim typically have whole sequences of different interpretations of one and the same Scriptural verse or phrase, each introduced with דבר אחר, 'Another thing', and there is a general principle, אין משיבין על ההגדה, that 'one does not contradict an aggadic opinion' (Tikkunei Zohar Chadash 166a).

It has often been remarked how differently Judaism and Christianity handle these two aspects – belief and practice – of religion. During the same period when the Church Fathers were drawing a razor-sharp distinction between correct doctrine and heresy, while taking a Paulinian, antinomian view about matters of law, the Rabbis were defining with the utmost precision what constitutes correct action, while permitting virtually unrestricted freedom of speculation in theology.

It follows, of course, that Aggadah is not to be viewed as having the same kind of authority as Halachah. Even apart from the great profusion of mutually exclusive opinions that reigns within it, much of it is in the nature of folklore and mythology, often derived from non-Jewish (especially Greek and Persian) traditions, although, as Louis Ginzberg has shown, not by way of direct borrowing (Ginzberg, 1955, p. 63). Furthermore, there are in the Aggadah not a few instances of tongue-in-cheek humour.

In spite of all that, the Rabbinic Aggadah has sometimes been taken with humourless seriousness. Even Tzvi Hirsch Chajes, who stood on the fringe of the *Wissenschaft* movement and was therefore not wholly unenlightened, could write of the Rabbis that they 'certainly did not fabricate these stories, rather they were transmitted to them as true stories' (Chajes, 1952, pp. 149f), and, 'The narratives which have come down from ancient times to Israel, with their miraculous events, were not pure inventions, God forbid, but were handed down to the Sages from early days' (p. 153). If Chajes could write in that vein, one wonders with what credulity the Aggadah is regarded in ultra-Orthodox and Chasidic circles!

It is less surprising that in the Middle Ages Nachmanides was widely criticised for having declared, in his famous disputation with Pablo Christiani, that the Aggadah is not binding. But it is significant that he felt able to make such a statement; and already before him, Maimonides had pointed out that the Rabbinic Aggadah is often to be understood poetically (*Guide of the Perplexed*, III, 43).

Perhaps the best comment on the matter was made by the modern Hebrew poet Chaim Nachman Bialik. In his celebrated essay entitled *Halachah and Aggadah*, he wrote: 'It is a sin against the Aggadah, committed by many generations and sects of Jews, that they have broken their living relationship with it. For any number of naïve persons among them have taken its words literally and regarded them as articles of faith, and many self-styled scholars have likewise understood it literally and therefore judged it to be so much nonsense. Both alike have been intellectually and aesthetically insensitive, and have viewed the Aggadah with blinkers which have blinded them to its poetic luminosity and metaphorical truth' (Bialik, 1951, p. 213a).

Some Characterisations

Claude Montefiore, in his Introduction to *A Rabbinic Anthology*, has this very perceptive description: 'Halakah and Haggadah, we are told, together constitute Rabbinic religion and literature. The interpretations of the Pentateuchal law, the enormous elaborations of it, the immense additions to it, the interminable discussions, arguments, disputations and counter-arguments, all this is Halakah. Upon Halakah all the regulated and orderly intelligence of the Rabbis was spent, all their logic and training. Haggadah was their relaxation and amusement; in Haggadah their fancy and imagination found its occupation. Then, too, their sermons to the congregation, their moral and religious teachings in our modern sense: the reports and records of all these are Haggadah. So, too, their prayers, though not their elaborate rules about prayer. All their vagrant and unsystematic thought and fancy about God and the relations between God and Israel, all that we read of their homiletic, imaginative, uncircumscribed and unregulated interpretation of Scripture on its non-legal side is Haggadah' (Montefiore and Loewe, 1938 edn, p. xvi).

Montefiore went on to explain why he had decided to include only Aggadah in the *Anthology*, and his collaborator Herbert Loewe, in his Introduction, while agreeing that Halachah does not lend itself to such treatment, tried to redress the imbalance by pointing out how important Halachah nevertheless is. 'Halakah', he wrote, 'is a necessary discipline for life.' Furthermore, 'Law needs accurate terminology, definite provisions. In the propounding of abstract principles, precision is uncalled for; in fixing rules of conduct there is no room for vagueness ... By-laws are not a burden; they are essential. Yet dull they certainly are. No one would take as his light reading a Memorandum on Public Health ... One cannot make an entertaining anthology out of ... Local Government By-Laws. In his choice of material, Mr. Montefiore was clearly right. Yet, in the past, history shows no such clash. Legislation and mysticism could go hand in hand' (ibid., p. xcv).

Similarly, Louis Ginzberg, the great authority on Aggadah, emphasised the importance of Halachah for a proper understanding of Judaism, and deplored the neglect of it by contemporary Jewish scholars. 'It is only in the Halakah', he wrote, 'that we find the mind and character of the Jewish people exactly and adequately expressed' (Ginzberg, 1958, p. 117). In the same vein, Rabbi Dr Louis Jacobs, when he gave the 1962 Claude Montefiore Lecture, remarked: 'It is in Halachah that you find Rabbinic thinking crystallised, not in Aggadah. I am quite sure that anyone who takes the trouble – and people ought to take the trouble – of going through the *Rabbinic Anthology* will have a very good idea of what many Rabbis have said. But if you wish to arrive at something like a consensus of opinion of Rabbinic thought, you go to the Halachah, not to the Aggadah' (Jacobs, 1962, p. 22).

But let the last word go once more to Bialik. 'Halachah and Aggadah', he wrote, 'are in reality two aspects of one thing ... The Halachah is the crystallisation, the necessary end-product of the Aggadah; the Aggadah is Halachah re-liquified ... As a dream yearns for its interpretation, the will to become deed, the thought to become word, the blossom to become a fruit – so Aggadah finds fulfilment in Halachah. Yet within the fruit there is already hidden the kernel from which a new flower is destined to grow ... So, too, a living and healthy Halachah is a former or future Aggadah, and *vice versa* ... The Halachah is therefore no less creative than the Aggadah. Its art is the greatest art of all: the art of living, and of the ways of life; its material is the living human being with all his passions; its methods, individual, social and national education; and its creation, an uninterrupted succession of days of living and of noble deeds ... The

Halachah, I say, is nothing but the sequel, the סיפא דקרא ['end of the verse'] of the Aggadah. גדולה אגדה שמביאה לידי הלכה, Great is the Aggadah, for it leads to Halachah … When Halachah and Aggadah, the two of them, go together, that is evidence of a nation's health and a testimonial to its maturity; and wherever you find a widowed Aggadah, there you may be sure that the people's will to action and means of action have become enfeebled, and are in need of healing' (Bialik, 1951, pp. 207a–b, 212b–213a).

Chapter 4

❖   ❖   ❖

THE NEED FOR A NEW APPROACH TO HALACHAH

The Most Important Question

Progressive Judaism has many great achievements to its credit. But it also has its weaknesses, and its gravest weakness is that, after one hundred and fifty years, it has still not achieved a satisfactory relationship with the Halachah.

It was the Pharisaic Rabbis who set themselves the gargantuan task of working out in every possible detail, and for every conceivable situation, what it means to do God's will. The Halachah is the answer of Pharisaic Judaism to the question, 'What does the Eternal One your God require of you?' (Deut. 10:12).

Surely that is the most important of all questions, and the attempt to answer it has stamped upon Judaism certain characteristics which we rightly applaud. First, its *practicality*, its foremost concern with deed rather than creed. Secondly, its *comprehensiveness*, its determination that all aspects of life, not just some of them, shall be guided and sanctified by religion. Thirdly, its *specificity*, the fact that it does not content itself with general exhortations, but goes into detail.

Finally, its *intellectuality*, for to evolve and constantly bring up to date such a system requires an enormous expenditure of mental effort. As Rabbi Dr Solomon Freehof never wearied of stressing, 'the real intellectuality of our people, their real brilliance, their full sounding of the depths of the human ability to think and to reason, is in the halacha. It is not an exaggeration to say that never in the story of mankind's intellectual effort has so large a proportion of one people produced so brilliant a succession of intellectual works' (Freehof, 1961, p. 9).

Any modern Judaism which ignores the Halachah therefore exposes itself to the danger of losing in some measure these precious characteristics – practicality, comprehensiveness, specificity and intellectuality; and it can hardly be denied that Progressive Judaism illustrates the point.

That is particularly true of the extremist tendency in nineteenth-century Progressive Judaism in Germany represented by the maverick Rabbi Samuel Holdheim, who declared that the entire Halachah had ceased to be authoritative.

The trouble, however, is that, as Progressives, we cannot accept the Halachah either – at least not in anything like its entirety. But if that is so: if we cannot wholly accept it and ought not wholly to reject it, then our attitude towards it must be an intermediate one between those extremes. We need some kind of a *via media*. The question is how to conceive and formulate it. It is a question to which Progressive Judaism has produced, as yet, no satisfactory answer.

'Biblical v. Rabbinic', 'Moral v. Ritual'

Attempts have, of course, been made to produce an answer. One attempted solution was to grant validity to Biblical law but not to Rabbinic law. This neo-Karaitic tendency manifested itself, vaguely, in nineteenth-century Germany and the United States and, more explicitly, in the David Woolf Marks days of the West London Synagogue. It was an unsatisfactory solution for several reasons.

First, the distinction between Biblical law and Rabbinic law is not so easy to draw. For the Halachah consists of several distinct strata. First, there is the Pentateuchal legislation. Secondly, there are the הלכות למשה מסיני ('laws of Moses from Sinai'), laws allegedly handed down by word of mouth, independently of Scripture, ever since Sinai. These two classes together comprise what the Rabbis call מדאורייתא ('from the Torah'), with the possible addition of a third and extremely large class, namely those laws which were derived from Scripture by המדות שהתורה נדרשת בהן ('the rules by which the Torah is expounded'), the rules of hermeneutic interpretation. Whether these should be considered מדאורייתא ('from the Torah', i.e., Sinaitic) or מדרבנן ('from the Rabbis', i.e., post-Sinaitic) is in doubt, a doubt probably reflected in the dispute between Rabbi Eleazar and Rabbi Jonathan as to whether the Torah is predominantly written or oral – רוב על-פה ומעוט בכתב or רוב בכתב ומעוט על-פה (Git. 60b).

In addition, there are all the גזרות and תקנות (preventive and ameliorative decrees) including some, like the institution of Purim, which, though recorded in the Bible, are obviously post-Sinaitic, as well as the innumerable law-court decisions (פסקי דין) and customs (מנהגים), all of which are of course מדרבנן ('Rabbinic', i.e., post-Sinaitic). But where exactly did the neo-Karaitic Reformers intend to draw the line? They never made that clear.

Secondly, it was an unsatisfactory solution because Biblical law is in many respects more primitive than Rabbinic law. The Bible, for example, gives women no rights in the matter of divorce, and ordains the death penalty for many offences, including בן סורר ומורה, the 'stubborn and rebellious son' (Deut. 21:18–21). In these and many other respects Rabbinic law is ethically more advanced than Biblical law.

Thirdly, the formula did not fit the facts. The neo-Karaitic Reformers *said* that they accepted Biblical law, but in reality they ignored many of its precepts, for instance the law of שעטנז ('mixed cloth', Lev. 19:19). Conversely, they *said* they rejected Rabbinic law, but in reality they followed it in countless respects. As Solomon B. Freehof wrote, 'The weakness of the position was primarily that the self-description of Reform as being solely Biblical was simply not true. All of Reform Jewish life in all its observances was actually post-Biblical in origin. None of the arrangements of worship, the hours of service, the text of the prayers, no matter how rewritten, was primarily Biblical. The whole of Jewish liturgy is an achievement of post-Biblical times. The religious calendar, based indeed on Scripture, was elaborated and defined in post-Biblical times. Marriage ceremonies and burial rites were all post-Biblical. The Bible, of course, was the source of ethical ideas, but the actual religious life was rabbinic' (Freehof, 1960, p. 16).

Another theory frequently found in the literature of Progressive Judaism is that the 'moral law' has authority but the 'ritual law' does not. The trouble here is, first, that this classification is far from exhaustive. It leaves out, for instance, the civil law, the matrimonial law, and the agricultural law. Secondly, ritual law has its importance. Even if we think that Rabbinic Judaism gave it exaggerated importance, the fact still remains that ritual plays a significant part in Jewish life, even Progressive Jewish life, and does involve decision-making.

The Conservative (or Traditionalist) Stance

Then there is an attitude which comes, in theory, close to accepting the Halachah. It maintains that the Halachah is in principle still valid; that we should adhere to it as closely as possible, and depart from it only in so far as modern circumstances, or the modern conscience, actually compel us to do so, and then, as far as possible, by the methods, and within the framework, of the Halachah itself. Given enough imaginativeness and liberality of interpretation, it is asserted, we can make the Halachah serve modern needs.

This theory seems to me untenable for several reasons. First, it assumes that the presuppositions underlying the traditional Halachah are valid for us. The most basic of these is תורה מן השמים, that 'the Torah is from Heaven' (San. 10:1). For the Rabbis believed implicitly and explicitly in the divine origin and authority of the Torah. They did indeed recognise that it had to be *interpreted*, and their interpretations of it were often remarkably liberal. They also claimed the right to modify Scriptural law in some respects, to build a 'fence' round it; to suspend temporarily (הוראת שעה) an individual provision which changed circumstances caused to operate to the detriment of the religion or of the people; and in some instances to legislate divergently from Biblical law by invoking the principle of הפקר בית-דין הפקר, that rabbinic courts have the power to declare property ownerless. But all these qualifications having been made, it remains true that the Rabbis believed in the inerrancy of Scripture, a belief which permeates all of Rabbinic literature.

This, however, is not our view as Progressive Jews. To us the Bible is a unique literature, produced under the impact of a unique revelational process. But it is human and history-conditioned, reflecting the social and intellectual milieu of the ancient Near East, often advancing magnificently beyond that milieu, but by no means always. Therefore many of the Biblical laws, for instance those governing the sacrificial cult, seem to us to have lost their validity, if they ever had any, long ago.

To us, the fact that a law is Biblical does not *ipso facto* make it valid. It has, in some sense, to validate itself. Therefore the question of טעמי המצוות, 'the reasons of the commandments', has for us a practical, not only an academic, importance. Rabbinic Judaism sometimes encouraged, sometimes discouraged, speculation concerning the טעמי המצוות, but it always maintained that the obligatory character of a Biblical law remained unaffected by our ability or inability to understand the reason for it. The Rabbis knew that there were seemingly irrational laws, notably those relating to אכילת חזיר (eating pork, Lev. 11:7), לבישת שעטנז (wearing mixed cloth, Lev. 19:19), חליצת יבמה (release from levirate marriage (Deut. 25:5–10), טהרת מצורע (purification of the leper, Lev. 14), שעיר המשתלח (the scapegoat, Lev. 16:6–10) and פרה אדומה (the red heifer, Num. 19). But it was precisely concerning such seemingly irrational laws that they said in God's name, אני יי חקקתים, ואין לך רשות להרהר בהם, 'I have ordained them, therefore you have no right to criticise them' (Yoma 67b) and again, הוקה חקקתי, גזרה גזרתי, אי אתה רשאי לעבר על גזרתי, 'I have ordained an ordinance and decreed a decree; you may not transgress my decree' (Num.R. 19:8).

For us, on the other hand, a Biblical law is obligatory only if its reason is discernible and can be shown to have a contemporary validity and relevance. Thus we feel under no obligation to observe the law of שעטנז (mixed cloth) because it makes no sense to us, or the law forbidding a כהן (priest) to marry a גרושה (divorcee) because, although we do understand the reason for it, it is not a reason that commends itself to us as valid or relevant.

The conservative approach to the Halachah further assumes that the Rabbinic interpretation of Biblical law is always to be affirmed. Now it is true that the Rabbis legislated as they did, not only under the constraint of the Scriptural text, which to them was sacrosanct, but also on the basis of their own ethical discretion; and in many cases their discretion does indeed commend itself to us.

For instance, they derived the principle פיקוח נפש דוחה שבת, that the saving of life overrides the Sabbath, from the word אך ('however') in the injunction אך את-שבתותי תשמרו, 'However, you shall keep My sabbaths' (Exod. 31:13; Yoma 85b). Again, they ruled that in a criminal case the junior member of the court must vote first. They obtained that principle from the phrase, ולא תענה על רב, 'You shall not testify in a lawsuit ...' (Exod. 23:2), by reading רָב ('master') instead of רִיב ('lawsuit') and so making the phrase mean 'You shall not contradict a master' (San. 36a). In cases such as these, the exegesis is quite unacceptable to the modern mind, but the principles obtained by means of it are excellent.

Nevertheless, the outlook the Rabbis brought to bear on their Scripture interpretations is by no means always sound from our point of view. For they lived in a mental world completely different from ours, and therefore held many beliefs which we would reject. For instance, they believed in the restoration of the Temple and its sacrificial cult, and in the laws of ritual purity and impurity. They classified women with slaves and minors as having, for most purposes, no legal personality. They accepted capital punishment, corporal punishment, slavery, and polygamy. These beliefs, so far removed from ours, underlie whole vast areas of Rabbinic legislation. How then can we say that we accept that legislation with only a few minor adjustments here and there?

Rigidification

Furthermore, the conservative approach overlooks or underestimates the extent to which the history of the Halachah is one of progressive rigidification. In the days of the Pharisees it still had considerable fluidity. But subsequently it became more and more rigid, and since the Shulchan Aruch (sixteenth century) it has been almost completely inflexible.

There are several reasons for this. First, it is a built-in handicap of any system that ascribes divine authority to ancient texts and traditions. Such a system can only grow 'at the edges', becoming more and more elaborate, and each elaboration reduces still further what room there is for manœuvre. Secondly, with the dissolution of the Sanhedrin, Rabbinic law ceased to have a legislature. In the words of Solomon Freehof, 'The unfortunate difficulty with Jewish law is that it has only one instrument, that of interpretation, but no longer possesses the instrument of legislation. Therefore, it can never make a new beginning with a new law ... It hops on one foot and therefore cannot walk' (Freehof, 1961, pp. 3f).

Thirdly, the Halachah has always been inhibited by its interpreters' veneration for their predecessors. The Amoraim deferred to the Tannaim, the Geonim (heads of the Babylonian academies) to the Amoraim, the Rishonim (earlier authorities) to the Geonim, and the Acharonim (later authorities) to the Rishonim. And the Acharonim of recent times have been the most timid of all. To quote Solomon Freehof again, 'The old rabbis feel that today they are beleaguered in a hostile world. If they dare be lenient and permit one thing, they will have to permit other things. So the best, the safest thing to do is always to say "no"' (ibid., p. 4).

In particular, they have been inclined to invoke the Mishnaic principle שאין בית דין יכול לבטל דברי בית דין חברו עד שיהיה גדול ממנו בחכמה ובמנין, that one court may not rescind the decision of another unless it is superior in wisdom and number (Eduyot 1:4). As Solomon Freehof has pointed out, that rule was intended to apply to *contemporary* courts, but 'Orthodoxy in recent centuries preferred, in its nervousness, to take the dictum to mean something that it was never intended to mean, namely, that no court of *any* generation can ever change the opinion of any other court, in whatever generation it lived, unless this modern court that wants to change the law can claim to be greater in number and in wisdom than the predecessor.' This 'psychology of self-deprecation', says Freehof, may show a commendable humility, 'but it did not help in adjusting Jewish law to life' (ibid., p. 5).

Not only, therefore, is the Halachah based on principles, such as the inerrancy of Scripture and the not-to-be-questioned authority of ancient traditions, which are foreign to our way of thinking, but it has been so rigid for so long that it can no longer be brought up to date without changing the 'ground rules'. The gulf is too wide. Consider, for example, that in an age which allows women to hold any office – even that of Prime Minister of Israel – the Halachah still declares women incompetent as witnesses. In this as in a number of other respects the Halachah has stood still so long that, instead of being ahead of Western civilisation, it lags behind it. To suppose, then, that, with a few minor adjustments, it can be brought up to date is surely an illusion. To quote Freehof once more, 'There is no possible stretching of the law or liberalizing of it that can enable it to roof over the realities of modern Jewish life' (Freehof, 1960, p. 13).

Need for a New Approach

What we need, therefore, is a new approach to the Halachah. This new approach cannot be one of acceptance, qualified or unqualified. Nor must it be one of rejection, qualified or unqualified. Nor again should it be a partial acceptance and a partial rejection on the basis of any artificial distinction, for instance between Biblical and Rabbinic or between moral and ritual law. We must re-examine the entire Halachah in a new spirit, respectfully yet critically, ready to learn but also prepared to differ from it.

The general character of this new approach has been well enough expressed by Solomon Freehof on many occasions; for instance: 'The law is authoritative enough to influence us, but not so completely as to control us. The rabbinic law is our guidance but not our governance ... Our concern is more with the people than with the legal system' (ibid., p. 22).

Accepting that as right in its general tenor, we need to ask ourselves whether we can spell it out in more detail.

I think we should first of all agree that the *whole* of the Halachah merits our attention: Biblical and Rabbinic, moral and ritual, matrimonial and civil. Secondly, we should approach all of it with the reverence due to a great heritage, and that our own. Therefore we should begin with the assumption that it has a certain kind of authority, and yet not a *conclusive* authority. *Presumptive* authority is the term I would suggest, by which I mean that we should approach the tradition with the expectation that we shall find what it has to say on any given subject acceptable rather than unacceptable.

But though this presumption applies to the literature as a whole, it does not necessarily apply to every section of it. If, for instance, a whole section is predicated on the belief in the restoration of the Temple sacrifices, or the importance of ritual purity, or the inferior status of women, then the presumption breaks down. Still less does it apply to every individual law. For we always need to ask two questions about it: a historical question, what the reason for it was when it was promulgated, and an evaluative question, whether that reason is both valid in itself and applicable in our time. Sometimes that will be easy, sometimes it will be difficult.

Often a law will commend itself to us with an immediate religious or ethical appeal. Thus the Bible says, אל־תּוֹנוּ אִישׁ אֶת־אָחִיו, 'You shall not wrong one another' (Lev. 25:14, 17). Splendid! Then the Talmud (BM 58b) and the Codes (e.g., Sh.Ar., Ch.M. 227–240) apply the principle to all sorts of particular situations that may arise in commercial and personal relations. Admirable!

Again, the Bible says, וְנָתַתִּי עֵשֶׂב בְּשָׂדְךָ לִבְהֶמְתֶּךָ וְאָכַלְתָּ וְשָׂבָעְתָּ, 'I will give grass in your fields for your cattle, and you shall eat and be satisfied' (Deut. 11:15). From this verse, because of its sequence, the Rabbis derived the rule that one should always feed one's animals before sitting down to one's own meal (Ber. 40a). A thoroughly praiseworthy injunction!

One more example: the Talmud tells us that a synagogue may be converted into a school (Meg. 27b), a principle reiterated in the Codes (Sh.Ar., O.Ch. 153:1). The implied idea, that study is a sacred activity, more so even than worship, is something we can readily appreciate.

Conversely, there are laws that offend our sense of justice. For instance, the Bible forbids a 'Mamzer' to 'enter the congregation of the Eternal One even after ten generations' (Deut. 23:3), which the Rabbis took to mean that a Jew born of an incestuous or adulterous union may not marry a fellow Jew who is not so tainted (Yev. 4:13). That children should be thus penalised through no fault of their own, seems to us grossly unfair, and indeed a violation of the ethical principle enunciated in the Bible itself when it says that children shall not be put to death for their parents (Deut. 24:16; cf. Ezek. 18).

Again, the Bible lays down that a Kohen (one of priestly descent) may not marry three categories of women (Lev. 21:7). We reject that law and its manifold ramifications for three good reasons. First, because we do not share the traditional hope for the restoration of a sacrificial cult performed by a hereditary priesthood. Secondly, because the division of the Jewish people into castes is undemocratic and, more specifically, contrary to the ideal of ממלכת כהנים וגוי קדוש, 'a kingdom of priests and a holy nation' (Exod. 19:6). Thirdly, because the implied slur on the categories of women forbidden to a Kohen, which include proselytes and divorcees, is unjust.

A third example is the ceremony of exemption from levirate marriage called חליצה ('taking off the shoe', Deut. 25:5–10). Here there are again three objections. First, the ceremony is ugly. Secondly, it has become meaningless, since it exempts from an 'obligation' which is no longer so considered. Thirdly, it empowers a vindictive brother-in-law, by refusing to co-operate, to prevent the widow from remarrying. Consequently this law violates the Bible's frequently reiterated concern for the protection of widows.

We have now considered two types of law: where the Halachah is plainly to be accepted, and where it is plainly to be rejected. Between them there is a third category, where the issues are not so clear-cut. There we need to apply a variety of considerations. For instance, does the law rest on an antiquated theological, ethical or scientific concept, such as an obsolete understanding of menstruation or sexuality? Again, is the subject one that really calls for legislation? For instance, do the minute rules and regulations concerning בדיקת חמץ (the searching for leaven before Passover) serve any useful purpose? Are there not areas of religious life, such as prayer, where more scope for individual choice would make for greater sincerity and spontaneity? Is it really necessary to forbid the opening of an umbrella on the Sabbath for the far-fetched reason that the action resembles that of erecting a tent, which is like building, which is one of the thirty-nine categories of forbidden acts, which the Rabbis derived from the Biblical account of the building of the משכן (the Tabernacle of the Wilderness)? In matters spiritual, are there not limits beyond which legislation becomes unnecessary and inappropriate?

A Proposal

These are some of the considerations which do, or which should, inform a Progressive approach to the traditional, Rabbinic Halachah. What they indicate is neither acceptance nor rejection but the need construct a new, post-Rabbinic, Progressive Halachah. To a considerable extent, that exists already: in Progressive Judaism's literature, especially its platforms, prayerbooks and responsa. The need now is to gather all that material, to present it as an orderly system, to clarify its premises and methods, to extend it into areas not yet covered, and to initiate an ongoing process by which it may be revised and further developed from generation to generation.

What are, or will be, the characteristics of such an evolving Progressive Halachah and, in particular, how will it differ from the Rabbinic Halachah?

1. It will re-examine the sources of the traditional Halachah reverently but not uncritically, respectfully but not subserviently. It will ascribe to them only a presumptive, never a conclusive, authority, and it will seek to understand them historically.

2. In addition to its historical understanding of the Tradition, it will tease out the valid ethical principles inherent in it, and bring into play considerations drawn from modern knowledge, thought and life.

3. It will therefore require the co-operation, not only of Halachists, but of historians and theologians, and of experts in relevant secular disciplines such as medicine, psychology, sociology, jurisprudence, etc.

4. It will lay special emphasis on *moral* law, which is the most enduringly valid and the most universally relevant. But it will also concern itself with civil law, which may guide us as we seek to make a Jewish contribution to the amelioration of society. And it will attend to ritual matters in so far as they call for legislation.

5. It will not claim finality, but its decisions will always be subject to alteration by subsequent generations in the light of their own researches, insights and judgments.

6. Wherever uniformity is not essential, for example in matters of personal and domestic observance, it will offer guidance rather than legislation.

7. Whenever there is a divergence of opinions it will record not only the majority view but the minority views as well, just as the Talmud did.

8. In all cases, it will record not only the conclusion reached, but the thought processes which led to it.

I am of course under no illusion as to the magnitude of the task involved, even though, as I have indicated, much of the groundwork has been done already. It may take generations before something clearly discernible as a Progressive Halachah, distinct from the Rabbinic one, emerges. But the attempt will do more than anything else to restore to Judaism generally its contemporary relevance, and to Progressive Judaism those qualities of practicality, comprehensiveness, specificity and intellectuality which it is in danger of losing.

The task is to take up again the most characteristically Jewish of all endeavours: to answer – in a new way, appropriate to our time, yet with the greatest possible precision – the age-old question: 'And now, O Israel, what does the Eternal One your God require of you?' And if that sounds daunting, let us be content to make a modest start, knowing that, as Rabbi Tarfon said, לא עליך המלאכה לגמור, ולא אתה בן־חורין להבטל ממנה, 'We are not required to complete the work, but neither may we free to refrain from it' (Avot 2:16).

Chapter 5

❖   ❖   ❖

RETHINKING OUR RELATIONSHIP
WITH HALACHAH

Restating the Case for a Progressive Halachah

There is a curious resistance in some quarters to the suggestion that
Progressive Judaism should establish its own Halachah, or even concern itself with Halachah at all: usually on the grounds that the modern Jew is troubled by questions of belief rather than of practice and
that in matters of practice the individual is autonomous and has no
need of legislation. This makes it necessary to restate the case for a
Progressive Halachah, beginning with first principles.

Judaism has historically concerned itself with two questions: what
individuals should believe and what they should do. It has sought to
influence both their inner state of mind and their outward behaviour.
The first enterprise is called Aggadah, the second Halachah. Of these
two, Judaism has tended to stress the second more than the first:
deed rather than creed. Its major concern has been to regulate conduct, and to do so from a particular point of view: 'What does the
Eternal One your God require of you?' (Deut. 10:12),

To pose this question is to presuppose that it is answerable, that
the will of God is knowable. That, too, has generally been affirmed, and Pharisaic-Rabbinic Judaism represents a particularly
strong form of the affirmation. The Rabbis were nothing if not
convinced that God's will is ascertainable with a high degree of
assurance, and not only in general terms but in every detail. For
they believed in תורה מן השמים, that the Torah, in both of its parts,
Written and Oral, is 'from Heaven'. On that basis they constructed
a system of Mitzvot (commandments) monumental in its comprehensiveness and precision.

The system, admittedly, is not quite as monolithic as is sometimes supposed. It does have its loose edges. There are questions which it answers only with יש אומרים ויש אומרים, 'some authorities say one thing and some say another', but that applies only to more or less peripheral matters. In the main, the system is definitive. To every conceivable question affecting human conduct it gives a clear answer in terms of the Divine Will.

Progressive Judaism cannot go along with that view. Our conception of God does not allow it; our conception of Revelation does not allow it; and our inspection of the contents of the supposedly revealed literature refutes it. God's will, we must say, is not knowable as fully, as clearly, as surely, as the Rabbis believed. But that does not mean that it is not knowable at all. It means that the task of ascertaining it is a great deal more difficult and complex than the Rabbis supposed. It involves consulting not only Scripture and Tradition, but also the relevant branches of modern knowledge, the conscience of the individual, and the consensus of the community, or of its leadership.

Moreover, none of these resources is an *infallible* guide. All we can do is to throw them together and let them interact with each other. What emerges from their interaction will fall short of certainty. All we shall be able to say about it is that, so far as we, in our fallible humanity, can judge, having considered the problem from every angle, such and such is the right course of action. Furthermore, the assurance with which we shall be able to say that will vary. In some cases it will be close to certainty, in some it will amount only to one degree or another of probability, and in still other cases we may have to heed the counsel of the Rabbi who said למד לשונך לומר איני יודע, 'Teach your tongue to say: I do not know' (Ber. 4a).

That being the situation, it may seem a hopeless task to construct a modern Halachah. But on the other hand, choices have to be made daily, both by individuals and by organisations, and it is surely desirable that those who make them should do so from the perspective, not of mere expediency or of some secular ideology, but of the question of God's will, however difficult it may be to puzzle out what that is.

Moreover, it is surely desirable that the decision-makers should take into account what the traditional Halachah has to say. For many of the questions that arise today have been considered by it; many of its answers are still valid; and even when we cannot accept a conclusion, we may still learn much from a study of the thought processes by which that conclusion was reached.

Then again, it has to be recognised that not everybody is equally well equipped to examine all the relevant data, especially not the halachic ones, embedded as they are in a literature that is inaccessible to the majority. Therefore it is right that individuals, while remaining free to make up their own minds, should, before doing so, seek guidance from those able to give it. To do so is not to relinquish personal autonomy but to exercise it in a responsible way.

Besides, it is not true that in Progressive Judaism all decisions are made by the individual. There is also the congregation, which, like any community, needs to have rules. These rules are, one hopes, democratically arrived at and always subject to amendment, but as long as they remain in force they are binding on individual members. And as the autonomy of the individual is circumscribed by the rules of the congregation to which he or she chooses to belong, so the autonomy of the congregation, in its turn, is circumscribed by the rules of the federation of congregations to which it chooses to be affiliated.

Thus decision-making, even in Progressive Judaism, cannot be avoided; and it happens at various levels: individual, congregational and communal. The question is not *whether* we have to make decisions but *how* we should make them, and, in particular, whether consideration of past decisions, as recorded in halachic literature, should play a part in the process. Those who would leave the traditional Halachah out of the reckoning seem to me, first, to show a regrettable lack of humility towards the wisdom contained in it; secondly, to overlook the considerable extent to which, as a matter of fact, it does govern our life; and thirdly, to ignore or underestimate the *communal* dimension of Judaism.

There is, after all, a Jewish people, whose strength derives in large measure from two factors: unity and continuity. Therefore, whenever our conscience does not dictate otherwise, whenever no question of right and wrong but only of style or etiquette is involved, we ought to give preference to those procedures which have been observed by the Jewish people in the past and which are capable of uniting it in the present.

In the light of these remarks, let us now consider a selection of the תרי״ג מצוות, the 613 Commandments, and ask ourselves to what extent they are relevant for us and should be affirmed by us.

Religious Mitzvot

We begin with a number of Mitzvot which concern the individual's relationship with God (בין אדם למקום) and may therefore be termed 'religious' in the narrower sense of the word. They include: לא יהיה לך אלהים אחרים, 'You shall have no other gods' (Exod.

20:3); לא תעשה לך פסל, 'You shall not make for yourself a graven image' (Exod. 20:4); לא תשא את־שם־יי אלהיך לשוא, 'You shall not swear falsely by God's name' (Exod. 20:7); ונקדשתי בתוך בני י שראל, 'I will be sanctified among the Children of Israel' (Lev. 22:32); and ואהבת את יי אלהיך, 'You shall love the Eternal One your God' (Deut. 6:7). Do we accept these Mitzvot? Surely we do.

Related to them are a number of prohibitions against practices which were thought to involve some derogation from God's sovereignty, some ascription of power to other supposed super-human beings. Examples of these are: ושם אלהים אחרים לא תזכירו, 'You shall not mention the names of other gods' (Exod. 23:13); מכשפה לא תחיה, 'You shall not allow a witch to live' (Exod. 22:17); לא תנחשו ולא תעוננו, 'You shall not practise divination or soothsaying' (Lev. 19:26); and אל־תפנו אל־האבת, 'Do not turn to ghosts' (Lev. 19:31, Deut. 18:10f). Here the position is not so clear. We certainly have misgivings about occultism in its sinister aspects, but we would urge the need to understand it rather than merely to condemn it, and we would not object to magic as a form of entertainment, whereas the issue of spiritualism is more problematic. Nevertheless, a study of the halachic discussions of these matters may well be helpful to clarify some of the issues involved.

Liturgical Mitzvot

We turn next to a number of Mitzvot which relate to worship and may therefore be designated 'liturgical'. They include a great many appertaining to the sacrifices (קרבנות). They, of course, ceased to be operative when the Temple was destroyed nearly two thousand years ago, but they still play a role in Orthodox Judaism, which maintains the hope that one day they will become operative again, and meanwhile commends their study, and makes many references to them in its liturgy. Here Progressive Judaism differs fundamentally, regarding the sacrificial cult as a past chapter of Jewish history which has no present or future relevance.

As for prayer, that is traditionally considered a Mitzvah, derived by verbal analogy (גזרה שוה) from the injunction ועבדתם את־יי אלהיכם, 'You shall worship the Eternal One your God' (Exod. 23:25), in conjunction with the phrase, ולעבדו בכל־לבבכם, 'to worship God with all your heart' (Deut. 11:13), this 'worship with the heart' (or mind) being understood to be prayer (Ta'an. 2a). Do we recommend prayer? Surely we do.

But then come all the details: how often? When? Where? How? Etc. All these matters are minutely regulated in the Rabbinic

Halachah. From our Progressive point of view all that is excessively legalistic. It makes for too much קבע (fixity) and too little כוונה (spontaneity). And yet the Pharisaic-Rabbinic prayer texts, and even the rules governing their recitation, do in fact play a large role in Progressive Judaism.

The same applies to קריאת שמע, the recitation of the Shema, derived from Deut. 6:7, ברכת המזון, Thanksgiving after Meals, derived from Deut. 8:10, the public reading of Scripture, and many other liturgical usages. The whole of the Progressive Jewish liturgy is to a large extent halachically determined as to content, form and manner.

Calendrical Mitzvot

Next, let us consider the sector of the Halachah that concerns the Sabbath and Festivals and may therefore be designated 'calendrical'. It is to be noted that the whole of our (Progressive Judaism's) sacred calendar is determined by the Rabbinic Halachah.

It is true that we do not insist on all the minutiae of Sabbath observance, and tend to give greater emphasis to the positive aspects of its observance, derived from זכור, 'Remember' (Exod. 20:8), such as Kiddush, than the negative aspects, derived from שמור, 'Keep' (Deut. 5:12), in the sense of abstention from prohibited activities. But we do try to make the seventh day of the week a day of rest and joy, holiness and peace. We even follow some of the detailed prescriptions of the Halachah, for instance, kindling the Sabbath lights first, then reciting the benediction, contrary to the general principle כל־המצוות מברך עליהן עובר לעשייתן, that the benediction should precede the action (Pes. 7b), and having two Challot (loaves of bread) on the table instead of just one. For though the technical reasons for these practices may not seem cogent to us, nevertheless we take the view that, where no question of right or wrong is at stake, we might as well follow the 'house style' of the House of Israel.

Similarly, with regard to the Festivals. It is true that we have for the most part discontinued יום טוב שני של גלויות, the Diaspora custom of observing an extra day. But we do celebrate the Festivals on their Biblically prescribed dates. We even follow the Pharisees against the Sadducees in celebrating Shavuot fifty days after the first day of Pesach, contrary to the plain sense of the relevant Scriptural phrase, ממחרת לשבת, 'on the morrow after the sabbath' (Lev. 23:15).

At the Seder table we follow the traditional 'order' in almost every detail; on Rosh Hashanah we sound the Shofar blasts according to their prescribed sequences; we build Sukkot and wave the Lulav in

compliance with the halachic specifications; we kindle the Cha-
nukkah lights from left to right. In all these and many other matters
our religious practices are largely governed by the Pharisaic-Rabbinic Halachah. We follow it, among other reasons, because when
there is no compelling reason to do otherwise, we wish to be at one
with our fellow Jews of the past and present.

Dietary Mitzvot

Progressive Judaism does not endorse the Dietary Laws *in toto*, but
leaves it to individuals to decide for themselves how far they will
go in observing them, so that the level of observance varies widely.
Nevertheless, the Dietary Laws are not *ignored* in Progressive Judaism. For one thing, the food served at its communal functions is
generally such as to cause no offence to the most observant. But pri-
vately, too, most Progressive Jews do not eat the Biblically forbidden species of animals (Lev. 11, Deut. 14), and it goes without saying
that they would not eat נבלה, an animal that has died of itself (Lev.
17:15) or טרפה, one that has been injured by a predator (Lev. 22:30),
let alone אבר מן החי, a limb torn from a living animal (Gen. 9:4, Deut.
12:23).

Above all, Progressive Judaism affirms the two essential principles involved in the matter of diet. The first is that the food we eat
should be good for us, since it is a sin to harm our health (Gen. 9:5,
Deut. 4:9, Yad, *Hilchot Rotzeach* 11:4f). That the Jewish Dietary
Laws, whatever their original purpose, have, at least in some respects, a hygienic value, is beyond doubt; but the extent to which
that is the case needs to be assessed in the light of the most up-to-
date medical knowledge.

The other essential principle is that, in so far as we do not opt for
vegetarianism, we have a duty to ensure that the animals we eat are
slaughtered in the most humane way possible. Whether the Rabbinically prescribed method of slaughter (שחיטה) satisfies that requirement
is, once again, a matter to be determined, not by traditionalist dogma,
but in the light of the best available scientific knowledge of our time.

Ecological Mitzvot

The Torah includes a number of provisions that are motivated, at
least in part, by concern for the welfare of animals. These include

שילוח הקן, the prohibition against taking a mother bird from its young (Deut. 22:6f); לא־תחרש בשור־ובחמר יחדו, against ploughing with an ox and an ass yoked together (Deut. 22:10), and לא־תחסם שור בדישו, against muzzling an ox when threshing the corn (Deut. 25:4). Similarly the Rabbis legislated, on the basis of the verse, ונתתי עשב בשדך לבהמתך ואכלת ושבעת, 'I will give grass in your field for your cattle, and you shall eat and be satisfied' (Deut. 11:15), that one should feed one's domestic animals before sitting down to one's own meal (Ber. 40a).

Do we, who are Progressive Jews, endorse these laws? Surely we do. Indeed, it is to be hoped that we go a great deal further: that we take to heart the *spirit* of these laws, and consider their implications for a whole range of contemporary problems, from vivisection to battery farming. Surely a Progressive Halachah should have a great deal to say about these issues.

But these laws for the protection of animals are only part of a still wider concern for the protection of nature, based on the principle that human beings are God's stewards, charged with the responsibility of preserving the bounty and beauty of the earth for future generations: a concern which the Halachah read out of and into the commandment בל תשחית, 'You shall not destroy' (Deut. 20:19), broadened from its immediate context, of the sparing of fruit trees when besieging a city, to apply to any wanton destruction (Maimonides, Sefer ha-Mitzvot, Prohibition 57). Here is an example of a Mitzvah which, far from being obsolete, has gained enormously in relevance in recent times.

Ethical Mitzvot

If the Halachah enjoins humanitarianism in the treatment of animals, all the more does it enjoin humanitarianism in the behaviour of men and women towards one another (בין אדם לחברו). On this ethical aspect of the Tradition, Progressive Judaism has always laid the greatest stress; in it, it has tended to see the very essence of Judaism. Halachically, it comprises two kinds of commandment: negative (מצוות לא תעשה) and positive (מצוות עשה).

The negative commandments include לא תרצח, 'You shall not murder' (Exod. 20:13); לא תגנב, 'You shall not steal' (Exod. 20:15), which the Tradition takes to mean 'You shall not kidnap'; לא תחמד, 'You shall not covet' (Exod. 20:17); לא תשא שמע שוא, 'You shall not spread a false rumour' (Exod. 23:1); לא תגנבו, 'You shall not steal' (Lev. 19:11); ולא תכחשו ולא תשקרו, 'You shall not deal deceitfully or falsely' (ibid.); לא־תעשק, 'You shall not defraud' (Lev. 19:13); ולא תגזל,

'You shall not rob' (ibid.); לא תקלל חרש ולפני עור לא תתן מכשל, 'You shall not curse the deaf or put a stumbling-bock before the blind' (Lev. 19:14); לא־תשנא את־אחיך בלבבך, 'You shall not hate your brother in your heart' (Lev. 19:17); לא־תקם ולא־תטר, 'You shall not take vengeance or bear a grudge' (Lev. 19:18); and the prohibition against insulting or humiliating a fellow human being, derived from the injunction ולא תונו איש את־עמיתו, 'You shall not wrong one another' (Lev. 25:17; BM 58b–59b).

The positive commandments enjoin ethical behaviour towards fellow human beings generally, summarised in ואהבת לרעך כמוך, 'You shall love your neighbour as yourself' (Lev. 19:18), but also expressed in specific injunctions, such as the exhortation to keep promises (ככל־היצא מפיו יעשה, Num. 30:3). With special emphasis does the Torah demand respect and kindness towards the most vulnerable members of society, such as strangers (וגר לא תונה, Exod. 22:20); widows and orphans (כל־אלמנה ויתום לא תענון, Exod. 22:21); the old (מפני שיבה תקום, Lev. 19:32); the poor (כי־פתח תפתח את־ידך לו, Deut. 15:8); and enemies (השב תשיבנו לו, Exod. 23:4). Needless to say, Progressive Judaism strongly endorses the traditional emphasis on גמילות חסדים (acts of kindness, Avot 1:2) and צדקה (charity, which is said to be 'greater than all sacrifices', Suk. 49b).

These examples, which are only a selection, will indicate sufficiently that here is an area of the Halachah which Progressive Judaism emphatically affirms.

Familial Mitzvot

Rabbinic matrimonial law is predicated on an ancient view of the subordinate status of women that cannot be reconciled with the modern emphasis on sex equality, endorsed by Progressive Judaism, and is to that extent antiquated, and in need of extensive revision, from its point of view. Nevertheless, some of its underlying principles are clearly to be endorsed.

These include its positive evaluation of marriage: 'It is not good for man to be alone ... Therefore shall a man leave his father and his mother, and cleave to his wife, and they shall be one flesh' (Gen. 2:18, 24). They include its emphasis on the importance of procreation – פרו ורבו, 'Be fruitful and multiply' (Gen. 1:28) – even though we would not wish to quantify the obligation, and would endorse responsible family planning. And they include much of what the Tradition has to say about the mutual obligations of parents and children (Exod. 20:12, Lev. 19:3, Kid. 29a–33b).

Parental obligations include circumcision (ברית מילה, Gen. 17:10–12), which Progressive Judaism maintains, and the redemption of the first-born (פדיון הבן, Exod. 13:2), which it does not. But the greatest parental obligation is the education of children, תלמוד תורה, derived from Deuteronomy 11:19, which the Rabbis declared to be as important as all the other positive commandments put together (תלמוד תורה כנגד כלם, Pe'ah 1:1). Here Progressive Judaism not only endorses the Rabbinic Halachah but vastly extends its scope by making it equally applicable to both sexes, so that mothers as well as fathers are responsible for the education of their children, and girls are included on a par with boys in the educational process, including the coming-of-age ceremonies (קבלת תורה, בת־מצוה, בר־מצוה).

Similarly, Progressive Judaism endorses the prohibition of incest and adultery (Lev. 18, Exod. 20:13) as well as the medieval decree forbidding polygamy, which, however, it carries further by declaring all bigamous marriages, on the part of either sex, void *ab initio* (לכתחלה), for so the Philadelphia Conference declared in 1869. However, Progressive Judaism does *not* go along with the special restrictions which the traditional Halachah applies in the matter of marriage to Kohanim (Lev. 21:7), Mamzerim (Deut. 23:3), and widows of childless husbands (Deut. 25:5–10).

As regards divorce, Progressive Judaism seeks in various ways to overcome the disabilities of women inherent in the Scriptural source (Deut. 24:1–4) and the legislation based on it. As regards the admission of proselytes, it follows the traditional procedures except that it does not insist on circumcision when exemption is indicated, and that there are different views in its communities as to the appropriateness of requiring ritual immersion (טבילה).

In the marriage service the traditional practices and customs are followed almost in every detail, but with the important qualification that the bride plays an active role in the ceremony, and that this is reflected in the text of the marriage certificate (כתובה).

Social Mitzvot

Under the heading of 'Social Mitzvot' we may group the whole vast corpus of Rabbinic civil and criminal law. Most of it has long ceased to be operative. Much of it is antiquated. Some of it, like its acceptance of slavery, and of capital and corporal punishment, lags behind modern ethics. And yet a good deal continues to have value, if only in terms of the general principles that motivated it, which in their turn may give us guidance as we seek to make a

Jewish contribution to the amelioration of the societies in which we live.

There is, for instance, the commercial law with its insistence on fair dealing (Lev. 25:14), true weights and measures (Lev. 19:35f), the considerate treatment of employees (Lev. 19:13) and the prohibition of usury (Exod. 22:24, Lev. 25:35ff, Deut. 23:30f) which is surely not irrelevant to the practices of modern capitalism. There is the law of inheritance, which already in Biblical times made some concessions, even though they fall short of equality, to the rights of women in this matter (Num. 27:8–11). There are the rules of law-court procedure, demanding the most scrupulous integrity on the part of judges, litigants and witnesses (Exod. 23:1–3, 6–8; San. 4:5).

Even on a subject such as capital punishment, much can be learnt from the aversion towards it, because of the sanctity of human life and the danger of false conviction, expressed in Rabbinic sources (Mak. 1:10). The whole area of medical ethics is illuminated by the Rabbinic principle that פִּקּוּחַ נֶפֶשׁ, the saving of life, overrides practically all other considerations (Shab. 132a, Yoma 85b, San. 74a). So, too, as has already been mentioned, is the hugely important area of environmental ethics by the prohibition, 'You shall not destroy' (Deut. 20:19).

Conclusion

The foregoing survey, which is far from exhaustive and yet fairly representative, has, I hope, abundantly demonstrated three things. First, that much of the Rabbinic Halachah *as a matter of fact* continues to govern or guide the life of Progressive, as of other Jews. Secondly, that a sympathetic but not uncritical study of its literature could yield many more insights than is generally appreciated of direct or indirect relevance to contemporary issues. Thirdly, that it is nevertheless impossible for Progressive Judaism to affirm the Rabbinic Halachah in its totality, or anything like its totality.

These propositions, taken together, clearly point to the need to evolve a new, alternative, Progressive Halachah, having much in common with the traditional, Pharisaic-Rabbinic Halachah, yet manifestly distinct from it, which is the chief contention of this volume.

Chapter 6

❖ ❖ ❖

TOWARDS A PROGRESSIVE HALACHAH

The presuppositions of the Rabbinic Halachah are three: that God exists; that God cares how we live; and that God's will is knowable. The first of these is a matter of common ground among religious Jews of all tendencies; the other two require closer scrutiny.

Judaism, it has often been said, seeks to regulate Jewish life in *all* its aspects, implying that *everything* we do is of concern to God. But is that really so? There are indeed מצוות עשה, positive commandments, and מצוות לא תעשה, negative commandments, which, between them, govern much of a Jew's life; but surely they nevertheless leave ample scope for freedom and multiple choice. As long as we observe the מצוות and avoid the עברות (transgressions), we may act as we please, with the implication that in this area of the מותר (permitted) it is a matter of indifference to God which of the options open to us we take.

In other words, the Halachah distinguishes, as it must, between *significant* and *insignificant* actions. Which then does it regard as significant? The short answer is: those which are the subject of legislation in the Torah. But that tells us nothing about their intrinsic character. Once that question is raised, it becomes apparent that they fall into two broad categories: moral and ritual.

Moral Mitzvot and Ritual Mitzvot

The *moral* Mitzvot are the מצוות שבין אדם לחברו, appertaining to human relations. Of course they can be further classified according to the nature of the relationship they involve: between person and person, husband and wife, parent and child, teacher and pupil, employer and employee, merchant and customer, judge and litigant, ruler and subject, and so forth. They also include the reciprocal obligations of individual and society, and of both to humanity as a whole, including future generations, namely the conservation of the environment. In this category we may also include, by way of extension, the avoidance of cruelty to animals, צער בעלי חיים.

All these areas of life are replete with opportunities to do good or evil, to act rightly or wrongly in the moral sense. Some of the obligations involved are capable of precise definition; others are דברים שאין להם שעור, unquantifiable, and therefore מסורים ללב, left to the individual conscience. Some call for action on the part of individuals, some on the part of society. There is no hard and fast distinction between moral law and civil law. Civil law is merely that part of moral law which demands, or lends itself to, governmental legislation and enforcement.

As for obligations in the area of *ritual*, they are traditionally characterised as מצוות שבין אדם למקום, appertaining to the relationship between human beings and God. But as that description implies, the word 'ritual' is insufficiently comprehensive, and 'devotional' would be better. For one thing, inward attitudes as well as outward actions are involved. For instance, in Maimonides' listing of תרי׳׳ג מצוות, the 613 commandments, seven of the first ten are: to acknowledge God's existence, to affirm God's unity, to love God, to fear God, to cleave to God, to imitate God's ways, and to sanctify God's name. For another thing, in so far as these obligations are fulfilled through overt actions, they are largely of a moral rather than a ritual nature. For example, to imitate God's ways is to be merciful, to visit the sick, and so forth. Thus the two categories, 'vertical' and 'horizontal', overlap. One of the ways – perhaps the chief way – in which we express our devotion to God is in our behaviour towards fellow men and women.

The two categories also overlap in the case of תלמוד תורה, the study of Torah. The whole of Jewish education has its halachic basis in that single one of the 613 commandments, which Maimonides lists as number 11: ללמוד תורה וללמדה, to learn Torah and to teach it. Here, too, the purpose is largely moral. It is in relation to moral duties – כבוד אב ואם וגמילות חסדים והבאת שלום בין אדם לחברו, honouring parents, acts of kindness, and making peace between person and person – that the Mishnah delivers the punch-line: ותלמוד תורה כנגד כולם, 'but the study of Torah is equal to them all' (Pe'ah 1:1). The purpose of Jewish education is, in large part, to produce lives of moral excellence.

Nevertheless, the majority of the 'Mitzvot towards God' are of a ritual kind in the accepted sense. They include private prayer, public worship, observance of the Sabbath and Festivals, and the celebration of the rites of passage. These actions, too, are traditionally considered significant, with the implication that God truly cares

whether and how we perform them. There is, according to the Rabbinic Halachah, a right and a wrong way of affixing a Mezuzah, making Havdalah, and building a Sukkah, just as there is a right and a
wrong way of behaving towards orphans, widows and strangers. But
it is obvious that in the two contexts 'right' and 'wrong' have entirely
different connotations.

It is well known to students of ethical theory that words like 'right'
and 'wrong' can be used in ethical or non-ethical senses. Thus we
speak of a 'right' and a 'wrong' way of using knife and fork, or
addressing an ambassador, or playing a musical instrument. These
uses are clearly non-ethical; they relate to etiquette, or protocol, or
efficiency, not to morality. So, too, ritual actions may be 'right' or
'wrong', but not in an ethical sense. They may be significant, but
they are of a totally different *order* of significance from moral actions.

Prophetic Distinction

The distinction between ritual and moral actions was well understood by the Prophets. The assertion, commonly made, that they
had no intention of minimising the importance of ritual, but merely
objected to its being made a *substitute* for right conduct, shows an
extraordinary imperviousness to their message. What Amos, Hosea,
Isaiah, Micah and Jeremiah said in the plainest language is that the
performance of rituals is not a way of pleasing or serving God at all,
that it simply does not feature among God's essential demands,
which are moral and nothing but moral.

Although Rabbinic Judaism is in many respects a continuation
and fulfilment of Prophetic Judaism, in this particular respect it is
not, for it makes little systematic distinction between moral and
ritual duties. It is true that it occasionally distinguishes between
מצוות חמורות, 'weighty' precepts, which are predominantly but not
exclusively of a moral kind, and מצוות קלות, 'light' precepts, which
are predominantly but not exclusively of a ritual kind. It is also
noteworthy that in the וידוי (confession) of the Day of Atonement
liturgy – and this applies both to the long version (על חטא) and to the
short one (אשמנו) – the emphasis is almost exclusively on moral
rather than ritual transgressions. Nevertheless, the Rabbis generally
discuss moral and ritual matters in the same 'tone of voice', bring to
both the same kind of seriousness. For they were essentially lawyers,
interpreting a constitution rather than evaluating its provisions.
Whatever the constitution (the Torah) contains is equally grist for
their jurisprudential mill.

On this issue our attitude, as Progressive Jews, is very different, and closer to the Prophets. Not that we wish to disparage ritual. On the contrary, we are much more conscious than the 'Classical Reformers' were of its importance as a means of cultivating our spiritual life, sanctifying our homes and strengthening our communities. But for all that, we still insist that ritual is not on the same level of importance as right conduct. It belongs to the realm of human conventions rather than divine imperatives. To us, therefore, it seems more than possible that some of the actions which the Rabbis considered significant enough to be worthy of legislation, are not so at all. It may well be, for instance, that whether we mix wool and linen, or meat and milk, is a matter of supreme indifference to the Almighty.

However that may be, it seems to me very clear that Progressive Judaism, with its emphasis on the Prophets, should concern itself primarily with the moral, and only secondarily with the ritual, aspects of the Halachah.

Is God's Will Knowable?

Let us now turn to the other presupposition of the Rabbinic Halachah: that the will of God is knowable. There are of course three possibilities: that it is knowable with certainty; that it is knowable with one degree or another of probability; and that it is not knowable at all. Of these, the first represents the view of the Rabbis.

They believed that the Divine Will could be determined with exactitude because it had been supernaturally revealed. The channels of that revelation are, first, מתן תורה, the Sinaitic theophany, and secondly, נבואה, prophecy. In both cases the recipients are deemed to be essentially passive; their human fallibility does not obtrude; they function as high-fidelity sound recorders. Therefore the record is undistorted. And that applies both to the Written and to the Oral Torah.

This whole epistemology, which is the rock-foundation of the Rabbinic Halachah, is light-years removed from modern thought. It belongs to the age of Scholasticism, which has long since ended. The modern view recognises the *human element* and the *historical circumstances* which shaped the literature on which the Rabbis relied. It insists that the Prophets, however inspired, and the Rabbis, however wise, were subject to the limitations both of their humanity and of the socio-cultural milieu of the ancient Near East in which they lived.

Consequently it is only too likely that the Rabbinic Halachah will sometimes be mistaken in what it asserts to be the Divine Will. From a Progressive point of view that applies to whole areas of the legislation regarding, for instance, sacrifices, ritual purity, the disabilities of women, and capital punishment. But let me offer two specific examples which will clinch the point.

The Torah forbids Jews to intermarry with Ammonites or Moabites, even if they convert to Judaism (Deut. 23:4). There is no mystery about the motive behind this law, which is explicitly stated: 'Because they did not meet you with bread and water on the way, when you came forth out of Egypt, and because they hired against you Balaam the son of Beor ... to curse you ... You shall not seek their peace or their prosperity all your days for ever' (ibid., vv. 5–7).

The motive is *all too human*! It is implacable vindictiveness towards an entire race on account of the alleged misdeeds of their remote ancestors. Now it is true that the Rabbis made this law inoperative in two stages: first, in order to exonerate Ruth, by confining it to *male* Ammonites and Moabites (Yev. 8:3), and secondly, by declaring that their descendants were in any case no longer identifiable (Yad. 4:4). What the Rabbis did not and could not do was to question the divinely revealed character of the law in the first place. But that is precisely what we must do if we believe in a just and righteous God; for then it is self-evident that such a law could only have emanated from a human misinterpretation of the Divine Will.

Furthermore, in the case of the textually adjacent and identically formulated law of the Mamzer (Deut. 23:3), the Rabbis made matters worse, not better. For by defining the term as referring to the offspring of incestuous or adulterous unions – in spite of strong indications that it had an entirely different meaning (Zech. 9:6; Neh. 12:23; J.Kid. 3:14; Yev. 76b) – they perpetuated the law indefinitely, outrageously unjust as it plainly is.

I have highlighted these defects (from a modern vantage-point) of the Rabbinic Halachah, not because I wish to denigrate it – on the contrary, in most respects it was far ahead of its time when first formulated, in many respects it is still unsurpassed, and I am a great admirer of it – but only to show that its perception of a perfect Torah yielding certain knowledge of God's will is unsustainable.

The *Via Media* of Progressive Judaism

If we reject the Rabbinic epistemology, does it follow that we then have no means whatsoever of ascertaining the Divine Will and must therefore abandon the halachic enterprise altogether? This all-or-nothing argument is often hurled at us by our opponents, but it is false. Indeed, it runs counter to one of the fundamental teachings of

Judaism: that human beings were created in God's image (Gen. 1:26f, 5:1). For what does this mean if not that they are capable, at least to some limited extent, of discerning between right and wrong, and hence between what is and what is not acceptable to God?

In fact, Rabbinic Judaism does sometimes acknowledge that human beings are capable of understanding the commandments, at least the משפטים ('ordinances') as distinct from the חוקות ('statutes'). There is, for instance, a Baraita which defines the former as דברים שאילו לא נכתבו, דין הוא שיכתבו, 'things such that, if they had not been written, it would have been appropriate for them to have been written' (Yoma 67b), implying that, even in the absence of revelation, human beings would have come to realise the need for them.

But if we are able to 'see for ourselves' what is right, and therefore what God requires, why do we need the Torah at all? The answer is in two parts. First: just as modern mathematicians benefit from a long mathematical tradition that elicits from their minds insights which they are unlikely, or less likely, to attain without it, but nevertheless maintain a critical attitude towards it, so we would be foolish not to draw guidance from our religious tradition, containing as it does the accumulated wisdom of our ancestors, even while reserving the right to appraise it critically.

Secondly, to reject the Rabbinic view of revelation is not to deny revelation altogether. We merely understand it differently, as an ongoing process rather than a once-for-all event: a process which did not cease after Sinai, or after Malachi, or after the destruction of the Temple. It is, rather, an interaction between God and humanity which, in varying degree, occurs, or can occur, in all lands and ages. But the degree *does* vary. There *are* in the history of revelation high moments, such as Sinai; the Prophets *were* giants of the spirit; and it *is* likely that Akiva's generation was closer to God than we are. So we stand in awe before the founders of our faith, as a modern mathematician may stand in awe before Newton; but we are not therefore obliged to switch off our critical faculty.

Consequently we are *not* compelled to accept the alternative that either God's will is knowable with certainty or it is not knowable at all. There is an intermediate view: that it is knowable with varying degrees of probability. For we have three sources of information which, though not infallible, are not useless. The first is Scripture; the second is Tradition as recorded in the literature of the Oral Torah; the third is our God-given human capacity for religious and moral discernment which we may call the Conscience.

That neither Scripture nor Tradition yields certainty has already been shown. But Conscience, too, is fallible; for there is always a danger of elevating personal prejudices or passing fashions into permanent principles. Yet we cannot dismiss the conscience as useless without denying the Jewish conception of humanity. Besides, the conscience can be trained. The more it is nurtured by the wisdom of the past, and the more it is checked against the consciences of others, the more reliable it becomes.

It is from the constant, dynamic, mutually corrective interplay of these three – Scripture, Tradition and Conscience – that correct answers to the question, what God requires of us, are most likely to emerge. These answers will always fall short of certainty. They will vary in probability from near-certain to highly problematic. Therefore they must always admit the legitimacy of conscientiously held divergent views, and they must always remain open to revision. The method, therefore, is not perfect. But there is no better method available to us. There is no escape from the human predicament of fallibility.

The unblinking acceptance of that ineluctable fact is Progressive Judaism's point of departure. The endeavour nevertheless to seek the best possible answers to the perennial question, what God requires of us, is Progressive Judaism's task.

Chapter 7

❖   ❖   ❖

Between Antinomianism
and Conservatism

Rabbinic Judaism

In the beginning God created the world in order that it should in time bring forth a species of autonomous creatures freely doing God's will. To that end God set in motion an evolutionary process which in due course produced human beings in the Divine Image, that is, with a capacity to discern between right and wrong. Then God chose one people to spearhead the process of the fulfilment of the Divine Purpose, entered into a Covenant with them, and sent them messages concerning the Divine Will. Eventually these messages became the subject of a book, and the book was canonised. That is to say, the priestly leaders taught the people to believe that it contained the actual divine messages rather than merely their ancestors' interpretations and misinterpretations of them.

When religious leadership passed to the Pharisees, they reaffirmed that myth and added to it another: that of an equally ancient and sacred oral tradition, explaining, elaborating and supplementing the book, and under the slogan of תורה מן השמים, 'The Torah is from heaven', made this twofold myth the foundation of post-Biblical Judaism.

On that foundation the Rabbis, who succeeded the Pharisees, built a superstructure of legislation phenomenal in its comprehensiveness, for it covered every aspect of life, and in its specificity, for they considered no detail too minute to merit attention.

This stupendous jurisprudential enterprise was not, indeed, the Rabbis' only activity. They also interpreted Scripture for edification; but the legal activity is what they took most seriously. To distinguish the two, they called the legal activity Halachah and the homiletical activity Aggadah.

The Rabbinic Halachah regulated Jewish personal, domestic and communal life for nearly two thousand years, until the Emancipation. Then, for most Jews, it lost its former authority: partly because the rabbinic courts no longer had the power to enforce it; partly because social pressure, having previously worked in favour of conformity to Jewish tradition, now encouraged conformity to the lifestyle of the non-Jewish environment; but most fundamentally because the very basis of Rabbinic Judaism, namely the myth of תורה מן השמים, that the Torah is 'from heaven', ceased to carry conviction.

Not, indeed, for *all* Jews. There were those, now called Orthodox, who barricaded themselves inwardly and outwardly against the encroachments of modernity. But they soon became a minority; and it was with the aim of keeping the *majority* within the Jewish fold that the Progressive movement came into being.

The Reform Movement

As with all such movements, the Reformers not only made changes but sought to justify them and to this end, paradoxically, often invoked the very tradition whose authority was now being questioned. But after some time that exercise was largely abandoned, both because its self-contradictory nature came to be perceived and because it became evident that no searching of the Rabbinic Halachah for permissiveness could justify the far-reaching reforms – such as the rejection in principle of priesthood and sacrifice, of Chalitzah and Mamzerut, and the granting of equal rights to women – that were deemed necessary.

Halachah was left to the Orthodox rabbinate, to whose jurisdiction one might make all sorts of concessions in practice, especially if one lived in a *Consistoire* or an *Einheitsgemeinde*, but it ceased to be a major concern of the Reformers. Progressive Judaism, especially in the English-speaking world, became *antinomian*. 'Halachah' and related words like 'Mitzvah' ceased to feature in its vocabulary. Instead, its expounders saw Judaism as consisting of 'beliefs' and 'practices'.

The 'beliefs' were drawn mainly from the Bible, especially the Prophets, embellished with apt quotations from the Rabbinic Aggadah. They included something called 'the Moral Law', which was, however, a philosophical rather than a legal concept. They also included social ideals, which inspired men like Rabbi David Einhorn to speak out courageously against slavery and prompted the CCAR to embark on an ambitious programme of 'social action', impressively recorded by Rabbis Albert Vorspan and Eugene Lipman in their volume *Justice and Judaism* (UAHC, 1956, revised 1959). As Eugene Lipman confessed, 'It is ... a source of pain to me that we have not used rabbinic sources ... in our social justice pronouncements' (Jacob, 1988, p. 133).

The 'practices' of Judaism were identified with 'ceremonies' or 'rituals' or 'observances', that is to say, the celebration of Sabbaths, Festivals and rites of passage in synagogue and home. Compared with the 'beliefs', they were considered of minor importance but nevertheless necessary, since every religion needs to have such 'frills'. Thus they, too, were not thought of as part of a halachic system.

The modern revival of interest in Halachah within Progressive Judaism owes much to the writings of Professor Jakob Z. Lauterbach and more to those of his disciple Rabbi Solomon B. Freehof, whose two-volume work *Reform Jewish Practice and its Rabbinic Background*, written during the Second World War, may perhaps be regarded as the watershed. But it was after the War that the shock of the Holocaust combined with the establishment of the State of Israel to bring about an intensified concern for Jewish unity and continuity and, with it, an enhanced appreciation of the significance of Halachah.

Since that time there has been a huge increase in the publication of Responsa by the CCAR Responsa Committee and especially by its former Chairman Solomon Freehof as well as his successor Rabbi Walter Jacob, who, in his contribution to *Liberal Judaism and Halakhah*, informed us that he was receiving over one hundred questions a year (Jacob, 1988, p. 93)! There has manifested itself in some of our movements, notably the RSGB, a new willingness to reinstate traditional halachic procedures in such matters as conversion. And Rabbi Moshe Zemer's numerous articles in the Israeli press have done much to show that the Halachah can be effectively invoked, not only to justify the policies of Progressive Judaism but also to give ethical guidance on burning social and political issues. (A collection of these articles was published under the title הלכה שפויה, 'A Sane Halachah', by Dvir in 1993.)

It must be said that there has also been a reaction against this renewed emphasis on Halachah, and there is certainly a wide range of opinions in Progressive Judaism as to what its relationship with the Halachah should be. In addition, there is unease in some quarters about existing divergencies of practice between different constituents of the World Union for Progressive Judaism, as highlighted by the 'patrilineality' debate.

Not surprisingly, these issues have tended to dominate the debate when international gatherings of Progressive Rabbis have taken place, usually in conjunction with World Union conferences. It was at these, especially in Jerusalem in 1976 and again in 1980, that the proposal was first discussed which ultimately led to the establishment in 1991 of the international Freehof Institute of Progressive Halakhah.

If this attempt to create a mechanism for international co-operation in the development of a Progressive Halachah is to succeed, there is an obvious need to establish a consensus as to what such a task involves and therefore to re-examine the diversity of attitudes to Halachah that exists in the Progressive Jewish world.

Antinomianism

At one extreme is the antinomianism to which I have already referred and which, though less typical of Progressive Judaism than it used to be, still exists, perhaps more commonly among lay people than among rabbis. But there is also a history of rabbinic antinomianism which stretches from Rabbi Samuel Holdheim to Rabbi Alvin Reines and his disciples.

Briefly summarised, the argument takes one or both of two forms. First, it is alleged, the Halachah has no authority for Progressive Judaism, which indeed recognises no external authority of *any* kind, since its greatest virtue and chief if not sole defining characteristic is its radical acceptance of individual autonomy. Secondly, it is asserted, the paramount need of the נבוכי הזמן, the 'perplexed of our time', is to rediscover God, and that is a matter of theology, or of spirituality, not of Halachah, which is therefore irrelevant as well as inappropriate.

The argument may sound plausible, but its implications, if they were taken seriously, would be disastrous. For to reject Halachah would be to reject one of Judaism's greatest assets. It is Halachah which has kept us mindful of the need to translate the theory of our faith into practice, and to apply it to all aspects of life. It is Halachah (though not only Halachah) which has preserved the unity of our people through a tempestuous history. And it is Halachah which has elicited the most strenuous intellectual exertions of our scholars for two thousand years.

To reject the Halachah would therefore be an act of unthinkable self-impoverishment, which being the case, we must go back to the antinomian argument and question its premises. Although the Halachah does not have a *decisive* authority for us, may it not have an *advisory* authority as a source of wisdom? Although the individual is indeed autonomous, do not individuals need *guidance* – from that source among others – so that they may exercise their autonomy responsibly? Does not a community, however liberal, need to have rules? And might not the very exercise of trying to puzzle out the Divine Will, with a respectful though not uncritical regard for tradition, be for many of the perplexed a means of finding their way back to God?

Conservatism

The opposite of antinomianism is fundamentalism, which demands total subservience to a tradition conceived as having divine and therefore not-to-be-questioned authority. That, however, is to be found in Judaism only in Orthodoxy; indeed it is the definition of Orthodoxy. Within the parameters of Progressive Judaism the opposite of antinomianism is, rather, *conservatism*, by which I mean those traditionalist and neo-traditionalist tendencies which resemble the stance of Conservative and Masorti Judaism, itself going back to the 'Positive-Historical School' of Rabbi Zacharias Frankel.

More specifically, I mean an attitude which rejects fundamentalism, but in muted tones; which hedges and wriggles rather than concede frankly that this, that or the other biblical commandment is not divine; which speaks of the Halachah as if it were authoritative, without need to question the intellectual assumptions or the historical circumstances that gave rise to a law; which claims that the traditional Halachah, properly understood and imaginatively interpreted, possesses all the flexibility necessary to make it serve contemporary needs, and on that basis claims to be in continuity with it.

I find that approach deeply unsatisfactory. First, because it fudges the key issue of the authority of Scripture, which needs to be faced squarely. It sounds pious to speak of Scripture as sacred; but some of its laws are so plainly human, and not even nobly human, that to hold God responsible for them, far from being pious, is a חלול השם, a 'profanation of God's name'. In this matter Rabbi Louis Jacobs has sometimes been more forthright than the neo-traditionalists in the Progressive camp. In his book *A Tree of Life*, for instance, he wrote with commendable candour: 'It can no longer be denied that there is a human element in the Bible' and that 'it contains error as well as eternal truth' (Jacobs, 1984, p. 242).

Secondly, the conservative tendency greatly overestimates the adaptability of the Rabbinic Halachah. The latter does indeed contain 'diversity, flexibility and creativity' (to quote the sub-title of *A Tree of Life*), and a great deal more than is generally realised, as Louis Jacobs demonstrates in that book. But the room for manœuvre in the traditional halachic system is nevertheless limited, and nowhere near adequate for present needs as Progressive Judaism perceives them. Solomon Freehof was surely right when he wrote: 'There is no possible stretching of the law or liberalizing of it that can enable it to roof over the realities of modern life' (Freehof, 1960, p. 13).

Furthermore, even if that were possible, it would still be inconsistent with Progressive Judaism's integrity, because it would involve pretending that the Halachah had an authority which, for non-fundamentalists, it cannot have. For all its sometimes surprising capacity for change, the Rabbinic Halachah is fairly and squarely based on the myth of תורה מן השמים, the divinity of the Torah. To quote Louis Jacobs again, 'None of the traditional Halakhists ever dared … to take issue with, for them, the basic doctrine upon which the Halakhic structure is reared, namely, the infallibility of Scripture in its rabbinic interpretation and the infallibility of the Talmudic rabbis as the sole and final arbiters of the Halakhah' (Jacobs, 1984, p. 237).

In many respects the premises of the Rabbinic Halachah are not our premises; its methods are not our methods; and the conclusions derived from those premises and by those methods are not our conclusions. Considering that whole vast areas of its contents relate to sacrifices and priesthood and ritual purity and male superiority and polygamy and Yibbum and Chalitzah and Mamzerut and corporal punishment and capital punishment – which list alone accounts for about half of the Taryag Mitzvot (613 Commandments) – for Progressive Jews to affirm such a system, subject only to a few cosmetic changes, is so bizarre that such a posture can only be assumed to be either a case of self-deception for emotional comfort or of propaganda for political advantage. Indeed, it seems to me that in the rhetoric of the neo-conservatives in Progressive Judaism the word Halachah is merely a synonym for 'tradition' and bears little resemblance to the kind of strenuous intellectual struggle to ascertain the Divine Will which I take the halachic process to be.

Rabbi Walter Jacob has written that 'no consistent philosophy of Conservative halakhah has yet emerged' (Jacob, 1988, p. 100). I would go further and say: it has not emerged because it cannot emerge, for to my mind the whole position is intellectually untenable, and there are signs that this is beginning to be recognised in conservative circles. At the 1980 Convention of the Rabbinical Assembly Rabbi Harold Kushner made the perceptive remark that 'the Conservative movement has owed itself a crisis on the issue of the authority of halakhah virtually since its inception' (*Proceedings*, p. 364). What has particularly brought the crisis to a head is the issue of women's rights. But there are other signs, too. For instance, the case for treating the children of mixed marriages alike, irrespective of whether the mother or the father is the Jewish parent, is so over-whelming that it has been adopted by the Reconstructionists and advocated by individual Rabbis within the Conservative movement, and it is surely only a matter of time before it becomes the accepted policy throughout the non-Orthodox world.

An Intermediate Position

If both antinomianism and conservatism are to be rejected, we need to adopt an intermediate position. There are two main options. One of them avoids the use of the word Halachah altogether but neverthe-less advocates a return to tradition, and speaks instead of 'Covenant' and 'Mitzvah'.

I have a great deal of sympathy with that approach, but feel un-comfortable with the centrality it gives to 'Covenant', which dimin-ishes God's universality, and its emphasis on 'Mitzvah', since that term is usually understood to refer to acts of ritual, which form only a small part (and the least important part from a Progressive point of view) of the totality of human life with which the Halachah has his-torically concerned itself. Besides, I see no good reason why we should deprive ourselves of the word Halachah. For the Pharisaic-Rabbinic Halachah is not the only one that has existed – the Karaites, for instance, had their own Halachah – or that can exist. Indeed, there already is a distinctive, Progressive Halachah, contained in hun-dreds of statements, resolutions, articles, responsa and prayerbooks.

Therefore the other option, which I have advocated for many years, is that we should come out into the open and say that we wish to continue to do, but to do more systematically, what we have in effect been doing ever since the Progressive movement first emerged in the first half of the nineteenth century, namely to evolve an alter-native, Progressive Halachah, consonant with our task as pioneers of a post-Rabbinic, post-medieval Judaism.

Chapter 8

❖   ❖   ❖

A GENUINELY PROGRESSIVE HALACHAH

Definitions

What is Halachah? It is one side of Rabbinic Judaism. What is Rabbinic Judaism? It is a particular kind of Judaism, pioneered by the Pharisees, which became normative after the destruction of the Second Temple, received its classic expression in the Mishnah, Talmud and Midrash, and its codification in the Middle Ages, and dominated Jewish life until the Emancipation.

Rabbinic Judaism has two sides: theoretical and practical. The theoretical side is called Aggadah, which means 'narrative'. It is a realm of legends and speculations in which there is virtually unrestricted freedom of thought and expression. The practical side is called Halachah, which is the Hebrew form of an Aramaic word for 'law'. Its aim is to regulate Jewish life. Therefore it demands conformity, and it does so on the highest possible authority, that of the Almighty, whose will it claims to represent.

How can it make such a claim? By virtue of its doctrine, fundamental to the system, of תורה מן השמים, that 'the Torah is from Heaven'. This means that the commandments of the Pentateuch, as well as the supplementary oral traditions assembled in such works as the Mishnah, emanate from God.

They do not always mean what at first sight they seem to mean. So they have to be *interpreted*: obscurities have to be clarified, contradictions resolved, new situations confronted. That process continues, and so there is still some fluidity along the edges of the system. But inevitably, it became more rigid from age to age, and since the Emancipation it has been 99 percent rigid.

The Rejectionist Attitude

To this heritage of Halachah, three different attitudes are to be found among Progressive Jews, of which the first is *rejectionist*. Halachah, according to this view, belongs to Orthodox Judaism: it has nothing to do with us. 'No Halachah, please: we're liberal! We live in the modern world, not the Middle Ages, and the hallmark of modernity is individual autonomy. Therefore we don't want anybody to lay down the law for us, thank you very much. There is no place for Halachah in our kind of Judaism.'

This rejectionist attitude is unacceptable for three reasons. In the first place it ignores the fact that a community without rules is a contradiction in terms. By the very fact of joining a community, we give up a portion of our individual autonomy, so that we may do things together with others according to common rules. A worshipping community, for instance, must agree where and when to worship and what liturgy to use. A community in which everybody does הישר בעיניו, what is right in their own eyes, is simply not a community at all.

Secondly, the rejectionist attitude ignores the fact that even in the most radical kind of Progressive Judaism, not only are there rules, but rules that derive from the Halachah. Therefore the rejectionist self-description of Progressive Judaism as non-halachic is simply untrue.

Thirdly, the rejectionist attitude rejects an extremely precious part of our Jewish heritage, in fact nothing less than one half of the Judaism that dominated the life of our ancestors from the first century through the eighteenth.

Whatever shortcomings the Halachah may have, the attempt which it represents to construct out of the data of Scripture, supplemented by the ancient oral traditions, a way of life monumental in its comprehensiveness and mind-boggling in the minuteness of its detail, must surely be accounted one of the greatest intellectual enterprises in the history of human civilisation. To dismiss it out of hand would be sheer vandalism.

The Traditionalist (or Conservative) Attitude

Just as total rejection of the Halachah does not really exist within the parameters of Progressive Judaism, since however much we may disown it, we are all governed by it to some extent, so the opposite attitude, of total acceptance, does not exist in Progressive Judaism either, but only in Orthodoxy. What does exist, however, is a certain kind of *traditionalism*.

According to this view, we stand within the tradition of Rabbinic Judaism and therefore of the Halachah. Why then are we not Orthodox? Because Orthodoxy, according to this view, is only *one* way of carrying on the Rabbinic tradition in the modern world, and an unnecessarily rigid one. In its heyday, so it is alleged, Rabbinic Judaism was imaginative and flexible. It adapted itself boldly to changing circumstances. That capacity for adaptation is still contained in the system, only the Orthodox, for various reasons, are afraid to make use of it. 'We, the traditionalist Progressives, mean to revive the dynamism inherent in the Halachah. We are the true heirs of the Pharisees.'

In practice this means that we follow the Halachah as far as we possibly can. Only when there is an incontrovertible religious or ethical objection do we deviate from it, and then by means which are themselves, as far as possible, in accord with the letter, or at least the spirit, of the Halachah.

All of which may sound very reasonable, but it does raise a number of problems. In the first place the Rabbinic Halachah is unequivocally based on the doctrine of *torah min ha-shamayim*, which, if Progressive Judaism means anything, is no longer credible from our point of view. And if we reject the very foundation of the Halachah, how can we say that it is authoritative for us?

Secondly, it is not only the foundation of the Halachah that is said to have divine authority, but also the methods it uses in dealing with new circumstances. Take, for instance, the 'legal fiction', the whole point of which is to change the law even while pretending that it has not been changed. How can we use such methods when there is no need to pretend since the sources are no longer sacrosanct for us?

Thirdly, just as the self-description of the rejectionists is untrue to the facts, so the self-description of the traditionalists, namely as followers of the Halachah in all but a few exceptional instances, is untrue. For the fact is that *whole vast areas* of the Halachah are rejected or ignored even by the most conservative Progressive Jews. As a rough estimate, I would say that applies to two-thirds of it. But how can you reject or ignore two-thirds of the Halachah and still claim to be a follower of it?

Fourth, the picture which the traditionalists like to paint of the dynamism that once characterised the Halachah and that is still inherent in it, is highly imaginative. It is based on a selective use of anthologies, not a serious study of the sources. For this is another characteristic of the traditionalists: that while they talk a great deal about the Halachah, very few of them take the trouble to study it.

What finally transpires, therefore, is that in the vocabulary of the traditionalists the word 'Halachah' does not generally stand for a thought-through theological position, but serves a psychological and political purpose. Psychologically, it relieves the guilt they feel about not being Orthodox. Politically, it is their way of claiming respectability, of bidding for the allegiance of the masses by reassuring them that Progressive Judaism is perfectly 'kosher' or at any rate not as 'treif' as its denigrators allege.

A Genuinely Progressive Attitude

Paradoxically, therefore, the rejectionist and traditionalist attitudes have this in common: that they both fail to take the Halachah seriously. Consequently we need to consider a third attitude, which does take it seriously: a genuinely Progressive attitude.

On this view, the task which the Pharisees took upon themselves and which their successors, the Rabbis, executed so brilliantly, namely to define the will of God for every human situation, is the most important of all human enterprises. Therefore the Rabbinic Halachah deserves our utmost admiration and demands our closest study. That having been said, however, we must go on to say that from our point of view it is flawed. It is flawed not only because recent generations of Orthodox Rabbis have lacked the courage to make such adjustments to the system as its limited flexibility allows, though that is also true. It is flawed because it is based on a premise, namely *torah min ha-shamayim*, which we know to be mistaken.

Therefore our approach to Halachah must necessarily be different from the Rabbinic one which Orthodoxy seeks to perpetuate. We do indeed begin where Orthodoxy begins, with the Biblical and Rabbinic texts. But we don't stop there. We go on to try to understand the texts *historically* and to evaluate them *ethically*, bringing to bear on the subject whatever source of knowledge may be relevant to it as well as the modern conscience.

Often our conclusions will endorse the traditional view. Sometimes they will differ from it. Always they will be offered, not dogmatically, as decrees, but humbly, as recommendations, representing the consensus of our membership, or of our leadership, as to what, in all probability, God requires of us in our time: a consensus which may well undergo change in the future as it has in the past. For the Middle Ages, with their grand illusion of certainty, are over. Precisely that is why Rabbinic Judaism has lost its credibility and why, for those to whom this applies, Progressive Judaism is needed to take its place.

That, in broad outline, is what a serious approach to Halachah, in the context of Progressive Judaism, involves: not the cavalier repudiation of the rejectionists, nor the sycophantic lip-service of the traditionalists, but a self-respecting, principled attempt to construct an alternative Halachah, responsive both to the values of the past and to the insights of the present: in short, a Progressive Halachah.

Chapter 9

❖   ❖   ❖

PRAYING WITH KAVVANAH

There is much discussion in the Halachah about something called
כַּוָּנָה in particular, whether it needs to be present in the mind of one
performing a Mitzvah, or reciting a prayer; and if so, whether the
requirement is an עִכּוּב, a *conditio sine qua non*, so that, in its absence,
the act is invalid, or whether it is merely required לְכַתְּחִלָּה, *ab initio* –
say, a *desideratum* or a counsel of perfection – so that בְּדִיעֲבַד, after the
event, the act 'counts', as it were, *faute de mieux*, even if it was performed without Kavvanah.

What then is Kavvanah? The word comes from a verbal root
which is well represented in the Bible, particularly in the *Niph'al* and
in the *Hiph'il*, and has a variety of meanings, including 'to direct', 'to
prepare' and 'to establish'. Particularly relevant for our purpose are
those occurrences in which the object or subject of the verb is the
heart (לב or לבב). Samuel, for example, appeals to the Israelites:
'Direct your hearts [הכינו לבבכם] to the Eternal One' (I Sam. 7:3).

There are many other Scriptural passages which, without necessarily using a form of the word, contributed to the idea of Kavvanah.
But the fully developed concept, which invariably employs a *Pi'el*
form of the root, is not found in the Bible. Nor does it occur in the
Dead Sea Scrolls. Probably it is a Pharisaic coinage. Claude Montefiore called it 'one of the fine religious creations of the Rabbis' (Montefiore and Loewe, 1938, p. 272).

Three more preliminary remarks are necessary. First, that the
verb is primary and the noun derived from it. Secondly, that the
object of the verb, whether explicitly stated or not, is the human
heart. Thirdly, that in Hebrew thought the heart is not chiefly the
seat of emotions (which is, rather, the function of the kidneys) but the
organ of thinking and willing, so that it is usually best translated as
'mind'. Kavvanah is consequently an orientation of the mind.

Kavvanah as Intention

Not surprisingly, therefore, one of the meanings of the word is 'intention'. The question of intention has an obvious importance in criminal cases. In Jewish criminal law, intention must be proved. There must be evidence that the defendant had been warned of the criminality of the act he was contemplating. Such a warning (התראה) is considered, theoretically at least, a precondition of conviction in a criminal case (San. 8b).

The important question for our purpose, though, is not whether intention is necessary to establish that a transgression has been committed, but whether it is necessary to establish that an obligation has been fulfilled. About that, there is a divergence of opinion. On the one hand the Mishnah cites a number of examples of laws which imply that the answer is yes. For instance, if a person overhears the blowing of the Shofar without realising that it is Rosh Hashanah, the rule is: אם כיון לבו יצא ואם לאו לא יצא, 'If he had the intention [of fulfilling the obligation of hearing the sound of the Shofar] then it counts; if not, it does not count' (RH 3:7). On the other hand we have the statement of Rava: לצאת לא בעי כוונה, לעבור בעי כוונה, that the fulfilment of an obligation does not depend on intention, but that the commission of a transgression does (RH 28b).

The conflict continued in post-Talmudic times. Joseph Caro, for instance, remarks: י״א שאין מצוות צריכות כוונה, וי״א שצריכות כוונה לצאת בעשיית אותה מצוה, וכן הלכה, 'Some authorities maintain that the Mitzvot do not require intention, and some maintain that they do, in order that the obligation in question may be fulfilled; and the latter is the correct view' (Sh.Ar., O.Ch. 60:4). But Abraham Gumbiner (Magen Avraham, Note 3) qualifies that by citing the Radbaz (Rabbi David ben Zimra) to the effect that it applies only to the Mitzvot of the Torah (מדאורייתא), not to those ordained by the Rabbis (מדרבנן).

Kavvanah as Attention: the Shema

Let us now turn to a particular Mitzvah: that of reciting the Shema. The Rabbis, on the basis of Deut. 6:6f, considered this an ordinance of the Torah (Ber. 2a). It follows, therefore, that intention is required. And, indeed, the Mishnah makes that point. It raises the question: if a man happens to be reading the Torah, including the Shema passages, at a time when it is incumbent on him to recite the Shema, has he fulfilled that obligation? And it answers, exactly as in the case of the Shofar: אם כיון לבו יצא, ואם לאו לא יצא, 'If he had the intention, yes; otherwise, no' (Ber. 2:1).

The Gemara, as a matter of fact, generalises from this very case and pronounces: ש"מ מצוות צריכות כוונה, 'From this you may infer that the Mitzvot require intention' (Ber. 13a). But then it goes on to ask: what does the Mishnah mean when it says 'if he had the intention'? Could it not mean simply that he intended to read Scripture? That may seem a silly question, for why would a man read Scripture unless he intended to do so? However, he might be proofreading – checking the correctness of the words without paying attention to their meaning. And so the possibility arises that in this context Kavvanah does not mean intention but attention: not the intention to fulfil a particular Mitzvah but attention to the sense of what is being read (ibid.).

Precisely that is what the word Kavvanah commonly means when the Mitzvah under discussion is one which involves not so much a physical act as the recitation of words. For what is a word? From one point of view it is only a blotch of ink which the eye sees or a sound which the ear hears. But if it is *only* that, it is not really a word. For a word is a symbol. It is of the essence of a word that it conveys meaning, and this presupposes a mind which comprehends the meaning. Therefore a recitation of words without attention to their sense is merely a series of meaningless noises.

In the case of the Shema, this general point is reinforced by the text itself, for it says: 'These words which I command you this day shall be *upon your heart.*' Accordingly, Rabbi Meir comments: אחר כוונת הלב הן הן הדברים, 'It is upon the attention of the mind that the recitation of the words depends' (Meg. 20a).

Nevertheless, the Rabbis were realistic. They knew that to attend to the sense requires a mental effort which it is difficult to sustain uninterruptedly for any great length of time. Therefore they limited the requirement. Thus the Tosefta, after laying down the general rule, הקורא את שמע צריך שיכוין את לבו, that one who recites the Shema must do so with an attentive mind, goes on to cite the opinion of Rabbi Judah ben El'ai that this is strictly necessary only in regard to the first paragraph (Tos. Ber. 2:2).

Even more lenient is the view of Rabbi Meir who held that only the first verse needs to be recited with כוונת הלב, mental attention, as an indispensable requirement (Ber. 13b). This view was subsequently codified. Thus Maimonides says: הקורא את שמע ולא כיון לבו בפסוק ראשון שהוא שמע ישראל לא יצא ידי חובתו, 'One who recites the Shema without concentrating on the meaning of the first verse, which is "Hear, O Israel ...", has not fulfilled his obligation' (Yad, Hilchot Keri'at

Shema 2:1). The same rule is found in the Shulchan Aruch (O.Ch. 60:5) which adds that it is conceded even by those who maintain that in general the Mitzvot do not require Kavvanah (O.Ch. 63:4).

Perhaps the reader should be reminded here that the question is, what are the *minimum* requirements that constitute a fulfilment of the Mitzvah. That it is desirable in principle (לכתחלה) that the *whole* of the Shema should be recited with mental attention, goes without saying.

Kavvanah as Attention: The Tefillah

Unlike the twice-daily recitation of the Shema, the three-times-daily recitation of the Tefillah (תפלה, 'prayer') – also known as עמידה, 'standing', and שמונה עשרה [ברכות], 'Eighteen [Benedictions]' – is not considered an ordinance of the Torah, but an enactment of the 'Men of the Great Assembly' (Ber. 33a). Therefore, if we accept the opinion of the Radbaz, quoted above, the principle that the Mitzvot require Kavvanah does not necessarily apply to it.

Nevertheless the Halachah does demand it, and not only *ab initio*, for the general reason, which applies to all liturgical recitations, that without Kavvanah they are meaningless noises. For the requirement is reinforced by the derivation of the duty to pray from two Torah verses: ועבדתם את־יי אלהיכם, 'You shall serve the Eternal One your God' (Exod. 23:25), and ולעבדו בכל־לבבכם, 'and to serve God with all your heart' (Deut. 11:13). From these phrases, taken in conjunction, the Rabbis inferred that God requires 'the service of the heart', which is prayer (Ta'an. 2a). In other words, the very concept of prayer, as the Rabbis understood it, has a built-in reference to the need for the involvement of the mind.

Two other verses were adduced by the Rabbis as supporting evidence. One comes from the First Book of Samuel, where we are told that Hannah, when she prayed for a child, מדברת על לבה, 'spoke in her heart' (1:13). On this verse Rav Hamnuna commented: מכאן למתפלל צריך שיכוין לבו, 'From here we learn that one who prays must do so with Kavvanah' (Ber. 31a). The same principle was deduced from the Psalm verse, תכין לבם תקשיב אזנך, 'You will direct their heart, You will cause Your ear to attend' (10:17), which the Tanna Abba Shaul interpreted to mean that only when a prayer is recited with Kavvanah does God attend to it (Tos. Ber. 3:6; Ber. 31a).

Maimonides clinches the matter by declaring: כל תפלה שאינה בכוונה אינה תפלה, 'Any prayer recited without Kavvanah is not a prayer at all' (Yad, Hilchot Tefillah 4:5).

However, as with the Shema, so with the Tefillah, the Rabbis recognised that to expect uninterrupted concentration from beginning to end would be a counsel of perfection. Accordingly they ruled that as long as the worshipper maintained full concentration during the first benediction of the Tefillah, known as Avot ('Ancestors'), the obligation is deemed to have been fulfilled (Ber. 34b; Yad, Hilchot Tefillah 10:1; Sh.Ar., O.Ch. 101:1).

Kavvanah as Comprehension

Obviously, the attention which Kavvanah requires is not merely to the *sound* of the words, or to their *appearance* on the printed page, but to their *meaning*. Therefore Kavvanah involves comprehension, and from this it would seem to follow that prayers must be recited in a language which the worshipper understands.

Such an inference was in fact drawn by the Halachah; but since that subject will be more fully discussed in the next chapter, it is mentioned here only so that our survey of the various meanings of the word Kavvanah may not be left incomplete.

Kavvanah as Affirmation

In addition to attention to the meaning of the words being recited, which requires comprehension, is it not also essential that the worshipper should *believe* what the words say? One would certainly have thought so; but there is very little discussion of the matter in the classical halachic sources, no doubt because such belief was generally taken for granted. That individuals might dissent from the theology of the liturgy is a modern problem which has few antecedents, unless we go back to a very early period, when Pharisees and Sadducees disputed the reference to תחיית המתים, the resurrection of the dead, in the second benediction of the Tefillah.

It is, however, stated in the Shulchan Aruch that on hearing a benediction recited one should respond 'Amen', and that one should do so with Kavvanah, saying to oneself, אמת היא הברכה שבירך המברך ואני מאמין בזה, 'True is the benediction which the precentor has recited, and I believe in it' (O.Ch. 124:6), which Abraham Gumbiner, in the name of Joel Sirkes, qualifies by adding that, while it applies to a benediction of the thanksgiving kind, in the case of a petitionary benediction, what one should rather say to oneself is: אמת היא ואני מתפלל שיאמנו דבריו, 'It is true, and I pray that his words will come true', while in a messianic prayer such as the Kaddish, one should pray that the hope expressed in it will come true in the eschatological future (Magen Avraham, O.Ch. 124:6, note 10). In other words, Kavvanah requires that the worshipper should mentally subscribe both to the affirmations and to the aspirations expressed in the liturgy.

But what if one does not? What if, in all conscientiousness, one cannot bring oneself to believe, for instance, in the existence of angels or in the rebuilding of the Temple? This problem, so far as I know, has never been seriously considered by exponents of the Rabbinic Halachah, presumably because they had too little contact, or too little sympathy, with such 'conscientious objectors', or because they preferred not to acknowledge their existence.

It was the Reformers who felt obliged to tackle the problem, and they did so by omitting or amending those passages in the traditional liturgy whose doctrinal content they personally found unacceptable and which they believed the congregations for which they intended their prayerbooks would find unacceptable.

Kavvanah as Reverence

The combination of attention, comprehension and affirmation, which Kavvanah connotes, is particularly stressed in regard to the name of God. Thus Jacob ben Asher writes: 'In reciting benedictions one should concentrate [ויכוין] on the meaning of the words one utters, so that, when one refers to God as *Adonai* one should ponder that God is the Sovereign [*Adon*] of the universe; when the divine name is written *Yah* [from the verb *hayah*, 'to be'] one should ponder that God was, is and will be; and when one reads the word *Elohim* one should ponder that God is strong and mighty, and the source of all power in heaven and earth' (Tur, O.Ch. 5).

This passage leads us to yet another nuance of the word Kavvanah. It connotes the proper mental attitude not only to the prayers, but also to the One to whom they are addressed. Thus Rav Abraham Kook, in his commentary on the prayerbook, points out: 'There is a particular Kavvanah, namely mental concentration on the words and concepts, and there is a more general Kavvanah, which is the focusing of the mind on the greatness of God' (Jacobson, 1968, Vol. I, p. 52).

For an early instance of the verb כון in this sense we may refer to the anonymous Baraita which says that a blind man or one who cannot tell the cardinal points, and who is therefore unable to direct himself bodily towards Jerusalem in prayer, as the law requires, should direct himself inwardly towards God (Ber. 30a). Of broader import is the saying of Ishmael ben Yosé that in praying one should lower one's eyes but lift up one's heart (Yev. 105b; Sh.Ar., O.Ch. 95:2). Relevant also is the story of the death-bed counsel of Rabbi Eliezer ben Hyrcanus to his disciples, which has inspired many inscriptions on synagogue arks: וכשאתם מתפללם דעו לפני מי אתם עומדים, 'When you pray, know before whom you are standing' (Ber. 28b).

Similarly, Maimonides asks, 'How is Kavvanah to be achieved?' and answers: 'The worshippers must empty their minds of all other thoughts and regard themselves as if they were standing before the very Presence of God' (Yad, Hilchot Tefillah 4:16). In the same vein, and more elaborate, is the following passage in the Shulchan Aruch, based on earlier sources: 'The worshippers should think of the Divine Presence as confronting them. They should therefore banish all distracting thoughts, until they have achieved complete purity of mind and motive. They should consider that since, if they were speaking to a human king, they would choose their words carefully and pronounce them with sincere feeling, how much more must they do so when addressing the supreme King of kings, the Holy One, ever to be praised, who searches the human mind. Accordingly, the faithful and saintly ones used to pray in solitude and concentrate until they became oblivious of the material world and attained a spiritual strength approximating to the condition of prophecy' (O.Ch. 98:1, 3).

The Practice of Kavvanah

In the course of the ages, while the ideal of Kavvanah has been maintained and even refined, the insistence on it as an indispensable requirement and a realistic expectation has tended to diminish. And this diminution, in turn, has been part of a general shift from greater spontaneity towards greater fixity.

In ancient times, for instance, the wording of the prayers was not rigidly determined but could be varied by the precentor or worshipper. Thus Rabbi Simeon ben Nathanel could say: 'When you pray, אל תעש תפלתך קבע, do not make your prayer something fixed' (Avot 2:13). Similarly Rabbi Eliezer ben Hyrcanus: העושה תפלתו קבע אין תפלתו תחנונים, 'If one makes one's prayer something fixed, it is not a true supplication' (Ber. 4:4). The Gemara asks what the Mishnah means, and cites an opinion that it refers to כל שאינו יכול לחדש בה דבר, 'anyone who is incapable of introducing

anything new into it' (Ber. 29b), on which Rashi comments: כהיום
כן אתמול כן מחר, that such a person's prayer is 'the same today, yes-
terday and tomorrow'.

The Decline of Kavvanah

Gradually, however, the liturgy became textually fixed, and even the
few slots originally intended for personal petition of a spontaneous
kind, such as the Tachanun ('supplication') slot at the end of the
Tefillah, were filled with standard formulations. (See the chapter
'Spontaneity and Tradition' in Petuchowski, 1972.)

As a result, the authorities became gradually less insistent on
Kavvanah. Thus the Mishnah exempts a newly married bridegroom from reciting the Shema on the ground that he may not be
able to give it his full attention (Ber. 2:5), but the Tosafot rescind the
exemption on the ground that 'we don't recite the Shema with great
Kavvanah at other times' and therefore the bridegroom, by not
reciting it, might appear to be boastfully implying that he was more
pious than other people (Tos. Ber. 17b). Similarly, Jacob ben Asher,
after recording the earlier law that one who has recited the first
benediction of the Tefillah without Kavvanah must say it over again,
adds: 'But nowadays we don't repeat it on that account, for the
chances are that even the second time it will be recited without
Kavvanah; therefore what is the point of repeating it?' (Tur, O.Ch.
101). Likewise, Joseph Caro faithfully records the older law that one
should not pray in a place or at a time unconducive to Kavvanah,
but then annuls it by saying: 'But nowadays we don't bother about
such things', מפני שאין אנו מכוונים כ'כ בתפלה, 'because we don't pray with
that much Kavvanah anyhow' (Sh.Ar., O.Ch. 98:2).

Though there is much emphasis on Kavvanah in medieval Jewish
literature, it becomes increasingly an ideal whose non-attainment is
wistfully regretted, and it is stressed more in pietistic than in halachic
writings. The more pious did indeed remember the example of the
ancient Chasidim, of meditating for one hour before praying, but
even that was redefined as שעה מועטת, 'a brief period' (Magen Avraham, Note 1, to Sh.Ar., O.Ch. 93). They might also practise the various aids to the attainment of Kavvanah which the halachic literature
recommends, such as raising the voice (Sh.Ar., O.Ch. 61:4; 101:2),
placing the hands over the eyes to avoid distraction (ibid., 61:5) and
bowing at various points (ibid., 113). But the general impression one
gets is one of greater emphasis on the correct performance of overt
acts rather than the devoutness of the accompanying state of mind.

The Renewal of Kavvanah

However, in two widely separated sectors of the Jewish world, significant attempts have been made to revive the former emphasis on Kavvanah. First, in kabbalistic circles, especially from the time of Isaac Luria (sixteenth century), and in Chasidism (beginning in the eighteenth century), with its elevation of prayer to the status of a cosmic force and its stress on spiritual ecstasy, aided by rapturous singing and dancing. It should be noted, however, that in the Lurianic tradition the word Kavvanah is given a new meaning, in that the worshipper is no longer required to concentrate on the plain sense of the prayers, but rather on esoteric, theosophical ideas, themselves called Kavvanot, which are only remotely connected with the liturgical texts.

At the other end of the spectrum, Progressive Judaism has sought to revive Kavvanah by quite other means: shorter services, so that the prayers can be recited sufficiently slowly for the mind to keep up with the lips, in accordance with the principle, טוב מעט תחנונים בכוונה מהרבות בלא כוונה, that 'fewer supplications with Kavvanah are better than many without Kavvanah' (Tur, O.Ch. 1); by employing the vernacular, along with Hebrew, so that what is said may be understood; by revising the doctrinal content of the liturgy, so that what is said may be believed; and by introducing instrumental and choral music, so as to create a reverential atmosphere.

How far these reforms have succeeded is, of course, another matter. It is certainly just as possible to pray without Kavvanah in a Progressive synagogue as in any other. But it can hardly be doubted that some people, some of the time, have been helped by the reforms to attain a high degree of Kavvanah.

Kavvanah as a Way of Life

Finally, Kavvanah is not only a way of prayer but also a way of life. It is the way of life of those who recognise that God demands, first and foremost, sincere dedication. As God said to Samuel, 'Human beings look at the outward appearance, but the Eternal One looks into the heart' (I Sam. 16:7), on which the Rabbis commented: הקדוש ברוך הוא ליבא בעי, that 'the Holy One, ever to be praised, demands the heart' (San. 106b). As the Rabbis were fond of saying, 'It matters not whether one does much or little, ובלבד שיכוין לבו לשמים, provided that one directs one's heart to Heaven' (Men. 13:11; Ber. 5b, 17a).

It is the way of life of those who are always conscious of God's presence and God's demands, so that every action of their waking life is dedicated to God's service.

At the very beginning of the Shulchan Aruch, Moses Isserles, basing himself on the Tur, quotes from the Psalm: שויתי יי לנגדי תמיד, 'I have set the Eternal One always before me' (16:8) and adds: הוא כלל גדול בתורה, 'This is a major principle of the Torah' (O.Ch. 1:1).

Chapter 10

❖   ❖   ❖

THE LANGUAGE OF PRAYER

In Ancient Times

'Take with you words, and return to the Eternal One; say to God: Forgive all iniquity, and accept that which is good; so we will render instead of bullocks the offering of our lips.' That Hosea verse (14:3) is a remarkable prevision of the revolution in the history of Jewish worship which occurred with the emergence of the Synagogue: the change, that is, from sacrifice to prayer, from gesture to speech, from priestly magic to a democratic and rational form of worship – 'rational' because the 'service of the heart' (Ta'an. 2a) is the exercise of the mind in the worship of God.

The vastly increased emphasis on *language* which this revolution entailed made it inevitable that, once Aramaic became the people's vernacular, the question should be raised whether it was permissible to pray in that tongue instead of Hebrew. For two reasons, one might expect the answer to be 'no'. The first is that Hebrew and Aramaic are closely related languages, so that the use of Hebrew by Aramaic-speaking Jews would involve no enormous problem of comprehension. In spite of that, the Mishnah informs us that in the ancient synagogues the public Scripture readings were regularly translated into Aramaic by an interpreter – one verse at a time in the case of the Torah, three verses at a time in the case of the Haftarah (Meg. 4:4). So anxious were the Rabbis that the Scripture readings should be fully, and not merely vaguely, understood by the people.

The other and more important reason why one might expect Hebrew to have been regarded as the only acceptable language for prayer is that it was, after all, לשון הקדש, the 'Holy Tongue'. That is not an expression we use much nowadays, but to the Rabbis it was very real. Hebrew, they seriously believed, was the language in which God had spoken to Moses and the children of Israel at Mount Sinai (Ber. 13a). And not only was it the language of *Revelation*; it was also the language of *Creation*, in which God had commanded the world to come into being, and which had been spoken by the original human inhabitants of the earth, before the confusion of their tongues at the Tower of Babel (Gen.R. 18:4; Tanchuma 58:19). It was the language in which the angels conversed with one another and daily sang God's praise. Indeed, according to Rabbi Yochanan they pay no attention to personal prayers offered in Aramaic (Shab. 12b)! That, admittedly, may be a reflection of a prejudice against Aramaic not unlike the disdain sometimes expressed, in modern times, by German Jews for Yiddish. Of Judah ha-Nasi it is said that he allowed only Hebrew and Greek, not Aramaic, to be spoken in his household (Sot. 49b; Meg. 18a).

Given the enormous veneration of the Rabbis for the 'Holy Tongue', one would hardly have expected them to countenance the use of any other language in the sacred act of prayer. But the evidence is otherwise.

The earliest passage dealing with the question, which occurs in the Mishnah, states categorically that the Shema, the Tefillah and Birkat ha-Mazon may be recited בכל לשון, 'in any language' (Sot. 7:1), and the context makes clear what motivated the Rabbis: they considered it essential that these prayers should be fully understood by those who recited them.

Similarly, we have in the Talmud a Baraita which tells us that Judah ha-Nasi, whom we have already encountered as a purist, was in a minority of one in wishing to insist that the Shema must be recited in Hebrew; his colleagues argued that, on the contrary, the very word שמע, 'Hear', implies that those who recite it must understand what they are saying (Ber. 13a; Sot. 32b).

The sole exception, so far as liturgy is concerned, is the Priestly Benediction, which, according to the Rabbis, must be recited in Hebrew because of the emphatic way in which the Bible says כה תברכו את־בני ישראל, '*Thus* shall you bless the children of Israel" (Num. 6:23; Sifrei Num. to Num. 6:23)

The Gemara endorses the permissiveness of the Mishnah, and makes some additional points. It asks, for instance, *why* the Tefillah may be recited in any language, and answers רחמי היא, that it is a plea for God's mercy (Sot. 33a), the implication being that such a plea makes no sense unless those who utter it understand what they are saying.

In Post-Talmudic Times

Judah he-Chasid ('the Pious', c.1150–1217), explains the point more fully in his Sefer Chasidim: 'Prayer takes place only when the mind understands, and if the mind does not know what proceeds from the lips, what good is that to the worshipper? Therefore it is better that [those who don't know Hebrew] should pray in a language they understand' (§ 588). And in another passage (§ 785) he quotes to the same effect an Isaiah verse which condemns those who honour God with their mouth and with their lips, while their minds are far away, and whose reverence for God is merely 'a commandment of human beings learnt by rote' (Isa. 29:13).

Maimonides (1135–1204), reiterates in his Mishneh Torah that the Shema may be recited in the vernacular but adds that, if so recited, it must be articulated no less meticulously than when it is recited in Hebrew (Hilchot Keri'at Shema, 2:10). He also makes the general point that prayer without Kavvanah (attention to the meaning) is not prayer at all (Hilchot Tefillah, 4:15).

Jacob ben Asher (1283–1340), the author of the Arba'ah Turim, agrees with the earlier sources that the Tefillah may be recited in any language, at least when one prays with the congregation. He does indeed mention two qualifications: that individuals, when praying on their own or, according to another view, when praying for their personal needs, should pray in Hebrew because individuals, unlike congregations, depend on the angels to transmit their prayers to God. But in the end he seems to endorse the view of his father, Asher ben Yechiel (c.1250–1327), who dismisses both these qualifications and advises only that Aramaic, because of the angels' proverbial aversion to it, should be avoided (O.Ch. 101).

Joseph Caro (1488–1575), the author of the Shulchan Aruch, repeats all the permissive rulings we have noted, with reference to the Shema (O.Ch. 62:2), the Tefillah (101:4) and Birkat ha-Mazon (185:1). And Abraham Gumbiner (1637–1683), author of the authoritative commentary Magen Avraham, adds that the same permissiveness applies, even without the usual proviso that the worshipper understands the non-Hebrew language being used, to Kiddush and Hallel as well as the short blessings traditionally recited before eating or drinking and before performing a Mitzvah (O.Ch. 62, §1).

Let me adduce one more witness, who will bring us to the beginning of the nineteenth century. Shneur Zalman of Lyady (1745–1812), the founder of Chabad, subsequently to become known as the Lubavitcher movement of Chasidism, wrote a code of law entitled Shulchan Aruch ha-Rav, which was published posthumously in 1814. There he repeats the general principle that one may pray in any language, and goes on to say that those who do not know Hebrew, even though it would be possible for them to learn the Tefillah by heart, would do better to pray in a language they understand with Kavvanah than to pray in the Holy Tongue without Kavvanah 'because prayer without Kavvanah is nothing at all' (Part I, 101:5).

Theory and Practice

Thus the entire Jewish Tradition, from the age of the Mishnah until the beginning of the nineteenth century, is unanimous that, with the sole exception of the Priestly Benediction, it is *permissible* to pray in the vernacular. Some of the sources even say that it is positively *desirable,* if not mandatory, to do so whenever comprehension, and therefore Kavvanah, depends on it.

To what extent this theoretical permissiveness was taken advantage of in practice, is indeed another question, and one on which evidence is hard to come by. As noted above, we do know from the Mishnah that in the ancient synagogues it was standard practice to employ an interpreter (מְתֻרְגְמָן) who would translate the Sidra, one verse at a time, and the Haftarah, three verses at a time, into the vernacular Aramaic (Meg. 4:4). But later that practice was discontinued, and Joseph Caro remarks: 'Nowadays we don't translate, for what would be the use of an Aramaic translation, since the people would not understand it?' (Sh.Ar., O.Ch. 145:3). Apparently, the logical solution, to translate into the appropriate vernacular, was not considered, or dismissed on the ground that only the Aramaic translation known as the Targum had been officially sanctioned or נתקן ברוח הקדש, 'instituted by the holy spirit' (Tur, O.Ch. 145).

We also know that in the early Rabbinic period some prayers were composed in the vernacular Aramaic for the precise purpose that they should be understood, the best-known example being the Kaddish (Tos. Ber. 3a), and the same happened again in the Gaonic age, from which we have, for instance, the Ha Lachma Anya and the Kol Nidre. We also know that individual rabbis sometimes used the vernacular, for the benefit of women and children, in domestic rituals. For instance, Moses Isserles (1525–1572), in his glosses to the Shulchan Aruch, informs us that Rabbi Jacob ben Judah, in thirteenth-century London, used to recite the Haggadah in the vernacular, which would have been Norman French, when he celebrated the Seder with his family (Sh.Ar., O.Ch. 473:6).

Women, before modern times, were generally excluded from Jewish education and therefore not expected to know Hebrew. But they

were certainly expected to pray, and did so, not only at home but
also in the section, gallery or annex of the synagogue reserved for
them. For this purpose they used prayerbooks with translations into
Yiddish, Ladino and other European languages, which began to
appear in the sixteenth century, and even collections of supplicatory
prayers called *techinnot* entirely in the vernacular. No doubt such
books were also used by men whose knowledge of Hebrew was
slight. So it would seem, for instance, from the introduction to a Yiddish translation of a prayerbook which appeared in Germany in
1544, in which the translator, Joseph ben Yakar, remarks: 'I consider
those people foolish who wish to recite their prayers in Hebrew
although they do not understand a word of it. I wonder how they can
have any spirit of devotion in their prayers' (Freehof, 1923, p. 382).

More generally, it is to be assumed that Jewish men did sometimes pray in the vernacular, not only at home but also in the synagogue, where much of the praying was in any case done individually,
though in the company of, and approximate synchronisation with,
the congregation, rather than in unison. But whether, before modern
times, the *sheliach tzibbur* or prayer leader ever *led* congregational
worship in any language other than Hebrew (with its Aramaic ad-
mixtures), I do not know. It seems likely enough, but I am not aware
of any evidence to prove it.

At any rate, the unequivocal statement of the Mishnah, that to
pray in the vernacular is permissible *in principle,* went unquestioned,
and was periodically re-affirmed, through all the centuries down to
the publication of Shneur Zalman's Shulchan Aruch ha-Rav in 1814.
But only five years later, in 1819, all of a sudden, a very different and
indeed wholly contrary note is struck. Clearly, something momentous must have happened during the intervening years. It did: the
Reform movement happened!

Reform and Reaction

It was in 1815 that the movement first attracted widespread attention,
shortly after Israel Jacobson (1768–1828) had settled in Berlin, when
regular Reform-style services were held in his home there, later to be
continued in the even more spacious home of Jacob Herz Beer
(1769–1825), father of the composer Meyerbeer. Since much of the
attention was critical, the leaders of the group commissioned one of
their number, Eliezer Liebermann, to solicit some rabbinical opinions in defence of their innovations. The result was a pamphlet entitled *Nogah ha-Tzedek* ('The Brightness of Justice', see Isa. 62:1),

containing three responsa by rabbis sympathetic to the Reform movement, to which Liebermann added a treatise of his own under the title *Or Nogah* ('The Light of Brightness').

The pamphlet was published in the year 1818, which also saw the establishment in Hamburg of the first major Reform synagogue, known as the Hamburg Temple, and both of these events prompted a number of rabbis of the old school to counter with a publication of their own, condemning the reforms, which appeared in 1819 under the title *Eleh Divrey ha-B'rit* ('These are the Words of the Covenant', see Deut. 28:69). It was a collection of twenty-two responsa, signed by forty rabbis, which set out to demonstrate that it is forbidden (a) to change the wording of any traditional prayer, (b) to pray in any language other than Hebrew, (c) to play a musical instrument in synagogue on Shabbat or Yom Tov.

The most famous of the contributors was Moses Schreiber (1762–1839), known as the Chatam Sofer (which was short for חדושי תורת משה, 'Novel Interpretations of the Torah of Moses', the title of his major work) who was the head of a great Yeshivah in Pressburg, as Bratislava, the capital of Slovakia, was then called. On the question of the language of prayer he says that the permissive ruling of the Mishnah applies only to the occasional prayer of an individual, but that to lead communal worship in the vernacular is completely forbidden, for otherwise the Men of the Great Assembly would have instituted the liturgy in Aramaic, since the Jewish people of that time did not understand Hebrew, as we know from the biblical account of how Ezra, when he conducted the public reading of the Torah, had it translated for their benefit (*Eleh Divrey ha-B'rit*, p. 10, alluding to Neh. 8:8).

The argument is neither historical nor logical, but it is typical of the kind of specious reasoning employed in this volume to 'prove' that what the Tradition has always permitted in the past is, on the contrary, forbidden. The whole *spirit* of the volume is different from anything that has preceded it, and is well summed up in the slogan with which the Chatam Sofer is associated, חדש אסור מן התורה, that whatever is new is forbidden by the Torah. We may therefore say that between 1814 and 1819 Orthodox Judaism was born.

The controversy did not end there. Israel Bresselau (1785–1839), one of the lay founders of the Hamburg Temple, replied with a satire in Hebrew verse under the title *Cherev Nokemet Nekam B'rit* ('The Sword that Avenges the Covenant', see Lev. 26:25); that, in turn, drew a rejoinder from Rabbi Meir Leib Reinitz which he called *Lahat ha-Cherev ha-Mit-happechet* ('The Flame of the Inverted Sword', see Gen. 3:24); and another Hebrew writer, David Caro of

Posen (c. 1782–1839), published a point-by-point refutation of *Eleh Divrey ha-B'rit* under the title *B'rit Emet* ('The Covenant of Truth', see Mal. 2:5f). All that in 1819 and 1820.

The prohibitive stance of the Chatam Sofer and his colleagues became normative for Orthodox Judaism, and is reflected in the subsequent halachic literature. For instance, Rabbi Yechiel Michael Epstein (1829–1908), in his codification of Jewish law entitled *Aruch ha-Shulchan*, states categorically that 'nowadays it is forbidden to recite the Shema or the Tefillah or any of the blessings in any language other than the Holy Tongue'. And he adds: 'So the world's greatest scholars have taught these past approximately eighty years' (O.Ch. 62: 4). That figure is significant, for since the *Aruch ha-Shulchan* was written about 1900, it amounts to a clear acknowledgement that it was the controversy surrounding the establishment of the Hamburg Temple which was the turning point.

All these attempts on the part of the opponents of Reform to prove that what premodern halachic literature has to say about the use of the vernacular does not mean what it appears to mean, must be considered a failure. Of course, even if they had been right, that would not necessarily have settled the issue for the Reform movement, since it did not consider itself *bound* by the Halachah. In any case, whether it is *permissible* to pray in the vernacular, is one question, to which the answer is plainly 'yes'; whether it is *desirable* to do so, and if so to what extent, is another.

Just that distinction was made in the great debate on the issue which took place during the Frankfurt Conference in 1845. At the end of the debate two questions were put to the vote. First, whether Jewish law positively requires the use of Hebrew in worship, to which the majority of the thirty-one participants, with four abstentions, subsequently reduced to two, answered 'no'. Secondly, whether the retention of Hebrew was nevertheless necessary on other than legal grounds, on which the Conference voted 'yes' unanimously.

It was during this Conference, and specifically on the issue of Hebrew, that Zacharias Frankel (1801–1875) dissociated himself from his colleagues to devote himself to the cause of what he called 'Positive-Historical Judaism', with a deeper commitment to Hebrew as belonging to the very essence of Judaism, which later gave rise to the Conservative movement in the United States. Even so, the majority view of the Conference, that in theory, as a universal religion, Judaism is not totally bound up with the Hebrew language, but that in practice, as a historical religion, it needs to continue to give it an important place in worship as well as education, has remained the position of Progressive Judaism, which has continued to debate only

the question of *proportion.* As to that, it may be said that, with some
exceptions, the tendency on the European Continent has been to
give considerably greater emphasis to Hebrew than to the vernacular, and in the United States to do the reverse, while in Britain the
Reform synagogues have tended to follow the European pattern,
and the Liberal synagogues the American one.

The Issues

Given the fact that the vast majority of Jews outside the State of
Israel know little Hebrew, the case for praying in the vernacular is
enormously powerful. How can there be Kavvanah without under-
standing? And prayer without Kavvanah, as the founder of the
Lubavitcher movement said, is 'nothing at all'; it is just a noise.
There seems to be no gainsaying that argument.

Yet the case for Hebrew is also very strong. It is, after all, the language of the Bible and, more generally, the chief language, though
not the only one, in which the spirit of the Jewish people has expressed itself in all lands and ages. A knowledge of Hebrew is the
key that unlocks the literature of Judaism; for no translation, however excellent, can convey the full flavour of the original; something
intangible but vital gets lost in the process. It should therefore be an
ambition of every self-respecting Jew to gain at least a fair degree of
competence in Hebrew; and the use of it in worship serves, among
other things, as an incentive to that end.

Above all, the cultivation of Hebrew is an act of identification with
the Jewish people in time and space. That is why there has been a significant increase of emphasis on it, even in Progressive Judaism, in
recent times. After the Holocaust and the establishment of the State
of Israel, itself a response to the Holocaust, how could it have been
otherwise? *Of course* these experiences have elicited from our people
an intensified desire to rediscover its roots and to reassert its identity.

However, there is one more point to be made. Although the use
of language in worship engages the mind, and although that is indeed its chief purpose and virtue, nevertheless it needs to be re-
membered that worship is not solely an intellectual activity. It also
operates on the level of emotion, intuition and mystical experience.
Therefore the change from Temple to Synagogue, from gesture to
speech, although it was an enormous advance, would not have been
a gain entirely without loss if it had not been for the introduction of
poetry, song and ritual capable of appealing to the non-rational side
of the human mind. To some extent the use of Hebrew can serve that

purpose. As long as its meaning is attended to *most* of the time, it may play an 'incantatory' role *some* of the time. (As a colleague has put it to me, 'there is a dimension in which language can be a mantra and a backdrop'.) I do not mean that it can ever be right for individual worshippers to mouth Hebrew words without understanding what they mean – that would be an offence against their own integrity as well as an affront to the One being worshipped. But during a service lasting an hour or more, it is permissible occasionally to relax, and allow the sound of the Hebrew, read by the Reader or sung by the Cantor or Choir, to 'wash over' one without attending to, or even necessarily understanding, the meaning of every word, so that, released from the rigour of propositional logic, the spirit is free to roam and to soar.

So the question of the language to be used in synagogue worship (except in the State of Israel, where Hebrew and vernacular are identical) poses a real dilemma, precisely because the case for both is so strong. To use the vernacular exclusively would be to stop up a life-giving fountain, and to disregard the fact that we are an ancient people with a wealth of memories and a worldwide constituency. To use Hebrew exclusively would be to restrict comprehension, to discourage those whose knowledge of Hebrew is slight, and to obscure the universalistic character of Judaism.

There is even spiritual danger in too great an emphasis on Hebrew, which all too easily fosters – if not the monstrous notion that the Creator of the cosmos is a monoglot – the illusion that it is more pious and virtuous to pray in Hebrew than to pray in the vernacular. That kind of holier-than-thou traditionalism, which fails to understand the truth that 'humans look at the outward appearance, but God looks into the heart' (I Sam. 16:9), poses as the servant of spirituality, but is actually its deadly enemy.

In the light of all these considerations, the only sensible solution is the one long adopted in Progressive Judaism: to use *both* Hebrew *and* the vernacular, each in significant measure, while leaving it to each synagogue to determine the optimal proportion in accordance with its own perception of the needs of its actual and potential membership.

'Take with you words, and return to the Eternal One; say to God: Forgive all iniquity, and accept that which is good ...' Whether we pray in Hebrew or in the vernacular, our best will never be good enough. But as long as it *is* our best, we may permit ourselves to repeat the prayer of the Psalmist: 'May the words of my mouth and the meditations of my heart be acceptable to You, Eternal God, my Rock and my Redeemer' (Ps. 19:15).

Chapter 11

❖   ❖   ❖

THE POSTURE OF PRAYER

Questions of Protocol

While the worshipper's spiritual attitude is obviously of paramount importance, most religions have also prescribed, or recommended, particular bodily attitudes as being appropriate or conducive to the act of prayer.

In Judaism there is, for instance, the ancient practice of facing towards Jerusalem during the more important prayers (I Kings 8:30; Daniel 6:11; Ber. 30a). Likewise, there are many references in the Bible to bodily postures such as prostration, bowing, kneeling, and lifting the hands (e.g., I Kings 8:54; Ps. 95:6; Neh. 8:6). Some of these are discussed in the Mishnah and Talmud (Shek. 6:1; Ber. 28b, 34b; Meg. 22b), but while they evidently played an important role in the Temple, there was a tendency to do without them in the Synagogue.

Among the practices that have nevertheless continued, especially in Orthodox synagogues, to this day, the following may be mentioned. (1) Bowing at certain points in the Tefillah: specifically, at the beginning and end of the first benediction (*Avot*) and again of the penultimate benediction (*Hodayah*). (2) Taking three steps backwards, as well as bowing again, at the end of the Tefillah; likewise of Kaddish. (3) Bowing on the part of the Reader when reciting *Bar'chu*, and on the part of the Congregation during their response. (4) Leaning forwards and sideways, by way of a kind of token prostration, during the penitential prayers known as *Tachanun*. (5) Prostration during the *Aleinu*, especially on Yom Kippur.

In Progressive synagogues these practices are not generally encouraged or emphasised. Nor do they necessarily require a definite policy, since individuals are free to follow their own inclinations, depending partly on their various backgrounds. Consequently they are not commonly perceived in Progressive Judaism as issues of הלכה למעשה, 'operative law'. But on one question decision-making cannot very well be avoided: that of sitting and standing, with which the rest of this chapter will deal.

It is not the most momentous of questions, or even a moral one. For though there are right and wrong postures in worship, as there are right and wrong ways of eating peas, it is obvious that in such contexts 'right' and 'wrong' do not have an ethical connotation: they are merely matters of convention or protocol. Yet even these need to be settled one way or another if it is desirable, as it is generally thought to be, that in public worship the congregation should act, at least to some extent, in unison.

How then does one set about answering such questions? The obvious starting point is to look up the traditional sources. They will at least tell us what the practice was in the past. Sometimes, but by no means always, they will give a reason. That, in turn, may be the 'real' reason, or it may be only a 'good' reason, invented to explain an existing custom of unknown origin; then we are free to speculate what the real reason might have been. In either case it may or may not be relevant today. If yes, well and good. If not, we may still wish to perpetuate the custom on the ground that, as a general rule, traditions should be maintained in the absence of a compelling reason to the contrary.

However, that is not a simple rule to apply. For one thing, there may be various customs in traditional Judaism. For another, Progressive Judaism has its own customs, going back many generations, which are also entitled to a hearing. It is a curious characteristic of its neo-traditionalists that they tend to ignore the history of their own movement, and count as 'traditional' only what is done by the Orthodox. Some of them even make a point of adopting the more stringent and exotic practices they have observed in Orthodox synagogues: a kind of supererogatory piety which the Rabbis called יוהרא ('shining' or 'ostentation') and did not like.

Then again, what constitutes a good reason for departing from a 'neutral' tradition? Is it legitimate to argue, for instance, that nowadays too much standing is felt to be irksome, and sitting more conducive to Kavvanah? How to steer a sensible course through this maze of conflicting considerations is a matter that must be left to the common-sense judgment of rabbis, synagogue councils and rites-and-practices committees. All that can be attempted here is to provide some of the relevant background information.

The Tefillah

The most obvious posture for prayer is standing, since it is a mark of respect. A subject stands before a ruler, a defendant before a judge, the young before the old (מפני שיבה תקום, 'You shall rise before the aged', Lev. 19:32); how much more should human beings stand when addressing their Creator! In many synagogues the words דע לפני מי אתה עומד, 'Know before whom you stand', derived from the Talmud (Ber. 28b), are inscribed above the Ark. Not surprisingly, the principal Jewish prayer is traditionally recited standing. Indeed, one of its names is 'Amidah', which means 'standing' (Soferim 16:12). Furthermore, the association between praying and standing can be traced back to a Rabbinic legend to the effect that Abraham instituted the morning service, since Scripture says that 'he rose up early' and 'stood' (Gen. 19:27), and explains that 'standing' refers to prayer, citing a Psalm verse (106:3) which is interpreted to mean that 'Phineas stood up and prayed' (Ber. 26b).

Standing to recite the Tefillah was not an absolute requirement; in some circumstances, says the Mishnah, one may even recite it without dismounting from one's donkey (Ber. 4:5). However, it was accepted custom to stand, as the angels did in worshipping their Creator (Ber. 10b, quoting Ezek. 1:7).

There is particular emphasis on standing for the angelological doxology called Kedushah ('holiness'), which is a central feature of the Tefillah when it is recited publicly (Sh.Ar., O.Ch. 95:4, 125:2). That recitation, like some other elements of the liturgy, traditionally requires a Minyan (quorum of ten men) on the principle, כל דבר שבקדושה לא יהא פחות מעשרה, that 'anything involving holiness requires the presence of at least ten' (Ber. 21b).

Closely related to that principle is another, כל דבר שבקדושה בעי למיקם ארגליו, 'For anything involving holiness one should stand on one's feet', which was at one time said to be stated in the Yerushalmi (Palestinian Talmud) and, though it is not found in current editions, evidently influenced usage (Sperling, 1957, p. 68).

And so the practice of standing for the Tefillah was codified. Jacob ben Asher cites the Yerushalmi to the effect that, since the Tefillah is a substitute for the daily sacrifice, one should stand for it as the priests stood when they officiated in the Temple (Tur, O.Ch. 127, referring to Deut. 18:5). Maimonides distinguishes between standing and correct body posture (feet together, eyes lowered, hands locked together over the heart) but makes it clear that both are *desiderata* rather than *sine qua non* requirements (i.e., they are required לכתחלה, ideally, not בדיעבד, indispensably; Yad, Hilchot Tefillah 5:2, 4).

In Progressive Judaism, practice varies. The radical tendency is, or used to be, to stand for the Kedushah only; the conservative tendency, to stand for the whole Tefillah; the intermediate tendency, to stand from the beginning of the Tefillah to the end of the Kedushah.

The Shema

The Mishnah records a controversy between the schools of Shammai and Hillel. The former believed, on the basis of the phrase, בשכבך ובקומך, 'when you lie down and when you rise up' (Deut. 6:7), that the Shema should be recited standing in the morning and reclining in the evening; the latter understood the phrase as alluding only to the times at which the Shema should be recited, leaving the matter of posture entirely optional (Ber. 1:3); one may, for instance, recite it while walking or at work (Ber. 11a). As usual, the Hillelite view prevailed.

However, great stress was laid on at least the first verse (Deut. 6:4) being recited with Kavvanah in the sense of undistracted concentration, so that, if one was walking, one should stop to recite it, while some Rabbis, including Akiva and Yochanan, held that this requirement applied to the whole section (Deut. 6:4–9); and Judah ha-Nasi's personal habit of shielding his eyes during its recitation (Ber. 13b) became the recommended practice (Sh.Ar., O.Ch. 61:5). It could therefore be argued that individuals who, in their private devotions, find it easier to recite the Shema when standing, rather than sitting, or *vice versa*, should do so.

As regards communal practice, it seems that in Gaonic times, and probably earlier, the Jews of Palestine used to stand for the Shema, those of Babylonia to sit (Levi, 1961, p. 142, citing Joel Miller's *Chilluf ha-Minhagim*). One suggested reason for the former practice is an alleged statement in the Yerushalmi that the recitation of the Shema is עדות, an act of 'testifying' to the unity of God (ibid., citing a thirteenth-century work, *Minhag Tov*), an idea which many prayerbooks express by highlighting the last letters of the first and last words of the first verse of the Shema so as to spell the word עד, 'witness' (Jacob ben Asher to Deut. 6:4).

However, the Babylonian Geonim, especially Amram ben Sheshna, denounced the Palestinian custom vehemently (see *Seder Rav Amram*, ed. Daniel Goldschmidt, 1971, pp. 16f, and Hoffman, 1979, pp. 46–49). *Inter alia*, they argued that the same principle which prompted an earlier generation to discontinue the daily recitation of the Ten Commandments, namely that it might lend credence to the view that the rest of the Torah was not authoritative (Ber. 12a and Rashi ad loc.), should count against giving the Shema undue prominence by standing for it.

In Progressive Judaism the predominant tendency has long been, nevertheless, to stand for the Shema, or at least for the first paragraph. Those who wish to defend that practice would argue (a) that it has, as we have seen, a precedent in ancient Palestinian custom; (b) that the Gaonic objection to it is far-fetched and irrelevant; (c) that the idea of עדות ('testimony') is, on the contrary, appealing; and above all (d) that the very nature of the Shema as 'the watchword of our faith' lends it a solemnity which makes Kavvanah particularly important, and standing appropriate.

Other Prayers

Other prayers which are traditionally, or according to some traditions, recited standing are as follows:

> The beginning and end of the section of the daily morning service known as פסוקי דזמרא, 'Verses of Song', that is to say, its opening benediction, ברוך שאמר ('Blessed be the One who spoke …'), Psalm 100, and from ויברך דויד ('And David blessed …', I Chron. 29:10–13) to the end of the section, including the concluding benediction, ישתבח, 'Let God be praised …' (Sh.Ar., O.Ch. 51:7, gloss; Sperling, 1957, p. 31, citing Mordecai Jaffe's *Levush*, 51:9, to the effect that these passages are 'the epitome of praise'; Klein, 1979, p. 17).
>
> The Bar'chu (Sperling, p. 68, says it is obvious since it involves קדושה, 'holiness').
>
> Avinu Malkenu, 'Our Father, our King', for which the Ark is opened (Klein, p. 27).
>
> The Aleinu (the *Kol Bo*, Chapter 17, points out that it is a great hymn of praise'; cf. Sh.Ar., O.Ch. 132:2, gloss, and Sperling, p. 111).
>
> The Kaddish (Sperling, p. 461).
>
> The last stanza of the Sabbath Eve hymn *L'chah Dodi* (Siddur Kol Ya'akov, p. 318).
>
> The Sabbath Psalm, Psalm 92 (Sperling, p. 128, citing Isaac Luria).
>
> The end of the *Hashkivenu* ('Cause us to lie down …'), from ופרוש עלינו (ibid.).
>
> *Va-yechullu* (Gen. 2:1–3) in the repetition of the Sabbath Eve Tefillah (Sperling, p. 132, because it testifies to God's Creatorship).

Hallel (Sperling, pp. 196 and 234, citing David ben Samuel
ha-Levi, who refers to Ps. 134:1).

As regards Sabbath Eve Kiddush, it is customary to stand for
the Genesis passage that traditionally precedes it, or at least for the
last two words of Chapter 1 and the first two words of Chapter 2
(יום הששי ויכלו השמים), whose initial letters spell the Tetragrammaton;
but otherwise standing is optional, and some authorities say that it is
preferable to sit (Sh.Ar., O.Ch. 271:10, quoting the Kol Bo). As for
Havdalah, according to Joseph Caro and Sefardi tradition, it is
recited sitting; according to Moses Isserles and Ashkenazi tradition,
it is recited standing (Sh.Ar., O.Ch. 296:6).

The Reading of Torah

It remains only to deal with the rituals surrounding the public reading of the Torah. Obviously, the congregation stands when the Scroll
is taken out of the Ark (הוצאה; Seder Rav Amram, ed. Goldschmidt,
p. 72; Tur, O.Ch. 146, quoting Sar Shalom Gaon), when it is elevated
(הגבהה; Sefer Chasidim, §778, on the principle of '… and give honour
to the Torah', Soferim 14:11), and when it is returned (הכנסה; Seder
Rav Amram, p. 72, and Tur, O.Ch. 146).

Likewise, the congregation stands for the prayers for the Community, the Government, the State of Israel, and ברכת החדש (the
prayer for the New Moon) during which the Reader holds the Scroll
(Magen Avraham to Sh.Ar., O.Ch. 417 says: 'by analogy with the
proclamation of the sanctity of the new month which used to be performed [by the Sanhedrin] standing).

During the actual reading of the Torah, the Reader stands but the
congregation sits (Sperling, p. 67; Solomon Ganzfried, Kitzur Shulchan Aruch, I, 23:5) However, when the Decalogue is read from the
Torah, the congregation stands (Sperling, p. 68), although Maimonides argued strongly against the practice 'since it encourages the
extremely dangerous opinion that some parts of the Torah are superior to others' (Jacobs, 1975, p. 46, quoting Maimonides' Responsum
No. 263 in Joshua Blau's edition).

Curiously, among Algerian Jews it was customary to stand for the
Exodus but not the Deuteronomy version of the Decalogue (Eisenstein, 1970, s.v. עשרת הדברות, p. 331). Finally, some communities used
to stand for the reading of Ezekiel's vision of the heavenly chariot
(מרכבה, Chapter 1) as the Haftarah on the first day of Shavuot (Sperling, p. 158).

If all these data are a little bewildering, here are two comforting thoughts. First, when in doubt, follow existing custom. Secondly, as already mentioned, no moral issue is at stake, and therefore, although some zealots may care passionately whether the congregation sits or stands, the One to whom its worship is addressed almost certainly does not. 'For human beings look at the outward appearance, but God looks into the heart' (I Sam. 16:7). Or, as the Rabbis put it, 'the Holy One, ever to be blessed, demands the heart' (San. 106b).

Chapter 12

❖　❖　❖

WOMEN AND WORSHIP

A Tragi-Comedy in Anglo-Jewry

Religious services conducted by women for women are not un-heard-of in the history of Judaism. Israel Abrahams tells us that 'by the end of the thirteenth century, and perhaps earlier, Jewish women had their own prayer-meetings in rooms at the side of and a little above the men's synagogue' in which they 'were led by female pre-centors, some of whom acquired considerable reputation'. He cites the case of one Urania of Worms whose epitaph records that she, 'with sweet tunefulness, officiated before the female worshippers, to whom she sang the hymnal portions' (Abrahams, 1932, pp. 39f).

However, in contemporary Jewish experience such services are something of a novelty. For in Progressive Judaism they are gener-ally considered unnecessary, since women participate equally with men in the regular services, while in Orthodox Judaism, where that is not the case, separate women's services are discouraged if not for-bidden. Therefore when it became known in 1992 that a group of women of the United Synagogue's Stanmore congregation intended to hold their own Shabbat services, the proposal seemed revolu-tionary, especially to those unaware that similar experiments had been going on in the United States for some time.

To say that all hell broke loose would be an overstatement. What followed was more like a tragi-comedy. First Chief Rabbi Dr Jonathan Sacks tried to stop the experiment. Then he issued a ruling forbidden such services on synagogue premises but allowing them elsewhere on condition that no Sefer Torah (Scroll of the Pentateuch) was used. Sub-sequently such services were successfully held in Stanmore, Pinner and Hendon.

Those outside the Orthodox community looked on with aston-
ishment. How can men presume to tell women what they may and
may not do by way of worship? How can women, with any self-
respect, submit to such impertinence? What is wrong with women
holding their own services, anyway? How can there *possibly* be anything wrong with it? What, more generally, do the sources have to say
about the role of women in Judaism and especially in Jewish worship?

The answer is a long story about which much has been written
recently, for instance by Blu Greenberg (Greenberg, 1981); Rachel
Biale (Biale, 1984); Judith Romney Wegner (Wegner, 1988); and
Michael Kaufman (Kaufman, 1993). What follows is a summary of
the salient facts.

In Bible Times

The opening chapter of the Bible tells us that man and woman were
created simultaneously, and both alike in the Divine Image (Gen.
1:27). From this it should have been inferred that men and women
are equal in dignity and status for all purposes. But theology made
only a limited impact on the roles of the sexes, which were largely
determined by economic and social conditions. Nevertheless, the
general picture is not a rigid one. The Matriarchs probably wielded
more influence than the patriarchal records permit us to glimpse,
and women could rise to high positions in society, as judges, queens
and prophetesses.

Especially relevant for our purpose are Miriam, who led the
women's chorus after the crossing of the Sea of Reeds (Exod. 15:20f);
Hannah, whose prayer at Shiloh later served as a proof-text for various liturgical rules (I Sam. 1–2; Ber. 31a-b); and Huldah, who
authorised the promulgation of the Deuteronomic law-book discovered during the restoration of the Temple in Josiah's reign (II
Kings 22:14–20).

Equally important is the emphasis on the inclusion of women in
the inauguration and confirmation of the Covenant between God and
Israel (Deut. 29:10, 31:12; Neh. 8:2). On the verse, 'Thus shall you say
to the house of Jacob and declare to the children of Israel' (Exod.
19:3), an early Midrash comments that the former phrase refers to the
women, the latter to the men, in that order (Mechilta ad loc.)!

From the involvement of women in the Covenant one might have
expected them to play an equal role with men in the twin pillars of
Jewish religious life: worship and education. But it was not so. The
duty of pilgrimage was laid only on men (Exod. 23:19). The priesthood

was hereditary and exclusively male. Therefore women, like men of non-priestly descent, could attend Temple worship only as spectators, not as participants. We even hear, though only in post-biblical sources, of a women's court (עזרת הנשים, Middot 2:5). But it is not therefore to be assumed that the sexes were always separated. For one thing, there is no evidence that such a court existed in the First Temple, or even in the earlier period of the Second Temple; for another, the sources show that men passed freely through the women's court (Epstein, 1967, pp. 78f). Only once a year, the Talmud tells us, was sex segregation strictly enforced, and that was on the Festival of Water-Drawing (שמחת בית השואבה), because of the levity it engendered, and the attendant danger of licentiousness (Suk. 51b-52a).

So far as education is concerned, we have little information on the period of the Bible, so that the question, whether its many exhortations to parents to teach their children (e.g., Exod. 13:8; Deut. 6:7, 11:19; Isa. 54:13) were meant to apply to both sexes – that is, whether in such passages the word בן was always meant in the sense of 'son' rather than 'child' – cannot be answered with certainty. It is, however, noteworthy that in the institution known as הקהל ('Assemble', i.e., the public reading of the Torah every seven years during the Festival of Sukkot, Deut. 31:12) women are explicitly included.

In Rabbinic Literature

It was the new phase of Judaism, pioneered by the Pharisees and developed by the Rabbis, which sought to define the role of women with legal precision.

General opinions about women in Pharisaic-Rabbinic literature (written by men!) vary from laudatory, for instance that they are compassionate (Meg. 14b) and more intelligent than men (Nid. 45b), to insulting, for instance that they are talkative (Kid. 49b) and weak-willed (Kid. 80b), and that they have the mentality of children and slaves (Yalkut Shim'oni to I Sam. 1:13). In their domestic role, as wives and mothers, they are praised to the skies; but their rights in matrimonial law, in spite of various alleviations, are minimal, and their role in society is one of almost total subordination to men. The accepted view is that their place is in the home. They gain merit, says the Talmud, by sending their sons to school and their husbands to college, and waiting for them till they come home (Ber. 17a). Like minors and slaves, with whom they are frequently juxtaposed, they lack 'legal personality' in the sense that they are incompetent to act as witnesses (Shevuot 4:1) or judges (J. Yoma 6:1). According to

Maimonides, they may not hold communal office (Yad, Hilchot Melachim 1:6).

The benediction a male Jew is required to say every morning, praising God for not having made him a woman (Men. 43b), implies exactly what it appears to imply, and all attempts to explain it away are transparent rationalisations. So, too, the often-heard assertion that in Rabbinic Judaism women have only a *different* role from men, not a lower status, is a manifest case of self-deception when it is not a deliberate lie. For a fair summary we might turn to Judith Romney Wegner: 'True, woman was never a complete person in mishnaic society, but neither was she always and only a chattel' (Wegner, 1988, p. 198); and to Rachel Biale: 'They have no public role and their proper sphere is the home' (Biale, 1984, p. 40).

What chiefly concerns us here is the position of women vis-à-vis the Mitzvot. The general rule is stated in the Mishnah: women are subject to all of them except those of a positive nature which have to be carried out within a specified time frame: מצוות עשה שהזמן גרמא (Kid. 1:7). According to the common explanation, the purpose of the exemption is to relieve women of the burden of having to perform rituals when they are likely to be preoccupied with wifely and motherly duties. But (a) not all women are married with young children and (b) the permitted time limits are very wide. The conclusion is therefore inescapable that the Rabbis were as much concerned to confine women to their domestic role as to make life easy for them. Hence, too, the tendency to interpret 'exemption' as 'exclusion', which has stultified women's role in Rabbinic Judaism ever since, may not be altogether contrary to the original intention.

Shema and Tefillah

The exemption is, however, only a rule of thumb which allows of exceptions and various interpretations. For instance, one of the Mitzvot from which women are exempt is the twice-daily recitation of the Shema (Ber. 3:3) – surprisingly, considering that the Shema is the Jewish people's declaration of loyalty to the Covenant. It is somewhat reassuring, therefore, that women were, nevertheless, to be *taught* the Shema, at least the first verse, so that they might 'take upon themselves the yoke of the Kingdom of Heaven' (Sh.Ar., O.Ch. 70:1); and there is little doubt that women have observed this devotional practice all through the centuries.

Conversely, according to the Mishnah, women are *not* exempt from the Mitzvah of Tefillah (daily prayer, Kid. 1:7) even though, as generally understood, it is subject to well-defined time limits (Ber. 4:1). One possible explanation, adopted by the Gemara, is that the Tefillah constitutes an exception because to recite it is to pray for God's mercy (דרחמין נינהו, Ber. 20b), which women, no less than men, need to do. Another, propounded by Maimonides (Yad, Hilchot Tefillah 1:1), is that the Mishnah refers to a general duty to pray, which is derived from the Torah (by גזרה שוה, verbal analogy, from Exod. 23:25 and Deut. 11:13; Ta'an. 2a) but not time-bound, and does not apply to the thrice-daily recitation of the particular, Rabbinically ordained prayer otherwise known as Shemoneh Esreh or Amidah, which is not incumbent on women.

Later commentators explain that from the point of view of the Torah it is sufficient if women say a spontaneous prayer first thing in the morning, and that this is 'possibly' all that the Rabbis of the Mishnah had in mind (Ba'er Heitev Note 1 to Sh.Ar., O.Ch. 106:1). More strongly represented, however, is the contrary view of Nachmanides, that the Mishnah refers to the recitation of the Amidah morning and afternoon, though not necessarily in the evening, since the evening prayer is not strictly obligatory even for men (Mishnah Berurah Note 5 to Sh.Ar., O.Ch. 106:1).

There is thus a range of opinions in the traditional sources regarding the exact nature of women's obligation in the matter of prayer. (See Yechiel Michael Epstein, Aruch ha-Shulchan, O.Ch. 106:7).

The Reading of Torah

Similar remarks apply to their position *vis-à-vis* the reading of Torah, which in turn relates to the Rabbis' attitude to women's education. That, alas, was mostly negative. Ben Azzai did indeed believe that Jewish fathers should teach their daughters Torah, but Rabbi Eliezer countered that to do so was tantamount to teaching them תפלות, frivolity or obscenity (Sot. 3:4). Tragically, Eliezer's view prevailed and was ultimately codified in the Shulchan Aruch, which states that it is not meritorious for women to study Torah in the same way as it is for men, and that they should really not be taught at all 'because most women are not motivated to be taught, and are liable to use words of Torah for vain talk because of the poverty of their intelligence' (YD 246:6).

Admittedly, contrary views are to be found. Individual women, such as Rabbi Meir's wife Beruriah, were highly respected for their learning (Pes. 62b). There is occasional emphasis on girls being taught at least the essentials they need to know to lead a Jewish life

(Sefer Chasidim §313). There have been significant advances in that respect in modern Orthodoxy. Even pleas for a complete reversal of the traditional attitude have been heard from 'mavericks' such as Yeshayahu Leibowitz, who has said: 'Barring women from the study of Torah is not freeing them from an obligation ... but rather a denial of a basic Jewish right' (quoted in Biale, 1984., p. 38). But much ambivalence remains.

Nevertheless, in view of the centrality of the ritual of the reading of Torah in Judaism, as well as its possible derivation from the Biblical institution of *hakhel*, which, as we have seen, applied to both sexes, one would expect women to be included in the duty of hearing it, if not the privilege of doing it. To some extent, that is the case. The Tosefta rules that all may be included among the seven men (called up on Shabbat morning to read from the Torah), even a minor and even a woman, but immediately goes on to say, without giving a reason, that it is not 'done' to call up a woman to read in public (Tos. Meg. 3:11/4:11).

A similar statement occurs in the Talmud, which adds that it is not done מפני כבוד הצבור, 'out of consideration for the dignity of the congregation' (Meg. 23a). What that phrase presumably means is that a visitor might think the men of the congregation were too ignorant to read from the Torah. (Similarly, it is considered a disgrace for a husband if his wife recites the thanksgiving after meals on his behalf, Ber. 20b).

According to Moses Isserles, however, the statement that 'it is not done' precludes only the calling up of women to the exclusion of men (Sh.Ar., O.Ch. 282:3). Similarly, Menachem Meiri cites an opinion that as long as one male Jew has been called up, the rest may be women (Beit ha-Bechirah to Meg. 23a).

There is furthermore a curious teaching that in a community that consists entirely of Kohanim (putative descendants of the ancient priests) women may be called up to the reading of the Torah in lieu of non-priestly Israelites (Beit Yosef to Tur, O.Ch. 135).

It should be added that the Mishnah does not exclude women from the reading of the Scroll of Esther (Meg. 2:4 and Maimonides' Mishnah Commentary ad loc.; Meg. 4a).

Divergent Attitudes

It is thus apparent that, on the role of women with respect to prayer, education and the public reading of Scripture, there is in the Tradition enough negativism to provide more than a little support for those who wish to discourage or prohibit women's services; and this has sometimes been thought to be reinforced by several further considerations. One is the view, held by some halachic authorities though not all, that a person who is not strictly obligated to perform a Mitzvah may not recite the blessing ('who has commanded us ...') that goes with it. Another is the halachic principle that such a person may not discharge the obligation on behalf of others. There is also an extreme puritanical (or should one say prurient?) attitude which regards the sight of a woman, and especially the sound of her voice, as sexually provocative or distracting to men. 'A female voice is seductive', says the Talmud (קול באשה ערוה, Ber. 24a; cf. Sh.Ar., O.Ch. 75:3). It is this mentality which led, though not before the Middle Ages, to the strict segregation of the sexes in the synagogue.

In addition, there is a common notion that women should not touch a Sefer Torah because they may be ritually impure through menstruation. That objection, however, is almost totally without foundation. For one thing, a Sefer Torah is not susceptible of ritual impurity. For another, Joseph Caro, in the Shulchan Aruch, states explicitly that all, including the ritually impure, may read from the Torah (O. Ch. 88:1; cf. Ber. 22a).

In the main, however, the view hostile to women's services is to be explained, not by what the sources say, but by the mentality of its proponents. Those of reactionary bent will adduce whatever they can find in the literature, provided only that it is stringent, prohibitive and illiberal. Hence Rabbis Moses Feinstein, Joseph B. Soloveitchik and J. David Bleich have opposed women's prayer groups; but other Orthodox rabbis have permitted or even advocated them (see Kaufman, 1983, pp. 293ff).

In 1974 the anonymous author of the 'Ask the Rabbi' column in the *Jewish Chronicle*, widely believed to have been Rabbi Dr Louis Jacobs, wrote: 'It is no doubt surprising but true that there is no specific religious law forbidding a woman to participate in the service or even to conduct the service' (27 December, 1974). Nobody contradicted him.

Thus the whole area of the participation of women in religious worship is one in which it is quite possible, if one is so inclined, to interpret the Tradition permissively.

But Progressive Judaism does not merely *interpret* the Tradition: it also questions its assumptions. How much validity, we must therefore ask ourselves, is there in these propositions: that women's place is exclusively in the home; that they have no legal personality; that all women must be exempted from certain rituals because some may be domestically occupied; that to be exempt means to be precluded;

that to teach women Torah is to teach them frivolity; that they are incapable of studying in the right spirit; that to call them up to the Torah is an indignity for the men of the congregation; and more generally that what is right for one period of history may not be wrong for another? Surely the answer is: none whatsoever!

That being so, one can only wonder at the time it has taken for women to attain their full rights even in Progressive Judaism. In 1837 Abraham Geiger wrote: 'Let there be from now on no distinction between duties for men and women unless flowing from the natural laws governing the sexes' (Plaut, 1963, p. 253). Yet it was 1920 before women were first permitted to conduct services at the Liberal Jewish Synagogue in London, and 1972 before the first woman rabbi was ordained in the United States. And even now Lily Montagu's challenge to the 1928 Conference of the World Union for Progressive Judaism, 'The women must come down from the gallery' (Philipson, 1967, p. 400), has not been fully answered in all Reform and Liberal, let alone Masorti, congregations.

Nevertheless, the situation in Progressive Judaism is sufficiently satisfactory for its women to feel no need to hold their own separate services except on special occasions. How many decades or centuries will it take before the same can be said of Orthodox Judaism? And will it still be Orthodox? If 'all is foreseen yet free-will is given' (Avot 3:15), God only knows.

Chapter 13

❖   ❖   ❖

ON SEEING HALLEY'S COMET

The appearance of Halley's Comet in 1985 prompted a colleague to ask: 'What blessing or blessings, if any, are appropriate on sighting the comet? Should they be repeated with each subsequent observation? What if the sightings are separated by weeks or months? By seventy-five years?'

Mishnah and Gemara

According to the Mishnah, the blessing to be recited on seeing זיקין, earthquakes, lightnings, thunders and storms is ברוך שכוחו וגבורתו מלא עולם, 'Blessed be the One whose strength and might fill the world' (Ber. 9:2).

The word זִקִּים occurs in Proverbs in the sense of 'firebrands' (26:15; cf. Isa. 50:11). The Gemara asks what the Mishnah means by זיקין and quotes the third-century Babylonian Amora Samuel (who was renowned for his knowledge of astronomy) to the effect that the term refers to כוכבא דשביט, literally 'a star with a rod', i.e., a shooting star (Ber. 58b).

Later sources expand the definition. For instance, the Shulchan Aruch explains: והוא כמין כוכב היורה כחץ באורך השמים ממקום למקום ונמשך אורו כשבט, 'It is a kind of star that shoots like an arrow across the length of the sky from place to place, and its light is drawn out like a rod' (O.Ch. 227:1).

The Mishnah goes on to say that on seeing mountains, hills, seas, rivers and deserts one should say: ברוך עושה מעשה בראשית, 'Blessed be the Creator of the world' (Ber. 9:2).

The Gemara records a disagreement concerning these two blessings between Abaye and Rava (both fourth century, Babylonia). According to the former, one should say both blessings in all the cases, since all of them are manifestations of God's creative power. According to the latter, on seeing mountains etc., one should say only the second blessing, for as mountains are stationary it would not be appropriate to say in regard to them that God's strength and power *fill* the world.

Later Authorities

Maimonides rules: 'For raging storms, lightning, thunder, a loud noise heard in the land, such as that made by large millstones, and the light sometimes seen in the sky that looks like falling stars racing from place to place, or like stars that have a tail – for any one of these one should say, "Blessed be the One whose strength and might fill the world"; and if one wishes one may add the blessing referring to the Creator of the world' (Yad, Hilchot Berachot 10:14).

Similarly, the Shulchan Aruch says that one may recite either of the two blessings, which are however given in the longer form, addressing God in the second person, i.e., beginning ברוך אתה יי אלהינו מלך העולם, 'Blessed are You, Eternal One our God, Sovereign of the universe' (O.Ch. 227:1).

The *Encyclopædia Talmudit* discusses the subject in Volume 4 (pp. 351) under the heading ברכות הראייה 'Blessings on Seeing'. It points out that since these are occasional rather than regular blessings, some of the Rishonim (earlier, i.e. pre-sixteenth-century authorities) hold that one should use the short form, without 'Eternal One our God, Sovereign of the universe' and referring to God in the third person (so, as we have seen, Mishnah, Talmud and Maimonides), but that most of the codifiers favour the longer version, addressing God in the second person (so, as we have seen, the Shulchan Aruch).

On the particular subject of meteors etc., it mentions a division of opinion among the Rishonim, some holding that one should say *both* blessings, while others, who are the majority, hold that one should say *either* of the blessings but not both (pp. 356f).

The Authorised Daily Prayer Book of the United Hebrew Congregations of the British Commonwealth recommends that 'on seeing lightning, or shooting stars, high mountains or vast deserts' one should say the blessing that ends עושה מעשה בראשית, while the blessing that ends שכוחו וגבורתו מלא עולם should be recited 'on hearing thunder' (1990 edn, pp. 747–750).

I have assumed all along that for our purpose a comet is to be likened to a meteor, since its appearance to the naked eye is similar.

As for Halley's Comet in particular, there is a possible reference to it in the Talmud, where Rabbi Joshua ben Chananya, on a voyage to Rome with Rabban Gamliel II c. 95 CE, mentions to the latter a star that appears every seventy years and leads sailors astray (Horayot 10a).

It may also be of interest that Israel Isserlein of Wiener Neustadt observed with great interest the appearance of Halley's Comet in 1456 (Trachtenberg, 1961, p. 252).

As for *repeating* the blessing, the sources I have referred to make it clear that it should be recited at every sighting except that there is no need to repeat it *on the same day* provided that לא נתפזרו העבים, the clouds are not dispersed between one appearance and another. However, there is an opinion that, while this applies to lightning and thunder, the blessing on seeing a comet is recited 'only if thirty days have elapsed since the phenomenon was last seen' (Nosson Scherman and Meir Zlotowitz, eds., *The Complete ArtScroll Siddur*, Mesorah Publications, Brooklyn, 1990, p. 228, first published 1984).

Progressive Judaism

In former times Progressive prayerbooks, regrettably, tended to omit the 'Blessings on Various Occasions'. The recent tendency, commendably, is to restore them. (See, for example, *Forms of Prayer for Jewish Worship* (Vol. I, RSGB, 1977), especially p. 273, 'On seeing the wonders of nature'; *Gates of the Home* (CCAR, 1977), especially p. 20, 'On seeing lightning or other natural wonders', and *Siddur Lev Chadash* (ULPS, 1995), especially p. 546, 'On seeing the wonders of nature').

While Progressive Judaism is not, of course, legalistic in such matters, it seems to me that it would accord well with its general outlook to regard the custom of saying an appropriate blessing on seeing a rare and remarkable sight such as Halley's Comet as a pleasant and religiously meaningful one which should be encouraged, while perhaps taking the above-mentioned view that *either* of the two forms of the blessing may be used with equal appropriateness. כן נראה לעניות דעתי.

Chapter 14

❖   ❖   ❖

Returning a Scroll to its Donor

In 1986 a colleague asked my opinion about a problem which had arisen in his community in that one of its prominent members, who had once donated a Sefer Torah (Scroll of the Pentateuch) to the Synagogue, but who, following a disagreement with its leadership, had resigned his membership, had requested that the Scroll be returned to him. The leadership was minded to accede to the request but wanted to know whether such an action should be accompanied by a religious ritual.

Is the Donor Entitled to Demand Return of the Scroll?

The first question is whether the donor of the Scroll is entitled to demand it back. Common sense suggests that, unless he made it clear at the time that he intended it to be a loan and not an outright gift, he has no such right.

That common-sense view is confirmed by Rabbi Solomon B. Freehof (Freehof, 1974, No. 22; also in *CCAR Yearbook*, Vol. LXXXIV, 1964, and in Jacob, 1983). Referring to Responsum No. 15 of the Maharshal (Solomon Luria, c. 1510–1573), Freehof writes: 'He says that once the mantle was on the Torah, it can no longer be returned or be sold even if the man who gave it claims he never intended to give it outright. Such a claim would be valid only if before he gave it, he declared formally, in the presence of two witnesses, that he is not giving the Torah as an outright gift, but is merely loaning it to the congregation. If he had not made such a formal declaration ... he may never take it back, whatever may have been his unspoken intention.' (Freehof also refers to No. 161 of the Responsa, first edition, of the Maharik, i.e., Joseph Kolon, c. 1420–1480.)

So far as I can see from the sources, the only qualification this statement requires is that, if there was an *established custom* in the congregation for members to provide it with Sifrei Torah on the unwritten understanding that they were only being loaned, then, even in the absence of a formal declaration before witnesses to that effect, the providers would retain the right of ownership and be entitled to demand the return of the Sifrei Torah they had loaned. In such a case, as Moses Isserles remarks, הולכים אחר המנהג, they follow the established custom (Sh.Ar., YD 259:2).

Is the Congregation Permitted to Return the Scroll?

Assuming, however, that the donor did *not* make it clear in writing or by a formal declaration before witnesses that he was merely loaning the Sefer Torah to the Congregation, and that there was *not* an established Minhag (custom) to that effect, then the second question that arises is whether in such circumstances the Congregation is even *permitted* to return the Sefer Torah to its former owner.

What is involved here is the principle, מעלין בקדש ולא מורידין, that it is permitted to upgrade but not to downgrade a sacred object (Ber. 28a, Yoma 12b, 73a, Meg. 9b, 21b, Hor. 12b; Sh.Ar., O.Ch. 153). The relevant point is that for a synagogue to sell a Sefer Torah in order to give the proceeds to an individual would be to downgrade it, and would not normally be permitted.

However, if the individual to whom it is given intends to give it to another synagogue, or intends that it should be used by a congregation worshipping regularly in his own home, then it would be permissible since the intended use would be no less holy than its previous one, all congregations being considered equal for such purposes.

Furthermore, it would even be permissible to give a Sefer Torah, or the proceeds of its sale, as an act of צדקה (charity), to an individual in need. That emerges from a responsum by Rabbi Solomon B. Freehof, which concludes: 'To sum up: *Sefer Torahs,* even when they are no longer an article of commerce in stores, etc., may still be sold. A man who can maintain his claim that he still owns the Torah used in the synagogue may, according to Isserles, sell it in order to ease his poverty. If, however, the Torah is owned without question by the synagogue itself, then clearly the rights of the poor, fostering the study of the Torah, and meeting a solemn obligation of the community fully justify the sale ...' (Freehof, 1977, No. 52).

It would seem, therefore, that much depends on the purpose for which the original donor of the Sefer Torah intends to use it when it is returned to him. However, even if he does not intend to give it to another synagogue, or have it used regularly by a congregation worshipping in his home, and even if he does not need it in order to sell it and use the proceeds to relieve his own or somebody else's poverty, even then it would perhaps be possible to justify the decision to return the Sefer Torah to its original owner, which, in this case, the leadership of the Congregation seems to have taken.

The justification, however, would have to be of an ethical kind comparable to the principle of צדקה (charity). For instance, if there is reason to believe that refusal of the demand would lead to bad feeling, litigation and unfavourable publicity which would do serious damage to the reputation of the Synagogue, and adversely affect its ability to fulfil its sacred role, then, it seems to me, that would constitute such an ethical ground; it would be in the nature of מפני דרכי השלום ('for the sake of peace').

A Ritual for Removing a Scroll from a Synagogue?

Assuming, then, that it has been decided to return the Sefer Torah, and that the decision can be justified on one or another of the grounds mentioned above, the remaining question is whether there is an established ritual for such an act. About this I can only say that, to the best of my limited knowledge, there is not. Even the rituals for the *installation* of a new Sefer Torah in a synagogue are, so far as I know, of relatively recent origin and matters of custom rather than law. Such rituals can be found in works such as Hyman E. Goldin's *Ha-Madrich* (New York, 1939) and in the rabbi's manuals of the American Conservative and Reform movements.

In the present case, what chiefly matters is that the Sefer Torah should be treated with all due respect and reverence until it passes out of the Synagogue's possession. Therefore, if the transfer is not to be made at the Synagogue but at the home of the donor, it would seem appropriate that it should be accompanied on its journey from the Synagogue by two or more leaders of the Congregation, who might also act as witnesses.

It would also be appropriate that there should be a little ceremony at the time when the Sefer Torah is taken out of the Ark of the Synagogue, for instance, a suitable prayer and perhaps something based on the סיום ('completion') liturgy which is to be found at the end of the every tractate of the Talmud. At the other end of the journey, before the Sefer Torah is handed back to its former owner, it might be appropriate to recite a suitable Psalm, such as Psalm 19 (especially verses 8–12) or the עץ חיים ('It is a tree of life ...') verses from the liturgy for the Reading of Torah.

Such a procedure would, I think, satisfy the requirement of כבוד ('respect' for the Sefer Torah) and make it clear that what is happening is no ordinary transfer of property. כן נראה לעניות דעתי.

Chapter 15

❖   ❖   ❖

RECYCLING OLD PRAYERBOOKS

In 1990 I was asked by a colleague what I thought about a proposal that had been made in his Congregation to dispose of old prayerbooks by recycling them.

The Tradition

Rabbi Solomon B. Freehof gives a very helpful survey of the relevant literature in the first of his many volumes of responsa (Freehof, 1960, No. 15). To summarise it briefly:

The book of Deuteronomy, after commanding the destruction of idolatrous shrines, adds: לא־תעשו כן ליי אלהיכם, 'You shall not do so to the Eternal One your God' (12:2). From this prohibition the Rabbis inferred that it is forbidden to destroy any writing that includes the Divine Name. Therefore, they said, a worn Sefer Torah should be buried in the grave of a scholar (Meg. 26b). The prohibition was subsequently extended to other sacred writings, including prayerbooks, which, in order to avoid destroying them, were commonly deposited in storerooms, called *genizot,* adjacent to the synagogue. But not all scholars took the view that the law applied to books other than Sifrei Torah, and in recent centuries it has been common practice to burn such books, lest they should fall into non-Jewish hands and be used for some degrading purpose or otherwise treated irreverently.

Nevertheless the custom in some Jewish communities, including Progressive ones, is to bury disused prayerbooks in the cemetery, preferably in the grave of a Torah scholar or other worthy individual.

The Suggestion

The suggestion that such books might be recycled is a novel one to me. My reaction to it is that since, according to some though not all halachic authorities, it is permissible to burn old prayerbooks for the *negative* reason that they should not come to be used for unworthy purposes, it is *a fortiori* permissible to recycle them for the *positive* purpose of making a contribution, even though it is little more than a symbolic one, to the conservation of nature.

Indeed, one could go further and say that, whereas the recycling of prayerbooks cannot reasonably be considered a violation of the intent of the law of Deuteronomy 12:1–4, which is indeed irrelevant, it is actually a fulfilment of the law of בל תשחית, 'You shall not destroy' (Deut. 20:18), which is highly relevant.

It is also appropriate to point out that, whatever respect is due to books, it hardly compares with the respect due to human bodies, yet Judaism, with some provisos, permits the donation of organs for medical research or transplantation, which is also a kind of recycling. (See further below under 'Organ Transplantation'.)

Even so, I would be inclined to make one qualification: that while we may recycle old prayerbooks, we should continue the practice of burying disused Sifrei Torah, so as to perpetuate at least that aspect of an ancient tradition which may be properly regarded as a meaningful symbol of reverence for Judaism's chief *sanctum.* כן נראה לעניות דעתי.

Chapter 16

MEDICAL CONFIDENTIALITY

Talebearing

The question of confidentiality arises in all human relationships. For in any communication between two persons, information may be conveyed which the giver would not wish the recipient to pass on to a third party. Sometimes the giver will make that clear by saying, 'I am telling you this in confidence' or by writing 'Confidential' at the head of a letter. At other times it will be *assumed.* In either case there is a general obligation on the recipient of the information to treat it as confidential. Let us call any information to which that presumption applies 'sensitive information'.

To investigate what Jewish tradition has to say on the subject, let our starting point be the commandment in the nineteenth chapter of Leviticus, 'You shall not go up and down as a talebearer among your people' (v. 16), re-emphasised in the book of Proverbs: 'A talebearer reveals secrets, but one of trustworthy spirit keeps a confidence' (11:13; cf. 20:19).

From the word רכיל for 'talebearer' Rabbinic Hebrew derived the abstract noun רכילות for 'gossip', and from the word סוד for 'secret', modern Hebrew has coined the abstract noun סודיות for 'secrecy' or 'confidentiality'.

Like 'gossip' in English, so *rechilut* in Hebrew has a negative connotation. It implies that what is disclosed is detrimental to the person to whom it refers: that it is what we have decided to call 'sensitive information'. It is therefore closely related to לשון הרע, literally 'evil speech', forbidden by the same Leviticus verse.

There are few sins which Judaism condemns more strongly: not because it is the most serious but because it is the most easily committed. As the Talmud says, 'Most people are guilty of robbery, fewer of unchastity, and all of slander' (BB 165a). And in the 'Great Confession' of the Day of Atonement liturgy there is repeated emphasis on the sins of speech.

Sensitive Information

How detrimental to its subject must the disclosure be to fall under this prohibition? What, in other words, constitutes sensitive information?

The extreme case is any disclosure which may lead to *fatal* consequences. Maimonides points out that the Leviticus verse continues, 'You shall not stand by your neighbour's blood', and comments: 'Talebearing is a grave sin, which is the cause of many deaths in Israel; that is why the prohibition against it is followed immediately by the warning, "You shall not stand by your neighbour's blood"' (Yad, Hilchot De'ot 7:1). In other words, the second half of the verse reinforces the first. As we shall see later, the juxtaposition can also be understood in a contrary sense.

By way of illustration, Maimonides refers to a story told in the First Book of Samuel about an Edomite called Doeg whose report to his master Saul about the support given to David by Ahimelech leads to the killing of eighty-five priests (22:9, 18).

But Maimonides goes on to say that the sin of *lashon ha-ra* is committed, not only when life is endangered, but whenever any damage is done to the individual concerned בגופו או בממונו, personally or financially, and indeed even להצר לו או להפחידו, by way of causing him distress or fear (Yad, Hilchot De'ot 7:5).

One opinion in the Talmud goes still further. According to this, whenever something is told by one person to another, the recipient of the information is forbidden to divulge it to a third party unless the informant gives him or her permission to do so, saying לך אמור, 'Go and tell' (Rabbah in Yoma 4b, q. Lev. 1:1).

Promises

Is the obligation of confidentiality strengthened when an actual undertaking has been given to observe it? What, in other words, is the status of promises in Jewish Law?

The key verse says that 'it is better that you should not vow than that you should vow and not pay' (Eccles. 5:4). But that can be taken in two ways. It can be taken as a warning against making any vows at all, lest we should find ourselves unable to keep them. According to this view, 'even those who make a vow *and fulfil it* are nevertheless called wicked' (Ned. 22a). Or the Kohelet verse can be understood as merely emphasising the sanctity of vows, so that we should indeed be careful not to make a vow if we have any doubt whether we shall be able to keep it, but it is nevertheless nobler still to make vows and to keep them (Midrash Tehillim to Ps. 116:14).

It is therefore highly questionable whether explicit promises of unconditional confidentiality should be given at all. But once given, they should certainly be treated extremely seriously. For of course Judaism disapproves of promise-breaking. 'The One who punished the generation of the Flood and the generation of the Tower of Babel will punish those who do not keep their word' (BM 4:2).

To put it another way, the obligation to keep sensitive information confidential exists whether or not a specific promise to that effect has been given, but when such a promise *has* been given, it undoubtedly reinforces the obligation.

The Hippocratic Oath

The key phrase of the Hippocratic Oath reads: 'Whatsoever things I see or hear concerning the life of men, in my attendance on the sick or even apart therefrom, which ought not to be noised abroad, I will keep silence thereon, counting such things to be sacred secrets' (*Encyclopædia Britannica*, Vol. 11, p. 827a). It is therefore clear that the promise of confidentiality is *not unconditional*: it applies only to those things 'which ought not to be noised abroad'. In other words, it applies only to *sensitive* information.

Since the obligation is not unconditional, there is no strong reason why a Jew should not take the Hippocratic Oath, or why those who have taken it should feel obliged to seek release from it. That is the view of even so conservative an authority as Rabbi J. David Bleich of Yeshivah University (Bleich, 1983, p. 80), though he does quote the more stringent view of Eliezer Waldenberg, Chief Rabbi of Haifa, that in certain circumstances the oath *should* be annulled (ibid., p. 79; see also Steinberg, 5738 [1977–1978], p. 230).

The Hippocratic Oath is not the only one of its kind. The British Medical Association's *Medical Ethics Today* refers to analogous ones in Hindu and Muslim sources (BMA, 1993, p. 319). In Jewish tradition we know of a physician called Asaf ha-Rofé who lived, probably in Babylonia, in the sixth century. He adjured his pupils, 'Do not disclose any secret which a patient has entrusted to you' (Dr Abraham

Steinberg, 'Medical Confidentiality' in *Assia*, Vol. III, Jerusalem, 5743 [1982–1983], p. 326; see also Jakobovits, 1975, p. 389, Note 85). A similar phrase is attributed to Amatus Lusitanus, a Jew born of Marrano parents in Portugal in 1511, who studied medicine at Salamanca, taught it at Ferrara, and practised it at Ragusa (Dubrovnik), Ancona and Salonica, where he died of the plague in 1568 (*Encyclopædia Judaica*, Vol. 2, p. 797).

Clearly, some of these formulations are too categorical; especially the International Code of Medical Ethics, which rules: 'A physician shall observe absolute confidentiality on all he knows about his patient even after the patient has died' (BMA, 1993, Appendix Two, p. 328; Bok, 1984, pp. 123f). In any case, these oaths merely reinforce an ethical obligation which exists independently of them.

There is a general belief that doctors are under a solemn obligation to treat any sensitive information about their patients in the strictest confidence. It is clearly important that that perception should be maintained. As the BMA's *Medical Ethics Today* puts it, 'There is … a strong public interest in enforcing the medical duty of confidentiality. In the absence of guarantees that their secrets will be protected, patients may withhold information important to their health care and possibly to the well-being of others, including health professionals' (BMA, 1993, p. 38).

Disclosure

Now we must ask whether, according to Judaism, it is ever permissible – or even obligatory – to disclose sensitive information, and so to breach whatever promise, explicit or implicit, has been given to the contrary.

The short answer is 'yes', if only because there are no absolute prohibitions in Judaism except the three forbidding idolatry, incest and murder (Yoma 82a). In all other cases, moral duties, if they come into mutual conflict, need to be weighed against each other in the light of the circumstances.

There is, however, one obligation which overrides all others except the three absolute prohibitions just mentioned, and that is פקוח נפש, the saving of life. For instance, it is a principle of the Halachah that the saving of life overrides the Sabbath (פקוח נפש דוחה שבת, Shab. 132a).

Furthermore, where the saving of life is concerned, Rabbinic Law does not require certainty or even a balance of probability; a significant chance is enough (אין הולכין בפקוח נפש אחר הרוב, Ket. 15b).

It follows that when we have a chance of saving somebody's life by disclosing a secret, we are not only permitted but *obligated* to disclose it, notwithstanding any implicit or explicit promise to the contrary which we may have given.

And here we may return to our key verse from Leviticus chapter 19, which (to repeat) consists of two clauses, the first being, 'You shall not go up and down as a talebearer among your people', and the second, 'You shall not stand by your neighbour's blood.' Earlier I quoted an interpretation which sees the second clause as *reinforcing* the first. But it can also be understood as, on the contrary, *qualifying* it. Then the whole verse would mean: 'You shall not tell tales; nevertheless you shall not stand by in silence when your neighbour's blood is in danger of being shed.'

That interpretation is found already in the earliest Rabbinic sources. For instance: 'How do we know that if you are able to testify you may not be silent? Because it says, "You shall not stand by your neighbour's blood"' (Sifra to Lev. 19:16).

In another context, the principle is already stated in Leviticus 5:1, which the New Revised Standard Version translates: 'When any of you sin in that you have heard a public adjuration to testify and – though able to testify as one who has seen or learned of the matter – does not speak up, you are subject to punishment' (see Spiro, 1959, pp. 95–191).

More generally, Maimonides says: 'Whoever is able to save a human life, and fails to do so, transgresses the commandment, "You shall not stand by your neighbour's blood"' (Yad, Hilchot Rotzeach 1:14; cf. San. 8:7; San. 73a; Sh.Ar., Ch.M. 426:1).

Since that is the case, an unconditional oath of confidentiality is an oath to go *against* the law which, therefore, cannot claim validity *in* the law. As the Mishnah states, 'If a person swears to violate a commandment, that is a vain oath' (Shevuot 3:8).

Rabbi Yechiel Michael Epstein (1829–1908) spells it out clearly: 'If a witness says, "It is true that I have information relevant to the present case, but I have undertaken not to disclose it", that amounts to nothing, and the court must rule that he shall testify, for it is a case of one who has sworn to violate a commandment' (Aruch ha-Shulchan, Ch.M. 28:5).

Of course a witness cannot in the last resort be *compelled* to testify. That also emerges from a passage in the Shulchan Aruch which, besides, widens the scope of the obligation to include cases where something less than the saving of life is at stake. The passage reads: 'If anybody is in a position to testify on behalf of his neighbour, and it is right that he should do so, and if his testimony would be *advantageous* to his neighbour, then he is obligated to testify if his neighbour asks him to do so ... And if he suppresses the evidence, though he cannot be prosecuted under human law, חייב בדיני שמים, he is liable to divine punishment' (Ch.M. 28:1).

Cases Calling for Disclosure

It is therefore permissible, and even obligatory, to disclose sensitive information whenever there are good grounds for believing that such disclosure would avert a serious danger of death or other harm. But *whose* death or harm are we talking about? There are three possibilities.

First, the beneficiary of the disclosure may be the patient. If, for instance, the patient suffers from a serious illness which can only be treated effectively with the co-operation of others, then those others must be informed: if possible, with the patient's consent; if necessary, without. Similarly, if the doctor becomes aware that the patient intends to commit suicide, it may be necessary to inform those best placed to prevent him from doing so.

Secondly, the beneficiaries may be other designated individuals. For instance, if it becomes known to the doctor that the patient intends to assault a third party, there is a clear duty to thwart that intention even at the cost of betraying a confidence. As Sissela Bok writes, 'Just as no one is granted autonomy when it comes to *doing* violence to others, so there is no reason to concede such autonomy ... for *plans* to do so, once divulged' (Bok, 1984, p. 128). Therefore 'patients who voice serious threats against innocent persons' cannot 'invoke confidentiality on the basis of their relationship with therapists or anyone else without asking them to be partially complicitous' (ibid. p. 129). Indeed, 'professionals should not then be free to promise confidentiality, nor should a client expect to be able to entrust them with such projects, any more than with stolen goods or lethal weapons' (ibid., p. 131).

Similar problems are discussed at length by Rabbi Israel Meir ha-Cohen (1838–1933), better known from the title of his principal work as the Chafetz Chayyim. Regarding the disclosure of sensitive information, he lays down five provisos: (1) that it is done only after due deliberation; (2) that the danger which it is intended to prevent is not exaggerated; (3) that the sole motive is the benefit of the person to whom the disclosure is made; (4) that this result cannot be achieved by any other means; and (5) that no real harm is done to the informant (Kagan, 5734 [1973–1974], II, 9, pp. 212–16).

One of the illustrations he gives concerns a young man who intends to marry but who suffers from a serious physical defect. If asked, should the doctor who knows this tell the bride, even though the engagement might then be broken off? Yes, says the Chafetz Chayyim (ibid., p. 232).

Similarly, Sissela Bok informs us, Catholic theologians have often discussed the question: 'What should a doctor do if he has a patient who suffers from an incurable and highly contagious venereal disease and who plans to marry without disclosing this fact to his fiancée?' According to many, she says, 'the doctor's obligation of secrecy would then cease' (Bok, 1984, p. 130).

She also cites the case of a middle-aged patient who suffers from a genetic kidney disease and who, with the agreement of his wife, decides to keep the information from his teenage children. Should they be told? It might depend, she says, on the *degree* of the severity of the illness and of the likelihood of its transmission (ibid., pp. 118f).

An unusual case is discussed by Rabbi Walter Jacob, Chairman of the Responsa Committee of the CCAR. A woman, who is engaged to be married, confides to her rabbi that she suffers from a rare, potentially fatal disorder, but threatens to commit suicide if he tells her fiancé. Rabbi Jacob concludes that if, in the judgment of the rabbi, the suicide threat is to be taken seriously, he should *not* divulge the information (Jacob, 1987, pp. 7f).

Thirdly, the beneficiary of the proposed disclosure may be society at large. A commonly discussed example is that of a patient who applies for a driving licence but conceals the fact that he is an epileptic. Then the patient's doctor is duty-bound to inform the licensing authority (Bleich, 1983, p. 36).

Similar problems may arise if a doctor is asked to give a medical report about a patient to a prospective employer or insurance company, or to testify in a court case. Above all, the public interest is involved, and requires the disclosure of sensitive information, if the patient suffers from a contagious disease, or is a drug addict, or liable to commit violence.

Who Decides?

These examples indicate the range of situations in which it may be permissible, and even obligatory, to disclose sensitive information. Obviously, it is necessary in each case to weigh the benefits of confidentiality against the benefits of disclosure, (a) for the patient, (b) for others and (c) for society at large. Equally obviously, that is a highly subjective process in which it is all too easy to make errors of judgment. Therefore we need, finally, to ask: who is to decide?

There are four possible safeguards against the irresponsible disclosure of sensitive information.

The first is legislation. To some extent, that is already in place; but I think the BMA is right to press for a more comprehensive code (BMA, 1993, pp. 63ff). For the danger of improper disclosure grows as medical information is increasingly computerised, and shared by an ever wider range of health professionals, including non-medical administrators.

Secondly, there is a need for statutory bodies which the Government may from time to time set up to regulate particularly difficult areas of medical practice. An example is the Human Fertilisation and Embryology Authority.

Thirdly, there is a need for professional codes of conduct. The guidelines of the General Medical Council and the BMA's Medical Ethics Committee serve that purpose.

Fourthly, there is need for local, hospital-based ethics committees to which doubtful cases can be referred for decision.

Nevertheless, the final safeguard is the educated conscience of the individual doctor or other health professional. As Kohelet says, עת לחשות ועת לדבר, there is 'a time to be silent and a time to speak' (Eccles. 3:7); but to differentiate between them is not always easy.

Chapter 17

❖ ❖ ❖

ORGAN TRANSPLANTATION

New Procedures

'A new heart will I give you, a new spirit put within you. I will remove the heart of stone from your flesh, and I will give you a heart of flesh' (Ezek. 36:26). Little did Ezekiel know that within two-and-a-half millennia his prophecy, though still lamentably unfulfilled in the metaphorical sense in which he meant it, would be fulfilled literally, or that the verb he used to describe the transplantation of a tree (Ezek. 17:23) would provide the Hebrew term, השתלה, for such a surgical procedure.

Since the 1950s, which saw the first kidney transplants, and especially since 1967, when Dr Christian Barnard performed the first heart transplant, this kind of surgery has made great strides, raising immensely complex ethical problems, which have recently been compounded by two new proposals: the use of pigs' hearts in cardiac surgery, and the implantation of human brain tissue into patients suffering from genetic neurological conditions such as Parkinson's Disease.

On the ethical issues raised by such operations there is now a widespread debate, involving doctors, legislators and theologians among others, to which Judaism has a significant and distinctive contribution to make. That it has begun to do so is evidenced by a growing literature of responsa and essays on various aspects of 'Jewish Bioethics', (e.g., *Jewish Medical Ethics* by Immanuel Jakobovits, first published in 1959, and *Jewish Bioethics*, edited by Fred Rosner and J. David Bleich, 1979.

Three Principles

The Jewish approach proceeds from three basic premises. The first is the concept of שותפות ('partnership'), that human beings are not merely playthings of external forces but God's partners in the work of creation-and-redemption and therefore divinely authorised to intervene – responsibly – in the processes of nature. With specific reference to the practice of medicine, this principle was stated in second-century Palestine by the School of Ishmael in the dictum שניתן רשות לרופא לרפאות, 'that the healer is permitted to heal' (BK 85a, interpreting Exod. 21:19).

The second principle is פקוח נפש, the saving of life. According to this, human life is so precious that to preserve it, and to prolong its duration as much as possible, is a positive obligation, and one that takes priority over all other commandments, including for example the observance of the Sabbath, and excluding only the three 'cardinal prohibitions'. In its particular application to medicine, the principle was formulated by the third-century Palestinian Rabbi Yochanan, who said: 'All means of healing are acceptable, provided only that they do not involve idolatry, incest or murder' (Pes. 25a).

Nor is it necessary that it should be *certain* that the proposed therapy will be successful: the mere possibility that it may save the patient from dying is sufficient to justify it. That is the third principle, articulated by the third-century Babylonian teacher Samuel, who said, אין הולכין בפקוח נפש אחר הרוב, that 'when it comes to the saving of human life we do not go by the majority', which also means that we do not go by considerations of probability (Ket. 15b).

Common Ground

These three principles are a matter of common ground between Orthodox and Progressive Jews, who nevertheless subscribe to them for subtly different reasons. From an Orthodox point of view it is sufficient that they were enunciated by great Talmudic sages and codified as law in the subsequent development of the Halachah, so that they are part and parcel of a Tradition that is guaranteed by a not-to-be-questioned divine authority. From the Progressive point of view, the Tradition is in large part human and consequently *could* be mistaken (as in some instances it has been shown to be); nevertheless, with respect to the three principles under discussion, not only is there no good reason to doubt their soundness, but they are self-validating in the context of Judaism's general life-affirming philosophy, which commends itself to Progressive, no less than to Orthodox, Jews.

It may even be said more generally that, because in this whole area of the application of Halachah to modern medical technology Orthodox scholars tend to invoke general ethical principles rather than legal precedents, therefore there is much similarity between their approach to these matters and that of the Progressives. On the subject of medical ethics, more than on some other subjects, Jewry can speak to a large extent with one voice.

The acceptance of the three principles has a wonderfully simplifying effect on the whole debate about transplant surgery, since it overrides at one fell swoop practically all counter-arguments. For instance, according to Jewish tradition it is normally forbidden to derive any benefit from the body of a deceased human being (AZ 29b), to mutilate it (Chul. 11b), or to delay its burial (San. 46b, interpreting Deut. 21:23); but when there is a chance of saving another human being's life, these considerations – like all other prohibitions (including much weightier ones) except for the three 'cardinal' ones – are simply set aside.

Determination of Death

There remains one major problem that affects all transplant operations in which the organ is taken from a human donor. For since one of the three cardinal sins which may not be committed even to save a human life is murder, the donor's death must be established beyond all possibility of doubt. How then is death to be defined? About that, too, there is now a widespread debate, the upshot of which will almost certainly be a more stringent definition than has hitherto been applied in either British or Jewish law. The tendency in the past has been to believe that when all breathing, or that and heartbeat, has ceased, the patient is dead (see J. David Bleich, 'Establishing Criteria of Death' in Rosner and Bleich, 1979). Recent advances in medicine will probably compel the legal systems to adopt a more comprehensive definition, including the cessation not only of respiratory and cardiac but also of cerebral activity ('brain death') and indeed the irreversibility of such cessation; in other words, there must be no possibility of resuscitation.

It is apparent that this tendency to greater rigour in the determination of death runs counter to the interest of the transplant surgeon, whose success depends on obtaining an organ that has been removed at the earliest possible moment, and it is therefore manifestly desirable that the law should require the donor's death to be certified by a doctor or team of doctors who have no direct involvement with the recipient.

The use of *animal* organs has a double advantage, in that it avoids the problem of a human donor, and that they are more readily available. Nevertheless the very thought of the implantation into a human being of an animal organ, especially if it is a pig's, tends to arouse revulsion. Does not this feeling of revulsion alone provide a powerful case against such operations? Do they not involve a 'mingling of diverse species' (כלאים)which the Bible forbids in other contexts (Lev. 19:19, Deut. 22:9–11)? These and other possible objections were carefully considered by Rabbi Dr Solomon B. Freehof as long ago as 1971 in a responsum entitled 'Transplanting a Pig's Heart Valve into a Human Body'. He concluded that if the operation is indispensable and has a reasonable likelihood of success, 'all the doubts ... must be set aside because of the general principle: 'Nothing must stand in the way of saving a life' (Freehof, 1971, pp. 322f). Not surprisingly, Orthodox rabbis, including Lord Jakobovits (*Jewish Chronicle*, 5 August 1988, p. 40), have come to the same conclusion. For the objections are emotional, whereas Judaism, especially on its halachic side, is a rational religion.

On the other hand, great caution is obviously required in this area. For instance, recent evidence that BSE (bovine spongiform encephalopathy) may be transmitted from cows to humans in the form of Jacob Creutzfeld Disease has given rise to concern that the transplantation of pigs' organs may involve a similar danger.

Brain Transplants?

The possibility of 'brain transplants' raises yet other issues. Until recently it was purely speculative. In a sermon I gave in January 1968, following the first heart transplant (a copy of which was sent to Dr Christian Barnard's brother Marius, who commented approvingly), I said: 'If at some future date it should become possible to transplant a human brain, or some other organ which would produce a fundamental personality change, then an entirely new problem would be created.' And in 1973 Rabbi Dr Louis Jacobs wrote: 'If one day, though it is extremely unlikely that this will ever happen, brain transplants will become possible, serious moral questions will have to be answered since the brain does influence the character' (Jacobs, 1973, pp. 322 f.)

Well, the unlikely has already become feasible, at least with respect to brain *tissues.* Here one problem is the way in which such tissues are obtained. With heart transplants the donor is usually the victim of a fatal accident. Brain tissues may also be obtained from foetuses that have been either aborted or produced by superovulation in the course of fertility treatment or embryological research. This is an area that bristles with moral difficulties which were considered in the Warnock Report in 1984. Clearly there is need for very stringent legal restrictions.

But even if the tissue is obtained by morally acceptable means there remains the problem referred to above as 'personality' or 'character' change, since the brain, unlike the heart, is the instrument of remembering and other mental processes. Strong objections have therefore been raised against such operations, not least by spokesmen of the British Medical Association (*Independent*, 7 May 1988), in so far as they would involve whole brains or major organs of the brain such as the cerebellum, the hypothalamus or the frontal lobes.

However, if we invoke again the guiding principles of the Jewish approach to medical ethics, these objections are not necessarily fatal. For even if we take the extreme case and suppose that it has become possible, which it is not yet, to transplant a complete brain, and even if that would indeed involve the transference of the donor's mind to the recipient's body, it would still be arguable that it is better that human life should continue in such a 'hybrid' form than that it should cease for donor and recipient alike.

Priorities

Finally, though, we must bring into play yet another principle of Jewish ethics, which has a bearing on all transplant surgery as well as other advances in modern medicine, and that is the extreme preciousness, not only of human life generally, but of all human lives *equally*. As the Rabbis put it, every human being is entitled to say, 'For my sake was the world created' (San. 4:5), the corollary of which is that no one may say to another, 'My blood is redder than yours' (Pes. 25b).

The relevance of this principle is that it raises the whole issue of *priorities*. For there is only a finite amount of human and material resources available for the development of any given branch of medicine. What then if the demand for the new techniques exceeds their availability? Who shall benefit from them? Is it tolerable that the rich should have greater access to them than the poor? Is it not possible that what is being expended on organ transplant research and surgery could be used to better effect – that is, to save more lives – if it were directed to other areas of medicine, or of public health, including preventive medicine, or to overseas aid? What is the relative cost of one heart transplant compared with the money needed to save a hundred children in the Developing World from death by starvation or epidemic?

There has been talk of setting up a national committee on medical ethics. Such a committee, or another one, should consider not only proper and improper procedures, but also proper and improper priorities, and ultimately such control will have to be extended to the international level.

If Progressive Judaism has a distinctive contribution to make to the present debate, it is not only thanks to its freedom from subservience to the past, and therefore its open-mindedness, but also by virtue of its characteristic emphasis, inspired by the Prophets, on the social and public, over and above the individual and private, dimensions of God's moral demands.

Chapter 18

❖   ❖   ❖

A Matter of Life and Death

The Relevance of Jewish Tradition

How precious is life? How imperative is the duty to prolong it? When does it cease? Why do we need to know? And what guidance can we obtain in these matters from Jewish tradition? Let us consider these questions in reverse order.

Jewish tradition comprises two strands: Aggadah and Halachah, or Theory and Practice. The question, What is life?, is a theoretical and therefore aggadic question. The question whether there is an obligation to prolong it in a given situation is a practical and therefore halachic question.

As traditionally understood, the Halachah derives from God's revelation, through Moses, to the Children of Israel at Mount Sinai: a revelation which was partly recorded in the Written Torah, comprising the 613 commandments of the Pentateuch, and partly transmitted by word of mouth to become the Oral Torah, which ceased to be oral when it was committed to writing in the Mishnah and, subsequently, the Talmud.

The twofold Torah yielded a legal system, covering every aspect of life, which has been elucidated, elaborated and updated ever since by a well-defined process of question-and-answer, interpretation and reinterpretation, codification and re-codification, commentary and super-commentary, by duly accredited teachers called rabbis. This legal system has a growing edge which tolerates differences of opinion, some more stringent, some more lenient; but in all essentials it is settled, and its authority is total.

In regard to Aggadah the situation is not so clear. There are literalists who regard every narrative of the Bible and Talmud as historical, and more relaxed interpreters who allow space for myth, legend and folklore. It is, at any rate, generally accepted that in matters involving only theory, not practice, different opinions may be allowed to stand side-by-side, without any need to harmonise them.

Progressive Judaism takes the liberal view where Aggadah is concerned and, as regards the fluid periphery of the Halachah, feels free to choose from the available range of opinions those which seem most appropriate to contemporary circumstances. But – and this is where it differs fundamentally from Orthodox Judaism – even the solid core of the Halachah is not, from its point of view, necessarily to be accepted in every instance.

What the writers of the Bible and the Talmud have to say is to be considered with reverential respect, for they were indeed the transmitters and interpreters of a divine revelation; but they were nevertheless human, and children of their various ages, and we may not therefore assume that they always 'got it right'. Indeed, we think we can point to quite a number of instances in which they 'got it wrong'. Therefore halachic questions settled long ago may be re-opened.

Perhaps I may clinch the point by quoting from a submission I made on behalf of the Council of Reform and Liberal Rabbis to the Government Inquiry into Human Fertilisation and Embryology (the 'Warnock Committee') in 1985. Our approach, I said, differs from that of Orthodox Judaism in the following ways.

'(1) We try to understand the Jewish Tradition *historically*, as interacting with its environment and undergoing change and development. (2) We seek from it guidance rather than governance, and find that it is often most relevant and helpful to us, not in its specific legislative enactments, but in the moral principles that motivated the legislators. (3) We cannot rule out the possibility that our ancestors may on occasion have been misled by their belief (which we do not share) in the inerrancy of Scripture and its ancient interpretations, or by the norms of their socio-cultural milieu, or for want of historical and scientific knowledge which has become available to us in modern times. (4) We are willing to admit the possibility that, with regard to some contemporary problems, definitive answers as to the Divine Will (which is always what concerns us) must be regarded as, for the time being, unattainable, and that we must therefore be content with tentative answers, or even suspend judgment altogether, pending further study and thought.'

The Need to Know

Why do we need to know, or decide, when life ceases? From a traditional point of view one reason is because as soon as life has ceased certain Mitzvot (obligatory observances) come into force, chief among them the duty of burial, which should be done without delay. That principle was inferred by a process of generalisation from a law in Deuteronomy (21:22f) which stipulates that the body of an executed criminal must not be left hanging overnight but buried on the same day. From a Progressive point of view that law has little relevance today, and though there are no doubt good psychological reasons for keeping the interval between death and burial (or cremation) reasonably short, nevertheless these have to be weighed against other considerations, for instance the need to allow time for an inquest, and to notify relatives who may have to travel long distances to attend the funeral. Therefore a delay, even of several days, may in many cases be quite proper.

Another reason, which is assuming ever greater importance, why it is necessary to determine with precision when life has ceased is because only after that is it permissible to remove organs from the body for transplant purposes – and even then of course only subject to the necessary authorisation. Traditional Halachists make a further stipulation: there must be evidence that the proposed transplant will save somebody else's life. That is because normally burial is considered a positive obligation, and post-mortem surgery a violation of the duty to treat the body of the deceased with respect, whereas the saving of life (פקוח נפש) supersedes these, as indeed practically all other requirements. There is also another principle involved, אין הולכין בפקוח נפש אחר הרוב, that when there is a chance to save a life we do not go by the majority (Ket. 15b), which is taken to mean that certainty is not necessary, probability is sufficient. But what constitutes a reasonable measure of probability is one of those 'grey areas' in which there are different opinions; Progressive Judaism inclines to the more lenient.

The Cessation of Life

When, then, *does* life cease? The Bible does not tell us, but we can perhaps guess what its legislators would have said. They clearly associated life with breath. When creating man, says the book of Genesis, God 'breathed into his nostrils the breath of life, and he became a living soul' (2:6). Indeed, both of the key words of that verse, נשמה and נפש, have the double meaning of 'breath' and 'life'. Similarly, the word רוח has the double meaning of 'wind' or 'breath' and 'spirit'. It is used, for instance, in the Psalm which says about 'the son of man': 'When his breath departs, he returns to his dust; on that very day his thoughts perish' (146:4).

There is also a recurring tendency to locate life in the blood (Gen. 9:4, Deut. 12:23), from which it might have been inferred that when the heart ceases to pump blood into the body, life ends. The heart is certainly regarded in the Bible as an organ of singular importance and, metaphorically at least, the *locus* of the chief mental processes such as thinking and willing – these rather than feeling, so that the Hebrew for 'heart' is often best translated 'mind'.

It is therefore highly probable that breathing and/or heartbeat would in biblical times have been considered the criteria of life, and just that is what we find when the issue becomes a matter of legal definition in Rabbinic times. The key passage occurs in a discussion about a collapsed building which asks: if there are people buried under the rubble, may one violate the Sabbath to dig them out? Yes, says the Mishnah (Yoma 8:7), if there is reason to think that they may still be alive. But how do you establish, asks the Gemara, whether that is the case? By pulling the body out far enough to uncover the nose, to test whether it is still breathing. But some say, adds the Gemara, far enough to uncover the heart, to ascertain whether it is still beating (85a).

This passage, and the medieval commentaries on it, have given rise to a complicated discussion in halachic literature as to whether *both* breathing and heartbeat must be tested or whether one suffices, how long one must wait after both have ceased before declaring the patient dead, and whether there are exceptional circumstances in which, though both have ceased, there is still muscular movement indicating life.

The argument has been well summarised by J. David Bleich, head of Yeshivah University, New York, in an essay entitled 'Establishing the Criteria of Death' (Bleich, 1977, chapter XVI; reprinted in Rosner and Bleich, 1979, chapter 17). His conclusions are that 'cessation of respiration constitutes the operative definition of death only because lack of respiration is also indicative of prior cessation of cardiac activity' and that 'death occurs only upon the cessation of both cardiac and respiratory functions' whereas 'the absence of other vital signs is not, insofar as Halakhah is concerned, a criterion of death' (Bleich, 1977, pp. 378f).

But what about 'brain death' and 'irreversible coma', which have been proposed in recent times as alternative criteria? Dr Bleich rejects both as halachically unacceptable. Thus he remarks that a number of instances have been reported 'in which patients have made either partial or complete recoveries despite previous electroencephalogram readings over an extended period of time which registered no brain activity' and quotes an impressive array of sources in support of that contention (ibid., p. 373). He concludes quite categorically: 'Brain death and irreversible coma are not acceptable definitions of death in so far as Halakhah is concerned. The sole criterion of death accepted by Halakhah is total cessation of both cardiac and respiratory activity' (ibid., p. 391); and in another essay he urges that any legislation re-defining death by neurological criteria would need to include an exemption clause to allow for conscientious objection by Jews (Rosner and Bleich, 1979, p. 312).

But Aaron Soloveichik, Head of Brisk Rabbinical College in Chicago, is less dogmatic. From a ruling by Maimonides (Yad, Hilchot Avelut 4:5) he deduces the opposite conclusion, not that respiration may continue after brain activity has ceased, but that brain activity may continue after respiration has ceased, so that 'the absence of spontaneous respiration does not in itself determine death' (ibid., p. 297). And he goes on to make the important, if obvious, point that death is usually *gradual*: 'Death is a process which begins the moment respiration ceases' and 'ends when all bodily functions emanating from a controlling center end. This means that when a person in whom death is imminent becomes devoid of respiration but other bodily functions such as the brain are potentially operative, such a person is no longer completely alive but not dead ... During this period, a person is in a state of semi-living'. But he goes on to indicate that there is a further question, whether a person in such a state is capable of resuscitation; if yes, 'one is prohibited from doing anything which may hasten his death'; if not, one may not desecrate the Sabbath to extricate him from the rubble (ibid., p. 301).

So much for the halachic debate. But from a Progressive point of view we need to ask ourselves whether there is any reason to suppose that the biblical or the talmudic or the medieval writers were privy to any information about the process of dying that is unavailable to us. Surely the *reverse* is the case, that *we* know more – even though we do not know everything! And what we know makes it clear that the ancients were mistaken in relating the life of the mind or soul to respiration or blood flow or heartbeat. All our knowledge indicates that mental activity is correlated with brain activity. Therefore as long as the brain is functioning there is human life; when the brain has ceased to function, even if other bodily processes such as respiration go on, what continues is not human but vegetative life.

The Preciousness of Life

It is customary to speak of the Jewish doctrine of the 'sanctity of life' as attested, for instance, by the Genesis teaching that human beings were created in God's image (1:27), the Deuteronomy injunction 'choose life' (30:19) and the declaration of the Mishnah that 'one who destroys a single human life is considered by Scripture as if they had destroyed a whole world, and one who saves a single human life as if they had saved a whole world' (San. 4:5). Some authorities have taken that doctrine very literally. For instance, Rabbi Dr Immanuel Jakobovits (as he then was) referred in his *Jewish Medical Ethics* (Jakobovits, 1975, p. 276) to 'Judaism's attribution of *infinite* value to human life', and went on to say: 'Infinity being indivisible, any fraction of life, however limited its expectancy or its health, remains equally infinite in value', from which a number of extremely rigorous consequences follow. But there is no need to press the sources quite so far; it is sufficient to take them to mean that human life is *immensely* precious, without introducing the ultimate concept of infinity.

What is chiefly deemed to follow from the 'sanctity' of life is the obligation to prolong it whenever possible and by all possible means. But here comes a paradox. In ancient times it was considered pious to submit oneself entirely to God as the ordainer of life and death, and, when ill, to pray to God for recovery, and it was therefore no simple matter for the Rabbis to sanction the practice of medicine. They did so by referring to a verse in the book of Exodus (21:19), which in a case of assault makes the assailant responsible for causing the victim to be healed, and concluding: מכאן שניתנה רשות לרופא לרפאות, 'Hence we know that a physician is permitted to heal' (Ber. 60a). Today, however, not only is it considered *permissible* for human physicians to encroach on what was once regarded as God's prerogative, but they are expected to go to extreme lengths to prolong life beyond the point at which, in the natural course of events, death would have supervened! Has this *volte face* perhaps gone too far? Just *how imperative* is the duty to prolong life?

The Prolongation of Life

Are there perhaps even circumstances in which there is, on the contrary, an obligation to *terminate* life? I raise this question only to clear the issue of euthanasia out of the way, partly because it is a whole big subject in itself and partly because in essence I accept the traditional Jewish view – not because it is traditional but because it seems right to me – that positive action with the intention of hastening death is wrong. In other words, I endorse, in a good sense, Arthur Clough's satirical rhyme, 'Thou shalt not kill but needst not strive / officiously to keep alive' ('The Latest Decalogue', 1862). Therefore the only question I wish to raise before I conclude is whether there are situations in which it is right to refrain from striving officiously to keep alive. Let me suggest that there are three.

First, where brain death has already occurred, so that what remains is only the 'semi-life' of a vegetative state, and it is certain beyond reasonable doubt that the coma is irreversible. In such a situation, not only is there no need to prolong life by 'heroic' measures, but if the point is reached *after* such measures have been initiated, it is then permissible to discontinue them, at least with the consent of the next-of-kin. Indeed, it is positively desirable, not only so as to free the expensive equipment for better purposes, but to spare the family unnecessary suffering. In this connection let me commend a moving article by Rabbi Daniel Jeremy Silver of Cleveland, Ohio, included in *Jewish Reflections on Death*, edited by Jack Riemer. Rabbi Silver recalls his experiences as a naval chaplain in the Korean War and mentions a neurological ward full of 'bodies of young men whose forebrain had been blown away'. Then he says: 'These vegetables suffered no pain, but think of the pain that was caused to their wives, children, and parents; not only the cruelty of losing a loved one in war but the cruelty of being in emotional limbo, having to visit a living corpse, having one's entire life stop for a year, and year and a half, all because medical science had kept certain organs pulsating' (Riemer, 1976, pp. 117f).

Secondly, there is the situation of multiple claims where a number of patients require life-saving and sustaining procedures but there is insufficient equipment for them all. On this subject there is an excellent responsum by Rabbi Solomon B. Freehof of Pittsburgh, Pennsylvania, entitled 'Choosing which Patient to Save' (Jacob, 1983, No. 75). He demonstrates from Jewish sources, first, that 'all people are alike in status as to the right to life', but secondly, that when a choice has to be made it may not be evaded by inaction, so that *all* the patients would die, when it would have been possible to save one or two, and thirdly, that the choice must be made on purely medical grounds, that is to say, in favour of the patient who is in greatest danger or who will benefit most.

Thirdly, there is the case of the terminally ill patient, who has no chance of recovery, and is in pain, and wishes to be allowed to die. In such a case it is of course permissible to administer a drug to relieve the pain even though it may slightly hasten death. For when the two duties of the doctor, to prolong life and to relieve pain, conflict, there is no need to take the view that the first must always take precedence. (On that subject, see Rabbi Walter Jacob's responsum in

Jacob, 1987, No. 83). But beyond that, there is no need to resort to 'heroic' measures to prolong the patient's life against his will. For although Dr Bleich denies it (Bleich, 1977, pp. 391f), I believe that there *is* a right to die with dignity.

In a responsum entitled 'Allowing a Terminal Patient to Die' (Jacob, 1983, No. 77), Rabbi Freehof refers to the famous story in the Talmud (Ket. 104a) of how a maidservant interrupted the prayers for Rabbi Judah ha-Nasi, who was dying in severe pain, and so enabled him to die without further suffering, which provided a basis in Jewish tradition for the view that in cases of hopeless suffering the physician is not duty-bound to force the patient to live a few days or hours longer. He also quotes the medieval authority Rabbi Nissim Gerondi to the effect that whereas normally 'it is our duty to pray for a sick person that he may recover, there comes a time when we should pray for God's mercy that he should die'. And he quotes a similar view from the *Sefer Chasidim*, where the author, Judah the Pious, bases himself on the words of Ecclesiastes, 'To everything there is a season, and a time for every purpose under heaven, עת ללדת ועת למות, a time to be born, and a time to die' (3:1f). In such cases, says Rabbi Freehof, to discontinue treatment is not to hasten death but to cease to delay it.

Similarly, Rabbi Silver remarks: 'We try to push off death as if death were always and ever an enemy … We've grown unaccustomed to death, and we tend to think that we must do anything and everything to keep death away from those whom we love. We've forgotten that, for many, death is a friend, a welcome visitor' (Riemer, 1976, p. 118).

Chapter 19

❖   ❖   ❖

Euthanasia

Jewish law has always prohibited active euthanasia – that is, deliberate action with the intention of hastening the death of a terminally ill patient. In modern times not only Orthodox but also Progressive rabbis have consistently taken that view. Therefore to permit active euthanasia would be a radical break with tradition. But the liberalism which Progressive Jews profess obliges them to be consider with open minds whether, in spite of the blanket prohibition of the tradition, active euthanasia might nevertheless be justified in some situations.

Such an exercise requires us not only to study the tradition, but also to look behind it to the values that motivated it, and then to ask ourselves whether they are valid for us. It is therefore not only a halachic investigation as traditionally understood, but also what Rabbi Moshe Zemer has called a 'meta-halachic' one.

In the Bible

The Bible does not discuss euthanasia at all, and records only one instance of it, relating to the death of King Saul, of which there are, however, two different accounts. According to one, Saul, faced with the prospect of being captured and tortured to death by the Philistines, asks his armour-bearer to kill him, and, when he refuses, kills himself (I Sam. 31:3f). According to the other, an Amalekite finds Saul still alive, impaled on his sword, and, asked by him to deliver the *coup-de-grâce*, does so, but is subsequently executed (II Sam. 1:1–16), with the implication that euthanasia is a criminal offence, even when done at the behest of a king of Israel.

Although we have no other directly relevant evidence to go on, I think it may be safely assumed that Biblical Judaism would have been wholly opposed to active euthanasia, for its whole philosophy was that God alone is the dispenser of life and death. As it says in Hannah's prayer, ה' ממית ומחיה, 'The Eternal One kills and revives' (I Sam. 2:6), and any human encroachment on that divine prerogative would have been considered sacrilegious. To which we must add the Biblical doctrine that humanity was created בצלם אלהים, in the Divine Image (Gen. 1:27), so that to destroy a human life is to destroy something of the utmost sanctity, as well as the general affirmation of the value of life which runs all through the Bible, as when it says, ובחרת בחיים, 'Therefore choose life' (Deut. 30:19).

In Rabbinic Literature

The same reverence for human life persists in Rabbinic literature. It is reflected in the daily morning prayer that begins, 'O my God, the soul which You have given me is pure; You created it, and formed it, and breathed it into me, You preserve it within me, and You will one day take it from me' (Ber. 60b), and in the great teaching of the Mishnah that one who destroys a single human life is considered as if they had destroyed a whole world (San. 4:5). It also finds expression in specific legislation. For instance, the Mishnah rules that to close the eyes of a dying person, because it could hasten death, is akin to murder (Shab. 23:5 and Rashi ad loc.; see also Semachot 1:4).

The attitude to suicide, however, is more lenient. Although there is a general assumption that it is wrong, it is not explicitly forbidden. Several instances of suicide – like the case of the four hundred boys and girls who jumped into the sea rather than fall into the hands of the Romans (Git. 57b) – are reported without disapproval. There is indeed a ruling that suicides are to be denied the usual burial rites (Semachot 2:1), but the subsequent tendency of the law is to qualify that in various ways, and to disregard it altogether whenever there are grounds for thinking that the suicide acted under duress (באונס) and not with deliberation (לדעת).

Similarly, there is some leniency about *passive* euthanasia, in the sense of abstention from, or even discontinuation of, some action which would artificially prolong for a short space of time the life of a dying patient. The story most often quoted in this connection is of the death of Rabbi Judah ha-Nasi. His colleagues prayed for his recovery, and his maidservant at first did likewise, but when she saw how he was suffering she threw a bucket down from the roof of the house. The clatter interrupted the prayers of the rabbis, and so the soul of Rabbi Judah at last had rest (Ket. 104a).

Another relevant story from the Talmud is that of the martyrdom of Rabbi Chananiah ben Teradion, who allowed his Roman executioner to remove a tuft of moist wool which was keeping the flames from his heart and prolonging his agony (AZ 18a).

On the basis of these and other passages the law was finally codified in the Shulchan Aruch as follows. First Joseph Caro rules: הגוסס הרי הוא כחי לכל דבר, 'A dying patient [which the Halachah generally takes to mean one who is not expected to live more than three days] is like a living person for all purposes.' Therefore we do not perform any of the last rites on him, and anyone who does so, הרי זה שופך דמים, 'is a shedder of blood'. Then Moses Isserles, in his gloss, adds: וכן אסור לגרום למת שימות מהרה, 'Similarly it is forbidden to hasten the death of a person who is dying', for instance by removing a pillow from under him. However, says Isserles, 'if there is דבר שגורם עכוב יציאת הנפש, a cause which delays the departure of the soul', such as a continuous noise, 'it is permissible to remove that cause, דאין בזה מעשה כלל, for that involves no positive action at all' (YD 339:1).

In Modern Judaism

A negative stance towards active euthanasia is maintained in modern times, as one would expect, by Orthodox rabbis. There is a variety of views only about passive euthanasia, from those who would disallow even that, to those who would go so far as to permit the withholding of food and drink, and even to argue that in some cases it is actually *forbidden* to prolong the life of a dying patient by artificial means (see Herring, 1984, pp. 81–86).

More surprisingly, Progressive rabbis have endorsed the traditional view. Israel Bettan, for instance, wrote in 1950: 'The Jewish ideal of the sanctity of human life and the supreme value of the individual soul would suffer incalculable harm if, contrary to the moral law, men were at liberty to determine the conditions under which they might put an end to their own lives and the lives of other men' (Jacob, 1983, p. 263).

Similarly, Rabbi Solomon B. Freehof wrote in 1969: 'If the patient is a hopelessly dying patient, the physician has no duty to keep him alive a little longer. He is entitled to die. If the physician attempts actively to hasten death, that is against the ethics of Jewish law (ibid., p. 260). And in a volume of Responsa dated 1971 he wrote about 'the limits of freedom of action of the physician in relation to the hopelessly dying patient' that 'he may not take any overt action to hasten death such as giving him, perhaps, an overdose of an opiate; but he may refrain from doing that which will prevent his dying' (Freehof, 1971, p. 202).

Even as recently as 1980, the Responsa Committee of the Central Conference of American Rabbis, headed by Rabbi Walter Jacob, concluded: 'We would not endorse any positive steps leading toward death. We would recommend pain-killing drugs which would ease the remaining days of a patient's life. We would reject any general endorsement of euthanasia, but where all "independent life" has ceased ... further medical support systems need not be continued' (Jacob, 1983, p. 274).

Re-opening the Debate

In the face of such unanimity, it requires more than a little audacity to re-open the debate; yet that is what we need to do.

As we have seen, the basic motive underlying the traditional opposition to euthanasia is the feeling that it is wrong for human beings to intervene in natural processes that are properly within God's prerogative. But that principle was breached long ago, when human beings resorted to hunting, cattle-breeding and agriculture, and, more relevantly, when the Rabbis decided that there was no need to rely on prayer alone in case of sickness, but that suitably qualified human beings were allowed to co-operate with God by practising medicine (Ber. 60a).

Similarly, Judaism has always allowed contraception in certain cases, and Progressive Judaism has extended these, and it could therefore be argued: if it is permissible to practise birth control, why not death control?

The other main ground for opposing euthanasia has been the doctrine of the sanctity of life. But that, too, was breached long ago, since the Bible sanctions both warfare and capital punishment. Both were indeed hedged about with many restrictions in the subsequent development of Judaism. But the principle remained that in some circumstances the general obligation to preserve life may yield to a more urgent purpose; and if such a purpose may be to resist aggression or to punish crime, might it not also be to diminish pain?

The Relieving of Pain

There is admittedly very little direct evidence in the classical Jewish sources that it was considered obligatory to relieve pain. But there is indirect evidence. For instance, the Talmud relates that it was standard practice to drug a condemned criminal before execution (San. 43a). It also repeatedly states the opinion that he should not be made to suffer more than necessary, since the commandment, 'You shall love your neighbour as yourself' (Lev. 19:18) obliges us to choose for him מיתה יפה, an easy death – literally 'a beautiful death', which is the exact equivalent of the term 'euthanasia' (San. 45a, 52a; Pes. 75a; Ket. 37a).

Certainly there is general agreement nowadays that it is a physician's duty not only to cure sickness but also to relieve pain: a duty that flows naturally from the commandment of neighbourly love and, more generally, from Judaism's emphasis on compassion.

Furthermore, there is a tendency among the more lenient interpreters of the Halachah to permit the administration of a pain-killing drug, even if there is a risk that it may prove fatal, provided that there is a fair chance that it may save the life of a patient who would otherwise die (Freehof, 1971, p. 199); and Reform rabbis have held that it is permissible more generally if the purpose is to relieve suffering, even though it may have the side-effect of shortening the patient's life (Jacob, 1987, p. 140).

The Question of Legislation

While 'mercy killing' is a criminal offence in Britain, it is nevertheless generally conceded that 'effective management of pain and distress which has the side-effect of curtailing life is an acceptable and indeed necessary option of ethical practice' (BMA, 1993, p. 157). Whether the law should be further liberalised is a question we must nevertheless consider.

Obviously, we are only talking about *voluntary*, i.e., requested, euthanasia. The idea of unrequested euthanasia, even in the sense of mercy-killing, let alone as practised by the Nazis from motives anything but merciful, is totally abhorrent. Equally obviously, any such legislation would have to have built into it the most stringent safeguards, and one of the tantalising questions is whether it is indeed *possible* to devise legislation which would not be unacceptably open to abuse or, more generally, likely to lower the threshold of respect for human life in our society.

That it is in principle desirable to liberalise existing legislation, is a conclusion hard to resist when one considers that there are circumstances in which suicide is commonly regarded as a legitimate, even honourable option, and that voluntary euthanasia is a kind of assisted suicide. Thus Dr Eustace Chesser wrote: 'Any man who chooses death rather than deny his beliefs or betray his friends proclaims to the world that the right to decide whether to live or die belongs inalienably to each one of us ... Modern medicine is so ingenious that life can be prolonged far beyond the time when it holds anything worth preserving.' Therefore patients are sometimes 'sentenced to life – and for some that is worse than death ... In my opinion the right to die is the last and greatest human freedom' (Chesser, 1967, pp. 110ff).

If we believe not only that it was right that, by the 1961 Act, suicide should have ceased to be a crime, but that in some cases it is not a sin either, and can even be morally right, then by what logic can we object *in principle* to voluntary euthanasia, which, as has been pointed out, is essentially assisted suicide?

Nobody would question that it is the doctor's duty to act in the best interest of the patient. But what is in the patient's best interest when his or her condition is not curable? *Always* the relief of pain, and *usually* the prolongation of life; but might it not *sometimes* be the diminution, not only of the intensity, but also of the duration, of the pain?

We know that God does not wish us to live for ever, and we also know that, being compassionate, God would not wish us to suffer excessively. Is it not then possible, even likely, that in some circumstances doctors are called upon to act as co-workers (משׁותפים) with God in both easing and shortening the process of dying?

Surely it must be so in theory. But how these circumstances are to be defined, and whether legislation can be devised which would not in practice do more harm than good – these are questions to which there are no easy answers.

Chapter 20

❖　　❖　　❖

BURIAL OF PROGRESSIVE PROSELYTE IN ORTHODOX CEMETERY

A colleague wrote: 'Our congregation has had the use of the cemetery belonging to the local Orthodox community from its creation until now. With the previous rabbi of that community there was a gentleman's agreement by which no question was asked … Lately there arose the case of a woman, a member of our congregation, converted by a liberal Beit Din, devoted to Judaism and to Israel, living a full Jewish life, who expressed the wish to be buried in the Jewish cemetery. Her burial there was refused. Can we find halachic justification for an Orthodox rabbi to authorise such a burial?'

The Refusal

It has to be admitted that the new rabbi is not necessarily bound by the gentleman's agreement his predecessor had with the community and, more generally, that agreements of such a nature, which are merely oral, have little weight in Jewish law. Nevertheless, his decision to disregard the agreement is, at worst, a sort of breach of promise, for which Jewish tradition expresses the strongest disapproval (cf. BM 4:2), and at best, an act calculated to sow disharmony where previously there was harmony, and therefore a violation of the spirit of Jewish unity on which our Tradition lays the greatest stress.

For both reasons, the rabbi's action would be most reprehensible unless he felt reluctantly *compelled*, out of loyalty to some principle of the most unambiguous clarity and overriding importance, to act as he did. On the basis of the injunction, הוי דן את כל־האדם לכף זכות, that we should always judge others charitably (Avot 1:6), let us assume that such was indeed the case, and, in particular, that the rabbi felt constrained by the following two considerations: (a) that the woman of the case is not Jewish and (b) that non-Jewish persons may not be buried in a Jewish cemetery. Let us examine these propositions in turn.

The Status of a Non-Orthodox Proselyte

It is well known that Orthodox Jewish authorities nowadays take the view that conversions performed by non-Orthodox Batei Din are invalid. But it is far from certain that they *need* to take that view. The reason generally given is that in such conversions the element of קבלת המצוות, acceptance of the commandments, is not present in the fullest sense. But there is considerable disagreement in the literature of the Halachah as to whether an explicit affirmation of such acceptance is required even לכתחלה, *ab initio*, let alone בדיעבד, *ex post facto*; there is even an opinion that intending proselytes should not be taught all the Mitzvot until *after* their conversion. It would therefore be perfectly possible for an Orthodox Beit Din, if it were so inclined, to rule that a person converted by a Liberal Beit Din is Jewish, at least בדיעבד, after the event, and by חזקה, presumption; and all the more so if, as in the case under discussion, the person has led a life of loyalty to Judaism and the Jewish people for a considerable time. At worst, there is a ספק, doubt, and in cases of doubt concerning matters of Rabbinic Law, which is what we are dealing with here, the rule is that one takes the lenient view: ספק דדבריהם להקל (Eruvin 45b).

It goes without saying that a proselyte such as the woman of this case would be considered Jewish by Liberal, Progressive, Reform, Reconstructionist and Conservative Judaism, accounting for approximately three million of the world's Jews; and it is likely that most secular Jews would take the same view. Likewise the State of Israel would have accepted such a person as Jewish for the purpose of the Law of Return. Only the Orthodox would question the woman's Jewishness, and they are, globally, a minority. In the United States they comprise under 10 percent of the Jewish population; in the State of Israel, less than 20 percent. And even the Orthodox, as I have pointed out, are not *compelled* to regard such a person as non-Jewish. If they do so, it is because they *choose* to do so, for reasons which have more to do with their political struggle against non-Orthodox Judaism than with a necessary interpretation of the Halachah.

Burial of Non-Jews in a Jewish Cemetery

Let me now turn to the second proposition, that non-Jews may not be buried in a Jewish cemetery. Is there a hard and fast law to that effect? The reason usually given in support of that assumption is that a Jewish cemetery is 'consecrated ground'. But the concept of 'consecrated ground' in that sense is Christian, and it could be argued that its application to a Jewish cemetery is a kind of חוקת הגוי, imitation of non-Jewish customs. It is true that there is a ceremony for the inauguration of a Jewish cemetery which is sometimes called a 'consecration' (see, e.g., Goldin, 1939, Section XXXII). But that is of relatively recent origin, and the term 'consecration' means nothing more than 'dedication'. Nowhere in Jewish tradition, so far as I know, is the term אדמת קדש, 'holy ground', applied to a cemetery. And even if a Jewish cemetery were 'holy ground', the suggestion that the burial in it of the body of a non-Jew would 'desecrate' it would be preposterous. Indeed, the whole concept of a communal cemetery has little basis in Jewish tradition, which only requires that a Jew should be buried בתוך שלו, in a plot belonging to him or his family (BB 102a).

On the contrary, there is a Baraita of the greatest importance for our purpose which states it as a positive duty that we should bury non-Jews as well as Jews: וקוברין מתי נכרים עם מתי ישראל מפני דרכי שלום, '... and we bury the dead of the Gentiles along with the dead of Israel for the sake of peace' (Git. 61a). It is true that Rashi comments: לא בקברי ישראל, 'not in Jewish graves', and that comment has sometimes been adduced as ground for refusing to bury non-Jews in Jewish cemeteries. But Rashi does not say that non-Jews may not be buried *among* Jewish graves – if he had meant that he would surely have said לא בין קברי ישראל – nor does his language imply a categorical prohibition. There is no need to infer from it any more than that *as a general rule* we do not bury non-Jews in our cemeteries. And that is indeed the case. Since Jewish cemeteries are established and maintained by Jewish communities for the primary purpose of burying their own dead, nobody would suggest that they should be available for the burial of non-Jews on a regular basis.

The only question is whether an *exception* may be made for a person whose Jewish status is technically questionable but who has a good claim to be buried among Jews; and nothing in Rashi's comment precludes that possibility. It should also be added that the greatest codifiers, including the Rambam (Maimonides), the Smag (Moses of Coucy, author of Sefer Mitzvot ha-Gadol) and Joseph Caro (author of the Shulchan Aruch) report the Gittin 61a Baraita *without* Rashi's qualification.

The only other ground on which it has sometimes been considered improper to bury non-Jews in Jewish cemeteries is the principle that 'we do not bury the wicked next to the righteous' (אין קוברין רשע אצל צדיק, San. 47a). That principle is indeed repeated in the Codes, e.g., Shulchan Aruch, YD 362:5, which adds that two persons who were enemies in life should not be buried together (אנשים שהיו שונאים זה לזה אין לקברם יחד, 362:6). But where that principle is stated, nothing is said about Jews and non-Jews. To apply it to that issue, to which it does not refer, would involve the monstrous proposition that all Jews are righteous and all non-Jews wicked, or else the equally monstrous proposition that Jews and non-Jews are necessarily enemies. And to apply such an argument to the case of a woman who has actually embraced Judaism and identified herself with the Jewish people, who is 'devoted to Judaism and to Israel' and 'living a full Jewish life' – that would be so outrageous as to constitute nothing less than a חלול השם, 'profanation of God's name'.

Conclusion

If the cemetery in question belongs to the Orthodox community, and if that community has given full authority to its rabbi to decide who may and who may not be buried in it, there is probably nothing that can be done to alter the situation unless the rabbi can be persuaded to change his mind. But to the question, whether he is *justified* in the stand he has taken, the answer in my view is an emphatic 'no'. There is no unambiguous and overriding halachic consideration that positively compelled him to act in a manner so insensitive to the wishes of a good woman and so harmful to communal unity.

I reiterate that the woman is clearly Jewish from any Jewish other than an Orthodox point of view, and even from an Orthodox point of view she should at least have been given the benefit of any doubt. But even if there had been a compelling reason to regard her as non-Jewish, which there was not, it would still have been proper to act in accordance with the spirit of the Gittin 61a Baraita, about which Maimonides wrote: 'Even with regard to non-Jews, the Sages commanded that we should visit their sick and bury their dead with our own, and to maintain their poor on the same basis as our own, for the sake of the ways of peace. For it says: "The Eternal One is good to all, and God's compassion extends to all God's creatures" [Ps. 145:9]. And it further says (of wisdom, understood as referring to Torah): "Its ways are ways of pleasantness, and all its paths are peace" (Prov. 3:17)' (Yad, Hilchot Melachim 10:12).

Chapter 21

❖   ❖   ❖

JEWISH IDENTITY

What are the Jews?

Before the Second World War the great debate about the Jews was: what are they? Are they a race, a nation, a people, a religious fellowship, a natural community, a civilisation? It was a passionate, confused and inconclusive debate which yielded more heat than light. In retrospect, we can see that this was partly because of a failure to understand the semantics involved. For to ask whether A is a B is to ask: given the facts about A and the usage of B, *how appropriate* is it to call A a B? If the protagonists had understood this, they would surely have realised that the debate they really wished to conduct was neither factual nor linguistic but programmatic, concerning the attitude to be adopted towards the Zionist enterprise.

Who is a Jew?

After the Second World War the debate fizzled out. The State of Israel had been established, and the need to support it was conceded, if not with equal enthusiasm, by all sorts and conditions of Jews; and if any doubts remained, they were dispelled by the Six Day War. But the old debate had hardly ceased when it broke out afresh in another form, expressed in the question: who is a Jew?

This new phase began with the Law of Return, which the Knesset passed in 1950, affirming that 'every Jew has the right to immigrate to the country', and the problem which soon arose over its interpretation. The decision of the Israeli government that all who declared themselves to be Jewish were to be so registered aroused a storm of protest which prompted Prime Minister David Ben Gurion to solicit the opinions of leading Jewish intellectuals around the world. The answers he received 'ranged from reaffirmation of the *halakhah* to acceptance of inner emotional choice and labeling by the outside world as valid forms of Jewish identity' (*Encyclopaedia Judaica*, Vol. 10, p. 63).

That was in 1958. Then, in 1966, there was the Brother Daniel case, when the Supreme Court ruled that an apostate could not claim Jewish status under the Law of Return, and in 1970 the Shalit case, when it ruled that the man's children could be registered as Jews, even though their mother was not Jewish and they had not been converted, but its ruling was subsequently overturned by the Knesset.

Three Camps

But these were only the first skirmishes. It is since the 1970s that the debate has escalated into a *Kulturkampf*, periodically re-ignited by the attempts of the religious parties to amend the Law of Return so as to restrict its application to those who are Jewish according to the Halachah (Rabbinic Law) as defined by the Orthodox authorities.

Once again, therefore, the debate is in reality neither linguistic nor factual but political, concerning the monopoly of Orthodoxy; but the main battle line is no longer between Zionism and non–Zionism. Instead, a threefold division has emerged.

First, there are the Orthodox, determined to assert the sole authority of the Halachah. They probably number no more than two million, but at least as many again if one adds those who, while not Orthodox themselves, nevertheless regard Orthodoxy as normative. According to them, only those may be accepted as Jewish who were born of a Jewish mother or have been converted to Judaism by an Orthodox rabbinic court.

Secondly, there are the various non-Orthodox religious movements: Liberal, Reform, Reconstructionist, Masorti and Conservative. Their combined membership is perhaps three million, to which an indefinite number of unaffiliated sympathisers needs to be added. They agree that Jewish status is a matter of birth or conversion but, as regards conversion, they have their own standards and procedures which fail to satisfy the requirements of the Orthodox, and, as regards birth, some of them accept patrilineality as well as matrilineality.

Thirdly, there is an indeterminate number, certainly running to several million, of Secular Jews who, though not religious, nevertheless regard themselves as belonging to the Jewish people on ethnic, national or cultural grounds. They tend to favour a broad, inclusive policy, with emphasis on self-identification, but have not come up with an agreed definition.

We are therefore witnessing a power struggle between three camps of approximately equal numerical strength, and it is impossible to predict how, when or whether it will be resolved. Meanwhile, however, it may be helpful to analyse the issues involved.

Not a Matter of Genetics

One thing at least is clear: that Jewishness is not transmitted genetically. It is indeed true that there are one or two rare medical conditions which are significantly more common among Jews, or some Jews, than in the general population. The incidence of Tay-Sachs Disease, for instance, is abnormally high among Ashkenazi Jews. But these are marginal phenomena which attest to nothing more than a high rate of endogamy in recent centuries.

It is also true that certain racial types – in terms of blood group, bone structure, skin pigmentation, colour of hair and eyes, etc. – are more common among Jews than in the general population of, say, China, Central Africa or Scandinavia. But they are hardly more common than among the Mediterranean peoples. To put it another way, a random sample of Jews would be found to be anthropologically almost, though not quite, as heterogeneous as a random sample of humanity.

For this anthropological fact there is a good historical explanation: that, even if the ancient Israelites were a 'pure' race, which there is no reason to suppose, they were soon joined, as the Bible testifies, by a 'mixed multitude' (Exod. 12:38); that in the Greco-Roman period large numbers of Gentiles converted to Judaism; and that throughout the ages there has been a constant intermingling through intermarriage as well as proselytism.

From this it follows (reverting for a moment to the pre-war controversy) that, given the facts about the Jews, and given the usage of the word 'race' not only in anthropology but also in general parlance, the degree of appropriateness of calling the Jews a race is very low.

It also follows that a newborn Jewish baby is genetically indistinguishable from a newborn non-Jewish baby except for the rather uninteresting fact that if an unidentified baby has 'Mediterranean' racial features it is *statistically* more likely to be Jewish than it would be if it had 'Scandinavian' racial features; the chances might be, say, one in three hundred compared with one in three thousand.

In addition to being almost totally inapplicable, the genetic part of the story is also irrelevant, since it tells us nothing significant about the nature of Jewishness.

Cultural Transmission

If Jewishness is not transmitted genetically, it must be transmitted culturally. What that means may be illuminated if we consider cultural transmission in its most primitive form: among animals.

On 28 October 1976 the *New Scientist* carried an article by Dr Richard Dawkins, then Professor of Animal Behaviour at Oxford, reporting the field work of fellow zoologist P.F. Jenkins, who had been studying a song-bird called saddleback on an island off the shore of New Zealand. Jenkins had discovered that the singing habits of these birds were not innate but learnt by imitation; also that an individual bird would sometimes vary the tune, and then the variation would be copied by other birds and become part of the repertoire of the flock. This, said Professor Dawkins, was an example of cultural transmission; and since an individual unit of genetic transmission is called a gene, he thought it would be useful to coin a corresponding term for an individual item of cultural transmission, and proposed the term 'meme', which he derived with a little licence from a Greek word meaning 'to imitate'. He was then able to speak of the song repertoire of the saddlebacks as their 'meme pool'.

We may, I think, adopt the same terminology when speaking of cultural transmission among humans. In that context, a meme or cluster of memes might be, for instance, a word or a phrase or a language; a tune or a song or a symphony; a gesture or a ritual or a dance; a memory or a prayer or a hope; a superstition or a theological doctrine or a political manifesto; a custom or a law or an institution.

We may then say that the different groups – nations, faith communities etc. – which constitute humanity have distinctive meme pools. Distinctive but not necessarily completely different, for there is much overlapping. Some memes may be specific to just one people, as igloos are specific to Eskimos; other memes, like Coca-Cola, may be universal! The distinctiveness lies in the configuration.

The Jewish Meme Pool

Judaism, if we use the term in its broadest sense, not merely as a religion but as a culture, may be said to be the meme pool of the Jewish people. Its component elements are all those memes or combinations of memes which have been distinctive or characteristic (though not necessarily in an exclusive sense) of the Jewish people in any period of their history and in any land of their settlement. But to say that is to recognise at once that no single Jewish individual or community has ever been in possession of the total meme pool. Each, by accident or design, appropriates and in turn transmits only a selection. In that sense there have been many Judaisms, each representing one configuration of Jewish memes.

Some memes, which we may call foundational or first-order, have indeed featured in all or most phases of Judaism. They include, for instance, ethical monotheism and the Hebrew Bible. It is difficult to imagine any kind of Judaism without them. Some, which we may call structural or second-order memes, have featured only in some phases of Judaism but, in these, have played a major role. For instance, the Temple with its sacrifices played a major role in Biblical Judaism; the Synagogue with its liturgy played a major role in Rabbinic Judaism. Still other memes, which may be called third-order, are (to continue the architectural metaphor) only ornamental. They feature in one kind of Judaism but not another, and their removal would do little damage to the structure. Thus Ashkenazi, Sefardi and Chasidic Jews, and even sub-groups and local communities of each, have distinctive customs and melodies which they may cherish but on which nothing much hinges.

Bearing these distinctions in mind, we may then ask, about the Jewish meme pool as a whole, how large a part has been played in it, for instance, by memes of a religious kind. Such an inquiry is of course highly subjective, But I will nevertheless venture these generalisations: that *in the main* Jewish history has been a religious history, Jewish literature has been a religious literature, Jewish beliefs have been religious beliefs, Jewish laws and customs have been religious laws and customs, the Jewish calendar has been a religious calendar, Jewish institutions have been religious institutions, Jewish leadership has been a religious leadership, and the only mode of entry into the Jewish community, other than by birth, has been the religious process of conversion.

Therefore (reverting once more to the pre-war debate) it does seem to me that to characterise the Jews as a religious community is a great deal more appropriate than to regard them as an ethnic or a national group. On the other hand the situation is fluid. Both the secularisation and the zionisation processes of the last century or two may yet produce a sea-change, transforming the Jewish people, for good or ill, into an entity significantly different from what they have characteristically been during the greater part of pre-modern history;

and there are some indications that that has already begun to happen. It may be, for instance, that Jewish culture, which in the past has been predominantly (though not exclusively) a religious culture, is in the process of becoming more of a secular ethnic or national culture in which religion is only an optional component. But whether, without the religious cement to hold it together, such a culture would long endure, remains to be seen.

Jewish-Making Characteristics

However, as has been pointed out, the current debate is not about the collective nature of the Jewish people, but about individual Jewish identity; and the best way to approach that is to ask: what makes a Jew a Jew?

What we have already said enables us to answer that question in terms of Jewish memes, or 'Jewish-making characteristics', as they may also be called, not indeed in the sense that any one alone makes a person Jewish, but that the more abundantly they are present, the greater becomes the appropriateness of describing the person in question as Jewish. *Jewishness, in other words, is a matter of degree.*

A few examples may help to make that clear. Belief in One God is a Jewish meme; yet it is not *exclusively* Jewish, for Christians and Muslims are also monotheists. Circumcision is a Jewish meme, but is also practised, among others, by Muslims. Regarding oneself as Jewish is a Jewish meme, but is also a claim made by Judeo-Christian groups such as 'Jews for Jesus'. Observing the seventh day as a sabbath is a Jewish meme, but applies also to Seventh Day Adventists. A knowledge of Hebrew is a Jewish meme; but there are also non-Jewish Hebraists. Belonging to a synagogue is a Jewish meme, but there are instances of non-Jews who have fraudulently obtained, or been inadvertently admitted to, synagogue membership. Going to synagogue, especially on occasions such as the Day of Atonement, is a Jewish meme, but is sometimes done by non-Jewish visitors. Liking Jewish food, laughing at Jewish jokes, and using Yiddish expressions, are Jewish characteristics, but are also found among non-Jews.

Nevertheless, if an individual not only believes in One God but is circumcised, regards himself as Jewish, observes the Jewish sabbath, has a knowledge of Hebrew, belongs to a synagogue, goes to synagogue on the Day of Atonement, likes Jewish food, laughs at Jewish jokes, and uses Yiddish expressions, then it is clearly fitting to consider such a person Jewish; and, as already pointed out, the more these examples are multiplied, as they could be a hundredfold, the more appropriate it becomes to classify the person as Jewish, and the more absurd it would be to do otherwise.

Reality and Law

What has been said so far relates to what constitutes Jewishness *in reality*. In reality, as should now be very clear, Jewishness is a matter of degree. In this context it makes sense to ask, *'How Jewish is X?'*, and the answer admits of an infinite variety of possible gradations, from 'completely' through 'borderline' to 'not at all.' In this context it makes no sense to demand peremptorily, 'Is X a Jew – yes or no?' To do that is to misunderstand the semantic situation.

However, for purposes of *law* it is sometimes necessary to make a hard and fast distinction between Jew and non-Jew. That oppressive regimes, such as Nazi Germany, have laid down precise definitions, is indeed nothing more than an obscene fact of history, which need not detain us. But Jewish communities themselves have naturally felt obliged to decide who shall and who shall not be regarded as Jewish for certain purposes, such as synagogue membership and entitlement to Jewish marriage and burial.

What needs to be clearly understood, though, is that in a legal context the question, who is a Jew, has an entirely different meaning. In particular, the verb 'to be' has a different function. To ask, in a legal context, who is a Jew, is to ask, who *shall be deemed to be* a Jew for the purpose of the law in question – precisely that and neither more nor less.

Now it is clearly desirable that there should be a correspondence – the closer the better – between reality and law. For if the legal definition excludes many people who, in reality, are plainly Jewish, and includes many who, in reality, are plainly non-Jewish, an unsatisfactory situation results in which those affected feel resentful and the law is brought into disrepute. On the other hand, it would hardly be practical to investigate the personal history of every individual in order to ascertain to what extent a Jewish identity has been established. Therefore in practice one has to make do with a legal definition that *approximates* to reality.

When Both Parents are Jewish or Non-Jewish

In the history of Judaism that *desideratum* has generally been satisfied by two simplifying assumptions: that where both parents are Jewish, Jewish identity will generally be transmitted, and the offspring may

therefore be deemed to be Jewish; and, conversely, that where neither parent is Jewish, no such transmission will normally take place,
and the offspring are therefore deemed to be non-Jewish.

There are only three exceptions to these general rules. One is the
case of the person born of Jewish parents who renounces Judaism
and converts to another religion; in other words, the apostate. The
general tendency in Judaism has been to regard an apostate as still
Jewish for *some* purposes but to require a formal act of reversion
before according to such a person *all* the privileges of Jewish status.

Conversely, there is the case of the person of non-Jewish parent-
age who converts to Judaism. Obviously, such a person becomes
Jewish by the act of conversion, and the only problem is one we
have already mentioned: that the authorities of Orthodox Judaism
refuse to accept as valid conversions performed under non-Orthodox auspices. The reasons they commonly give for their refusal
are: that non-Orthodox (Progressive and Conservative) Jewish rabbinic courts lack the competence to perform conversions; that they
perform them incorrectly; and that they do not obtain from their
candidates an undertaking to observe *all* the commandments which
Orthodox Judaism considers obligatory.

This disagreement about the validity of conversions causes much
distress both in Israel and in the Diaspora. There is, however, no reason why the Orthodox authorities should not re-convert those whom
they consider to have been inadequately converted, and in many
instances they do so.

The third exception is the case of a baby born of non-Jewish parents being adopted in infancy by Jewish parents and therefore receiving from the start a normal Jewish upbringing. In such a case
Orthodox Judaism would require conversion (in so far as it permits the
conversion of infants, which is, from its point of view, a problematic
issue) but the more radical branches of Progressive Judaism would
accord Jewish status to such a person without need of conversion.

When Only One Parent is Jewish

What happens, however, when one parent is Jewish and the other is
not? In such a case the genetic consideration, even if it were relevant,
which it is not, would leave the issue undecided, since genetically, as
we know (though the ancients did not know it), a child inherits as
much from one parent as from the other. The question, therefore, is
what is likely to happen culturally – whether the father or the mother
is likely to exercise the stronger influence – and whether a simplifying

assumption can be made about that. The answer to that question has to be given in three historical stages.

In biblical times such a simplifying assumption does indeed seem to have been made: in favour of patrilineality. For the Bible mentions many individuals who, though born of a non-Jewish mother, were evidently regarded as Jewish by virtue of having been born of a Jewish father. They include Manasseh and Ephraim, sons of Joseph and Asenath, an Egyptian; Gershon and Eliezer, sons of Moses and Zipporah, a Midianite; Rehoboam, King of Judah, son of Solomon and Naamah, an Ammonite; and Ahaziah, King of Israel, son of Ahab and Jezebel, a Phoenician.

In post-biblical times, however, this policy was reversed in favour of matrilineality. The earliest clear statement of this volte-face is to be found in the Mishnah (Kid. 3:12), and it must therefore be assumed to date from the first or second century CE. No reason is given. Subsequently the Talmud sought to justify it by an artificial interpretation of a Pentateuchal proof-text (Deut.7:3f; Kid. 68b).

About the real reason, there has been much speculation. Suggested explanations include the fact that maternity is easier to prove than paternity, especially in times of war; the influence of Roman law, under which the children of a mixed marriage followed the mother as regards citizenship if there had been no legal marriage; and the desire to discourage Jewish men from marrying non-Jewish women, intensified by the wave of anti-Gentile feeling following the Maccabean and Roman wars.

Whatever the reason may have been, matrilineality became the accepted principle by which the status of the offspring of mixed marriages was determined in Rabbinic Judaism. That principle remained unchallenged in the ensuing centuries – partly, it must be surmised, because out-marriage among Jews was sufficiently rare not to make it seriously problematic.

In recent times, however, the rate of intermarriage between Jews and non-Jews has risen dramatically, and demonstrated that whereas in some such cases the mother's religious influence prevails, in quite as many the father's prevails, while in yet other cases the children receive a mixed religious upbringing, or none at all. In other words, no simplifying assumption, either patrilineal or matrilineal, can any longer be made as to what is likely to happen to the children of mixed marriages, and consequently a yawning gap has emerged between reality and law – the reality of how such children are brought up and the insistence of Rabbinic Law that their maternity alone is determinant.

This unprecedented situation has prompted the more radical branches of non-Orthodox Judaism to deviate both from Biblical

Judaism, with its emphasis on patrilineality, and from Rabbinic Judaism, with its insistence on matrilineality, by accepting *either* as conferring Jewish status on the children, provided that they are brought up to identify themselves with the Jewish people, and do so.

Such has long been the policy of the Central Conference of American Rabbis, of the Union of Liberal and Progressive Synagogues, and more recently also of Reconstructionist Judaism. It is known that there is, as one would expect, much sympathy for it among secular Jews, some among Traditionalist-Progressive and Conservative Jews, and a little even among Orthodox Jews. Whether and when it, or something like it, will become the generally accepted policy throughout the Jewish world, it is impossible to foresee.

Conclusion

For the time being, therefore, the Jewish world will remain untidily, uncomfortably and sometimes fractiously divided over this one aspect (apart from the acceptability of non-Orthodox conversions) of Jewish identity, relating to the quandary of how to determine the religious status of the children of mixed marriages. But if this difference cannot at present be resolved, at least it may help to understand clearly what is at issue: namely, how far it is desirable, and how far it is possible, to close the gap between law and reality that has manifested itself in recent times.

In any case, the disagreement should not be allowed to obscure the large measure of agreement that exists about other aspects of Jewish identity, and indeed what essentially constitutes Jewishness.

Besides, over and above the question, who is a Jew, there is another: who is a *good* Jew? About that, too, there will inevitably be different opinions in the different streams of Judaism. But there is one definition which, in its deceptively simple and seemingly circular way, expresses a profound thought: 'A good Jew is one in whose life being Jewish is a constant influence for good' (Israel I. Mattuck, quoted in ULPS, 1995, p. 191). That thought would, I hope and believe, commend itself to most Jews as constituting, at least, an important part of the answer.

Chapter 22

❖   ❖   ❖

CONCEPTION AND CONTRACEPTION

Fertility Then and Now

'And God blessed them, and God said to them: Be fruitful and multiply, and fill the earth' (Gen. 1:28). 'I will greatly bless you, and I will surely multiply your seed as the stars of heaven and as the sand on the seashore' (Gen. 22:17). 'Your wife will be like a fruitful vine within your house; your children will be like olive shoots around your table. Thus shall the man be blessed who fears the Eternal One' (Ps. 128:3f).

To our ancestors, as these verses illustrate, and to the ancients generally, human fertility, like the fertility of cattle and soil, seemed an unmixed blessing and a token of divine favour. This is not surprising, for the world in those days was sparsely populated; the infant mortality rate was high; the economy was simple; the educational process was short; a large family meant a large labour force and therefore a promise of prosperity; woman's chief role was childbearing; and little was known about genetics.

Today the world is over-populated, or threatening to become so, with potentially disastrous consequences in terms of overcrowding, mental stress, social tension, and damage to the environment; the infant mortality rate is low; the economy is complex; the educational process is long; a large family is no longer conducive to prosperity, often the reverse; women have other ambitions besides motherhood; and we know a great deal about heredity.

In these radically changed circumstances, human fertility is no longer necessarily a blessing. Beyond certain limits, it can become an oppressive burden upon the individual family and a grave threat to the survival of humanity as a whole.

Christian Responses

This novel situation poses a challenge to the old-established religions whose moral codes received their classical formulations at a time when the problem, in so far as it existed at all, had an altogether different context and complexion, and it has not been easy for them to come to terms with it.

Christianity has had to cope, additionally, with a strand in its tradition that is less than wholly positive about marriage in general and its physical aspect in particular. (Consider, for instance, the celibacy of Jesus and Paul, of the monastic orders, and, in the Catholic tradition, of the priesthood; the juxtaposition of 'the world, the flesh and the devil', and the allusions to marriage as a concession to human weakness, in Christian liturgy.)

The Protestant Churches have nevertheless issued statements in favour of responsible contraception, but the Catholic Church adheres to its prohibitive posture, allowing only the so-called 'natural' method of birth-control, i.e., abstention during fecundity. Pope Paul VI, for example, in his 1968 encyclical *Humanae Vitae*, while conceding that marital intercourse has a 'unitive' as well as a procreative function, nevertheless insisted that these two functions are 'inseparable', so that 'each and every marriage act must remain open to the transmission of life'.

Classical Jewish Teachings

Unlike Christianity, Judaism has never seen any intrinsic virtue in celibacy. On the contrary, it has regarded marriage as highly desirable: divinely ordained because it is good, and good because divinely ordained. In Jewish law marriage has the status of an obligation from which there are exemptions only in special cases (Sh. Ar, EH 1:2, 4), and an obligation especially urged upon the High Priest and the precentor (Lev. 21:13; Yad, Hilchot Issurey Bi'ah 17:13; Ta'an. 2:2).

The obligation to marry is indeed closely linked to the obligation to beget children, which is its most obvious purpose. 'Be fruitful and multiply' is, in the Genesis narrative, God's first commandment to humanity. For God formed the world 'to be inhabited' (Isa. 45:18) by human beings, created in the Divine Image. Therefore, to refrain from procreation is to 'diminish the Divine Image' and to frustrate God's purpose (Sh. Ar., EH 1:1).

This is not, however, an *unlimited* obligation. According to the school of Hillel, whose view was accepted, it is satisfied when a man has begotten one boy and one girl, just as God created humanity 'male and female' (Gen. 1:27; Yev. 6:6). Thereafter, further procreation is commended but not commanded.

To continue to beget children is commended on the basis of a statement in the Talmud which so interprets the verse, 'In the morning sow your seed, and in the evening do not withhold your hand' (Eccles. 11:6). Accordingly, some medieval authorities, including Alfasi, Maimonides and Asheri, consider it Rabbinically (מדרבנן) though not Biblically (מדאורייתא) obligatory, while others, including Nachmanides, Isserlein and Isserles, do not regard it as a requirement (Yev. 62b; Yad, Hilchot Ishut 15:16; Sh.Ar., EH 1:3, gloss, and 1:8 and Ba'er Heytev *ad loc.*).

On the more lenient view, therefore, once a man has fulfilled the Scriptural obligation of begetting two children, one of each sex, he may refrain from further procreation. According to some authorities, he may even marry a woman incapable of childbirth (Sh.Ar., EH 1:3, gloss). But this does not mean that he may then abstain from marital intercourse, for Judaism has always recognised that this has a 'unitive' as well as a 'procreative' purpose. 'It is not good that man should be alone; I will make him a helper fit for him' (Gen. 2:18). Marriage is also for mutual help and companionship, love and devotion. It establishes a relationship which is to be valued for itself, as potentially the deepest, happiest and most beautiful of all human relationships. No higher compliment could be paid to this relationship than its use in the Bible as a metaphor for God's Covenant with Israel, which is founded upon mutual חסד, loving loyalty (Isa. 54:5, Jer. 31:30–33, Ezek. 16:8, Hos. 2:21f, Mal. 2:14–16).

In this husband-wife relationship, sexual intercourse plays a vital role, as the chief expression, on the physical level, of marital love. Besides, it is more than merely physical. It engages the whole personality, and it has a sacred quality. 'When a man cohabits with his wife in holiness, the Shechinah is with them' (*Iggeret ha-Kodesh*, a thirteenth-century kabbalistic work traditionally attributed to Nachmanides, Ch. 2, Mossad Harav Kook, 1963, Vol. 2, p. 326).

Furthermore, it is a deep human need, the satisfaction of which is one of the basic obligations owed by husband to wife (Exod. 21:10; Ket. 5:6; Yad, Hilchot Ishut 12:1f; Sh.Ar., EH 69:1f). It is an obligation which Talmudic law defined in detail and which does not cease when procreation is no longer obligatory or (e.g., after menopause) no longer possible. In other words, the 'procreative' and 'unitive' functions of marital intercourse are *not* inseparable.

Ambiguities

In the light of these general teachings, there ought to be no objection to the practice of birth control by married couples who have fulfilled the duty of procreation. Nevertheless, it is uncertain whether the Rabbis of old would have taken that view. We cannot be sure because they do not tell us. The only explicit statement is to the effect that three categories of women – minor girls, pregnant women, and nursing mothers, because it was believed that childbirth might endanger their life or that of their offspring – 'use a contraceptive absorbent' (קטנה, מעוברת ומניקה :שלוש נשים משמשות במוך, Yev. 12b, 100b, Ket. 39a, Ned. 35b, Nid. 45b).

It is not clear whether this means that they *must* do so, with the possible implication that other women *may*, or that they *may* do so, with the implication that other women *may not*. The former inter-pretation was ingeniously and forcefully argued in 1927 by Jakob Z. Lauterbach, Professor of Talmud at the Hebrew Union College (Lauterbach, 1927, pp. 369–84). But there are general considerations which make it doubtful whether the Rabbis would have approved of birth control so generally: among them their strong commendation of procreation even beyond the legally defined minimum; the crude and unreliable nature of the contraceptives then available; and a reluctance, more common in pre-scientific times than now, to inter-fere with the normal processes of nature.

There is also a further complication. The Bible relates that Judah's son Onan refused to fulfil his levirate duty with his brother's widow; instead, 'he spilled the semen on the ground, lest he should give offspring to his brother; and what he did was displeasing in the sight of God' (Gen. 38:9f). On the basis of this story, Rabbi Yochanan taught: כל המוציא שכבת זרע לבטלה חייב מיתה, 'Whoever ejac-ulates semen in vain commits a deadly sin' (Nid. 13a). This state-ment, in turn, was elaborated in the medieval law codes under the influence of a strongly felt abhorrence for what was considered the evil practice of masturbation (cf. Sh.Ar., EH 23).

From a common-sense point of view, this objection is irrele-vant. For Onan's action (which gave rise to the term 'onanism') was reprehensible because its purpose was to circumvent an oblig-ation; and, equally obviously, contraception is not comparable with masturbation.

Orthodox Attitudes

The objection that contraception involves 'the spilling of semen in vain' has been adduced by Orthodox rabbis since the eighteenth century as a ground on which to prohibit it. Some have made exceptions for cases where the prevention of conception is medically indicated; others have, like the Catholic Church, shrunk from making even that concession. According to Rabbi Immanuel Jakobovits, 'the opinions for and against the use of some artificial methods to prevent conception where danger to life may otherwise ensue are about equally balanced' (Jakobovits, 1975, p. 169).

The reluctance of Orthodox rabbis to sanction contraception needs to be understood, however, in the light of their general disposition, since the Emancipation, to adopt a prohibitive stance, not only in marriage law, but in all matters. For they have tended to see in the modern world an enemy rather than a friend; to be apprehensive of innovation; quick to prohibit, slow to permit; and inclined to judge new problems on the basis of an atomistic legalism rather than a general assessment of ethical principles and contemporary needs.

Progressive Attitudes

However, Progressive rabbis, and even Conservative rabbis, have long held favourable views about birth control, provided that only medically approved methods are used, and that the motive is not to evade the responsibility of parenthood (see Mattuck, 1953, pp. 120ff). Worthy motives are: to safeguard the health of the potential mother or the potential offspring; to prevent the transmission of a hereditary disease; to ensure that the parents are economically and otherwise able to give their children the best possible upbringing and education; and to play one's part in keeping down the world's human population to a viable level.

Where one or more of these motives is present and applicable, the responsible practice of birth control is not only permissible but positively commendable and even a moral duty; and it is so, not only on common-sense grounds, and not only from the sectarian standpoint of a new-fangled version of Judaism, but in the light of the general drift, correctly understood, of the relevant religious and moral teachings of Judaism generally, as embodied in its classical sources and as applied to contemporary circumstances.

God formed the world to be inhabited. It will continue to be inhabited only if we learn to multiply intelligently. That, too, although not explicitly stated in the ancient sources, is among the divine statutes and ordinances by doing which humanity shall live (Lev. 18:5).

Chapter 23

❖   ❖   ❖

From Unilateralism to Reciprocity
A Short History of Jewish Divorce

Traditional Jewish marriage law is predicated on a fundamental disparity of status between men and women which has been mitigated
in the course of the ages but, except in one branch of modern
Judaism, never fully rectified. This chapter will sketch the history of
that disparity, with special reference to divorce, then discuss various
attempts to remedy it.

Biblical Times

Biblical matrimonial law was polygamous. More precisely, it allowed
a man to have several wives (polygyny) but regarded the reverse
(polyandry) as unthinkable. This is reflected in the process of marriage, which was unilateral. That applies both to the act of betrothal,
for which the verb ארש was used, and to the marriage proper, for
which the usual verb was לקח, meaning 'to take' and 'to buy'.

That very point is made at the beginning of Tractate Kiddushin,
which opens with the Mishnah statement, האשה נקנית בשלוש דרכים, that
'a wife can be acquired in three ways', the first and most usual being
בכסף, 'with money'. Then the Gemara comments that the same verb
לקח which is used in the story of the Machpelah, when Abraham offers
Ephron the purchase price for the field, saying קח ממני, 'Take it from
me' (Gen. 23:23:13), is used in Deuteronomy about marriage when it
says (22:13), כי יקח איש אשה, 'If a man takes a wife' (Kid. 2a). Essentially,
therefore, the bridegroom 'bought' the bride from her father.

The same inequality is reflected in divorce, which was likewise
unilateral, only the husband having the right to dissolve the marriage. Admittedly, information about Biblical divorce is sparse. Virtually the only relevant passage is Deuteronomy 24:1–4, and that is an

oblique reference, for it is really about remarriage: that of a man to his former wife, whom he has divorced, which is permitted only if she has not been married to another man during the interval. Nevertheless it shows clearly enough that the procedure was unilateral. The key phrase is: וכתב לה ספר כריתות ונתן בידה ושלחה מביתו, 'he writes her a bill of divorce, hands it to her, and sends her away from his house' (v. 1).

A husband's right to divorce his wife was unrestricted except if he had falsely accused her of premarital unchastity (Deut. 22:13–19) or if he had raped her before marriage (Deut. 22: 28f); in both these cases לא־יוכל לשלחה כל־ימיה, 'he may not divorce her as long as she lives'. It is not known how the biblical bill of divorce was worded, but it is likely to have included some such phrase as כי היא לא אשתי ואנכי לא אישה, 'She is no longer my wife and I am no longer her husband' (Hos. 2:4).

There is no reason to suppose that divorce was common, or viewed with approval. Malachi makes God say כי־שנא שלח, 'I hate sending away' (2:16), where, incidentally, the same verb is used as in the key Deuteronomy passage. Above all, it follows from the frequent Prophetic use of marriage as a metaphor for the Covenant between God and Israel (e.g., Isa. 54:5, Jer. 31:30–33, Ezek. 16:8, Hos. 2:21f) that marriage was regarded as *ideally* permanent.

Second Temple Times

It seems that in the fifth-century BCE Jewish military colony at Elephantine in southern Egypt women enjoyed greater rights. For the Aramaic papyrus manuscripts that have been found there include three marriage contracts, of which two stipulate that the husband may not marry a second wife (Yaron, 1961, p. 60), and one of these indicates that the wife could take the initiative, for it states: מחר ויום אחרן תקום מפטחיה בעדה ותאמר שנאת לאחסור בעלי..., 'Tomorrow or another day, if Miftachiah should stand up in the congregation and say, "I divorce Aschor my husband …"' (Cowley, 1923, p. 45; Yaron, 1961, pp. 53f).

According to Josephus, Queen Salome divorced her husband Costobarus, but, as he explains, her action 'was not in accordance with Jewish law. For it is (only) the man who is permitted by us to do this … Salome, however, did not choose to follow her country's law but acted on her own authority' (*Jewish Antiquities*, Book XV, 7:10; Loeb Classical Library, verses 259f).

Pharisaic sources concede no such right to the wife but do seek to discourage hasty divorce and show concern for a divorced woman's economic security. Hence the Ketubbah ('marriage contract') was instituted by Simeon ben Shetach in the first century BCE כדי שלא תהא קלה בעיניו להוציאה, 'so that a husband may not regard it as a light matter to divorce his wife' (Tos. Ket. 12:1; J. Ket. 8:11; Ket. 11a). It entitled the wife to financial compensation from her husband's estate if he should divorce or predecease her.

Tannaitic Times

In Tannaitic times, polygamy was still permitted, and marriage remained unilateral. A Baraita emphasises that the Torah says כי יקח איש אשה, 'When a man takes a wife' (Deut. 22:13), not כי תלקח אשה לאיש, 'When a wife is taken to a man' (Kid. 2b), because he alone is permitted to take the initiative. A third possibility, that the Torah might have said, כי תקח אשה איש, 'When a woman takes a husband', is not even contemplated.

The verb ארס, now spelt with a *Samech* instead of a *Sin*, continued to be used for 'to betroth', referring to the first stage of the process of getting married, and gave rise to the noun אירוסין for 'betrothal', but was often replaced by the verb קידש, meaning 'to set apart' or 'consecrate', which yielded the alternative noun קידושין for 'betrothal' and gave its name to the Mishnah tractate on that subject.

For the second stage, the marriage proper, in addition to לקח, the verb נשא, which means 'to lift', 'to carry' and 'to take', was also used. It is found already in late Biblical passages, as in Ezra 9:2, כי-נשאו מבנותיהם להם ולבניהם, 'For they have taken of their daughters for themselves and for their sons', and gave rise to the noun נישואין for 'wedding'. Yet another verb is קנה, 'to acquire' or 'to buy'; it is used, as we have seen, in the opening statement of Mishnah Kiddushin, האשה נקנית בשלוש דרכים, that 'a wife is acquired in one of three ways'. All three terms clearly indicate an act of acquisition by the husband.

Similarly, divorce remained unilateral: אינו דומה האיש המתגרש לאשה המתגרשת, שהאשה יוצאה לרצונה ושלא לרצונה ,והאיש אינו מוציא אלא לרצונו, 'The husband who divorces is not like the wife who is divorced, for she is divorced with or without her consent while he divorces her only if he wants to' (Yev. 14:1).

Again we notice a change in terminology. Whereas in the Bible the verb for 'to divorce' was שִׁלַּח, 'to send away' or 'dismiss', in Rabbinic literature it is usually גרש, 'to expel', or הוציא, 'to cause to go out'.

Divorce, though permitted, was looked upon as regrettable. On the Malachi verse, כי-שנא שלח, that God hates divorce (2:16), Rabbi Eleazar ben Azariah made the famous comment, כל המגרש אשתו ראשונה,

אפילו מזבח מוריד עליו דמעות, 'Whenever a man divorces his first wife, the very altar weeps over him' (Git. 90b).

In addition to the biblical restrictions we have noted, a husband was no longer allowed to divorce his wife if she became insane (Yev. 14:1) or if she was taken captive (Ket. 4:9). Conversely, although the right to effect a divorce continued to be vested exclusively in the husband, nevertheless, in certain situations a wife could sue for divorce, in the sense of asking the court to bring pressure on the husband to release her. Such grounds included refusal of conjugal rights (Ket. 5:6), impotence (Ned. 11:12) and unreasonable restriction of freedom (Ket. 7:2–5).

Moreover, an attempt was made to restrict the husband's right to divorce his wife so that he would be able to do so only if she had committed a matrimonial offence. What constitutes such an offence was disputed between Beit Hillel and Beit Shammai according to their divergent interpretations of the key phrase ערות דבר in Deuteronomy 24:1. The former understood it very broadly, the latter as referring only to adultery, which was also the view of Jesus according to one Gospel tradition (Matt. 5:32, 19:19). Rabbi Akiva, however, on the basis of the phrase, אם לא תמצא חן בעיניו, 'If she does not find favour in his eyes' (Deut. 24:1), would allow a husband to divorce his wife even in the absence of a matrimonial offence, אפילו מצא אחרת נאה הימנה, if he had fallen in love with another woman (Git. 9:10).

The biblical *sefer keritut* for 'bill of divorce' was now called *get* (גט), an Aramaic word for a legal document, apparently derived from a Sumerian term meaning 'oblong object' (Tigay, 1996, p. 221), or, more fully *get ishah* (גט אשה), 'woman's document'.

As for its wording, an anonymous Mishnah states that its essential formula was הרי את מותרת לכל אדם, 'You are free to remarry' (Git. 9:3), and this was codified. But the Mishnah adds a minority opinion, in the name of Rabbi Judah ben El'ai, that the correct formula is an Aramaic one which reads: ודין דיהוי ליכי מינאי ספר תרוכין ואגרת שבוקין וגט פטורין, למהך להתנסבא לכל גבר דתצביין, 'Let this be to you from me a document of release, a letter of dismissal and a bill of divorce, so that you may go and marry any other man you wish' (ibid.). In the subsequent development of the text, both phrases were included.

Regarding the language of the Get, the Mishnah makes it clear that it may be written in Hebrew or Greek (Git. 9:8), which was taken to mean that it may be written בכל לשון, in any language (Git. 19b).

The Mishnah also raises the question whether divorce documents executed in a Gentile registry (העולים בערכאות של גוים) are valid; 'no' was the majority view, but Rabbi Simeon ben Yochai thought 'yes', אף על פי שחותמיהם גוים, even if the signatories were non-Jews (Git. 1:5).

Amoraic Times

During Amoraic times, polygamy was still permitted, but viewed with disfavour. Marriage remained unilateral. Admittedly, the bride's consent was now considered mandatory. As the Talmud puts it, מדעתה אין, שלא מדעתה לא, 'With her consent it is valid; without her consent it is not valid' (Kid. 2b). Nevertheless the bride's role in the marriage ceremony was passive, as it remains in Orthodox Judaism to this day.

Divorce likewise remained unilateral. But the feeling persisted that it was a serious matter. Accordingly, divorce proceedings were made increasingly elaborate, necessitating expert supervision, and it became a principle that כל שאינו יודע בטיב גיטין וקדושין לא יהא לו עסק עמהן, 'anyone who does not understand the nature of divorce documents and betrothals should have nothing to do with them' (Kid. 6a).

The greatest precision was required regarding the process of writing, witnessing and delivery; the writing materials; the תֹּרֶף, i.e., the 'variables' such as the date, the place, the names of the parties, and the signatures of the witnesses; and the טֹפֶס, or the 'constants', which were now in Aramaic, with only the essential phrase stipulated by the Mishnah in Hebrew.

This process of elaboration took place principally in the Babylonian academies throughout the Amoraic period. Details of wording and even of spelling were still debated between Babylonian rabbis of the fourth and fifth centuries (see, e.g., Git. 82a–88b).

The wife could still take the initiative in asking the rabbinic court to coerce the husband to divorce her if she had objective grounds for complaint, which now included his refusal to support her (Ket. 77a). Indeed, she could apparently do so even in the absence of such grounds, if he had become repulsive to her, provided that she was willing to forgo part of her alimony; for the Palestinian Talmud (Ket. 7:7) cites a Ketubbah clause to that effect, similar to the Elephantine one quoted above (see Riskin, 1989, pp. 31).

Gaonic Age

The wife's right in certain circumstances to sue for a divorce was maintained throughout the Gaonic period and, as we shall see, beyond. This is confirmed by a tenth-century Ketubbah, found among the manuscripts of the Cairo Genizah, which again includes a clause similar to the Elephantine one (Riskin, 1989, pp. 79f). But of course the husband alone could instruct the Get to be written.

Although all the necessary prescriptions and ingredients are already present, somewhat scattered, in the Talmud, the full text of the Get is first found in the attempts to codify talmudic law which began during the Gaonic Age. The most important early work of that genre is *Halachot Gedolot* ('Great Laws') commonly attributed to Simeon Kayyara but of disputed authorship, probably compiled in Babylonia in the eighth or ninth century. It gives a text of the Get which is virtually identical with that subsequently found in the medieval law codes (ed. Mekitzei Nirdamim, Hilchot Gittin, p. 339).

Middle Ages

Several important developments took place during the Middle Ages. First, by a decree attributed to Rabbenu Gershom ben Judah (tenth–eleventh centuries) polygamy was forbidden (Sh.Ar., EH 1:10). However, Ze'ev W. Falk has shown that the attribution is incorrect, and that the decree actually dates from the twelfth century (Falk, 1966, pp. 1, 13–34). Moreover, it was not immediately accepted by all communities, and there were various views as to whether it admitted of exceptions, and whether it remained in force only until the end of the fifth millennium, which was the year 1240 (EH, 1:10). In any case, prohibition is not the same as abolition. Thus a man's bigamous marriage, though forbidden, remained valid *ex post facto* (בדיעבד) and any children resulting from it were unblemished (כשר), whereas a woman's bigamous marriage was considered void (אין קדושין תופסין) and the children of such a union were illegitimate (ממזרים) – which remains the position in Orthodox Judaism to this day.

Secondly, contrary to the Mishnah statement quoted above (Yev. 14:1), a husband was no longer allowed to divorce his wife without her consent. This decree was also attributed to Rabbenu Gershom (Sh.Ar., EH 119:6); but it, too, has been shown to date from the twelfth century (Falk, 1966, p. 119).

Thirdly, 'divorce was no longer a private act by the husband, for it was subject to public supervision by a tribunal, or by representatives of the community' (Falk, 1966, pp. 122f). Indeed, there was a tendency to require the Get to be authorised, not only by the individual Beit Din, but by larger communal authorities. Rabbi Jacob Moellin (the Maharil, fourteenth–fifteenth centuries) reports: 'The custom of the three communities of the Rhineland [Speyer, Worms and Mainz] was: … when they intended to give a Get in one of these communities they would first obtain the agreement of the other two, so that the Get might be given with their authorisation' (Sefer Maharil, 68a).

Thus Jewish divorce was now mainly by mutual consent, but not reciprocal, for it was still the husband who initiated it by instructing a scribe (סופר) to write the Get before a rabbinic court (בית דין) in the presence of witnesses (עדי חתימה). The delivery, too, took place before the court and in the presence of witnesses (עדי מסירה). However, on the principle that 'a person's agent is like himself' (שלוחו של אדם כמותו, Ned. 72b), the husband could appoint an agent to deliver the get (שליח להולכה) and the wife could appoint an agent to receive it (שליח לקבלה).

There were, however, some exceptions to the principle of mutual consent. If, for instance, either party wished to condone adultery or apostasy on the part of the other, or if the marriage had been contracted in contravention of the so-called 'negative prohibitions' (איסורי לאוין), as when a Kohen (man of putative priestly descent) had married a divorcee – in all these cases the Beit Din could, in theory, 'enforce' a divorce by bringing pressure on the husband to give the Get to his wife against the wishes of either or even of both parties.

As for the wife's right to petition for a divorce, that too continued, at least until the twelfth century, when Rabbi Jacob ben Meir, known as Rabbenu Tam, argued against the practice of rabbinic courts coercing husbands to divorce their wives; and his influence was so great that he 'single-handedly changed the course of the halakhic attitude' (Riskin, 1989, pp. 94, 134).

The wording of the Get became standardised, with only minor variations, chiefly between the Sefardi and Ashkenazi traditions. Following the pattern of the Gaonic *Halachot Gedolot*, which we have already mentioned, it can be found in medieval law codes such as the *Halachot* of Isaac Alfasi (1013–1103; Git. 89a) and the Mishneh Torah of Moses Maimonides (1135–1204; Hilchot Gerushin 4:12). The Shulchan Aruch of Joseph Caro (1488–1575) devotes a whole appendix to the rules and regulations pertaining to the writing of a Get (*Seder ha-Get*, appended to chapter 154 of Even ha-Ezer). Here, according to the standard Ashkenazi text, is a translation of the key phrases, the man apostrophising the woman:

> I, of my own free will and without being under any constraint, release, dismiss and divorce you, my wife …., who have been my wife hitherto. I dismiss, release and divorce you, so that you may have permission and authority over yourself to go and marry any man you wish, and no person may prevent you from this day and for ever, and you are free to marry any man, and this shall be to you from me a document of release,

a letter of dismissal, and a bill of divorce, according to the law of Moses and Israel. (See, e.g., *Encyclopædia Judaica*, Vol. 6, p. 131; *Encyclopedia Talmudit*, Vol. 5, p. 656; Klein, 1979, p. 479).

A final point to be noted is that after the delivery of the Get to the wife or her agent it was returned to the Beit Din, which defaced it by cutting it crosswise (שתי וערב) and stored it away. Instead, the wife or her agent received a certificate (פטור or תעודת גירושין) to the effect that the Get had been executed.

The Modern Situation

The Emancipation changed the situation in several respects. First, the affected Jewish communities lost their juridical autonomy. Secondly, the secularisation of Christian countries led in most of them to the institution of civil divorce of which Jews could now avail themselves without *necessarily* obtaining a Jewish divorce as well. Thirdly, there occurred a steady, and in the end massive, increase in marriage breakdown and divorce among Jews, as among non-Jews. Fourth, since many of those concerned divorced civilly only, this resulted in a corresponding increase in the number of Jewish women who remarried without a Get, with serious consequences for the status of any subsequent children.

These developments have brought into prominence a twofold problem which always existed in Rabbinic Law but now occurred on a vastly increased scale: that of the Agunah and that of the Mamzer.

The Agony of the Agunah

The term Agunah derives from a verb which occurs only once in the Bible, when Naomi advises her widowed daughters-in-law to go home rather than wait in vain for her to bear more sons for them to marry, for, as she says, הלהן תעגנה לבלתי היות לאיש, 'Should you on their account debar yourselves from marriage?' (Ruth 1:13). Since the key verb is a *hapax legomenon*, it is impossible to know precisely what it meant, but in Rabbinic Hebrew it meant 'to tie down', so that an Agunah may be said to be a 'tied' or 'chained' woman.

In the case of Orpah and Ruth, the disability would have been a self-imposed commitment to marry Naomi's hypothetical future sons – a wildly extravagant feature of the story which was no doubt meant to be humorous. But in the real world the status of *iggun* (cf. Git. 3a) results from any one of three quite different causes.

The first is the disappearance of the husband in circumstances that leave room for doubt whether he is alive or dead. He may have deserted his wife or gone abroad, or he may have died but there is insufficient evidence to prove it. Such cases are relatively rare in normal times but tend to become numerous in times of war or persecution.

A second possible case is that of a widow whose husband has died without issue. According to the biblical law (Deut. 25:5–10), her brother-in-law is then obligated to marry her ולא־ימחה שמו מישראל, 'that his name may not be blotted out from Israel', such a levirate marriage being known as *yibbum*, or else to obtain release from that obligation through the ceremony of *chalitzah* ('taking off the shoe'). Until *yibbum* or *chalitzah* has been performed, the widow is said to be זקוקה, 'bound' to her brother-in-law. But if he refuses both *yibbum* and *chalitzah*, then she is, additionally, an Agunah.

The third and commonest cause of *iggun* is the case of the 'recalcitrant husband' who refuses to free his wife to remarry by giving her a Get.

There is indeed also the converse problem of the 'recalcitrant wife' who refuses to free her husband to remarry by accepting a Get from him. But if the husband nevertheless remarries (e.g., civilly), then, as we have previously observed, his second marriage is valid *ex post facto*, since polygamy was only forbidden, not abolished, by the twelfth-century decree, and any children resulting from it are unblemished (כשר), whereas, if the civilly divorced woman remarries without a Get, her second marriage is void (אין קדושין תופסין) and any children resulting from it are branded Mamzerim.

The Misery of the Mamzer

The relevant verse occurs in Deuteronomy and says that 'a Mamzer may not enter the congregation of the Eternal One even in the tenth generation' (23:3). The meaning of the word Mamzer is, however, uncertain (Jacobs, 1984, pp. 257–65).

The very next verse, which uses the identical formula about an Ammonite and a Moabite, suggests that it might have been the name of a pagan tribe – a conjecture which can draw some support from the fact that in the only other occurrence of the word in the entire Bible (Zech. 9:6) it is associated with a geographical region, that of Ashdod.

Indeed, the exact meaning of the word was still disputed in Rabbinic times (see, e.g., Yev. 49a–b), but it was eventually defined as the offspring of an incestuous or adulterous union.

According to Rabbinic law, a Mamzer, so defined, is forbidden to marry a Jew not similarly tainted. Furthermore, since 'even in the tenth generation' was taken to mean 'for ever', the disability perpetuates itself indefinitely, both in the male and in the female lines, on the principle that 'the child follows the more blemished parent' (הולד הולך אחר הפגום; Yev. 76b; Sh.Ar., EH 8:4).

The tragedy of the Agunah, therefore, is not only that, in Orthodox Judaism, she is forbidden to remarry, but that if she remarries in a non-Orthodox way, her subsequent children and children's children until the end of all generations, are burdened with the stigma and disability of Mamzerut.

It is worth reiterating that this twofold problem stems from two quite separate causes: (1) the inferior status of women in Rabbinic matrimonial law, which preserves the *ex post facto* validity of male polygamy, even though it is no longer permitted, and makes the procedures of marriage and divorce unilateral, and (2) the law of the Mamzer.

We shall now look at various attempts to solve or alleviate this twofold problem, within the parameters of Rabbinic Judaism.

Purification of the Mamzer

If it were possible to remove the stigma and disability of Mamzerut, although that would not *solve* the problem of the Agunah, it would take the sting out of it.

Already in the Tannaitic period, an ingenious suggestion to that end was made by Rabbi Tarfon: that the Mamzer should be advised to marry a slave-girl, whose children would then be slaves rather than Mamzerim and, if subsequently converted to Judaism, would be as unblemished as any other proselyte (Kid. 3:13). But such a circumvention of the law became unavailable when slavery ceased.

Another way out, not mentioned in the sources but allegedly practised in various times and places, is for the rabbinic authorities to turn a blind eye to the problem by allowing the Mamzer to go and merge into another community where the circumstances of his birth are unknown. Such a policy would be humane but hardly honest.

The only other way of dealing with Mamzerut is the drastic one of retroactively annulling the woman's first marriage, so that her subsequent marriage will not, after all, have been adulterous, and therefore any children born from it will not, after all, be Mamzerim.

Retroactive Annulment of Marriage

Such annulment of marriage is called הפקעת הקדושין and is based on the statement in the Talmud, כל המקדש אדעתא דרבנן מקדש ואפקעינהו רבנן לקדושין מיניה, 'When a man marries, he does so under rabbinic authority; therefore the rabbis may annul such a marriage' (Ket. 3a, Git. 33a, 73a). But in the Talmud the principle is invoked only in precisely defined and unusual circumstances, and in post-talmudic times there was a general reluctance to invoke it at all. (See *Encyclopedia Talmudit*, Vol. 2, pp. 137–140; Elon, 1994, Vol. 2, pp. 631ff; Freimann, 1964, pp. 285f).

It would in any case be inconsistent with any kind of integrity retroactively to annul a marriage except when there are genuine grounds for doubting its initial validity, for example, when there is reason to think that one of the parties was at the time insane or not Jewish, or that the marriage ceremony did not satisfy the indispensable requirements of Jewish law. Therefore, as Louis Jacobs points out, this remedy offers no solution 'in those many cases in which the first marriage cannot really be questioned as to its complete validity' (Jacobs, 1984, p. 274).

It may, however, be asked: if a rabbinic court can in some instances retroactively *annul* a marriage, why can it not *dissolve* a marriage? Other legal systems do give such power to the courts, just as they empower them to declare a missing person dead. But Rabbinic Law is quite clear that nothing can terminate a marriage except either a Get willingly given and received, or the death of one party, incontrovertibly attested.

Conditional Betrothal

Since there is, to all intents and purposes, no *cure* either for the problem of the Agunah or for that of the Mamzer, rabbinic authorities have generally concentrated their efforts on *prevention*.

An early example of this is the 'conditional betrothal', קדושין על תנאי. This device was allegedly used in Alexandria in Second Temple times. In order to avoid the risk of a betrothed woman being 'snatched up' by another man before being married, the betrothal included a conditional clause in which the bridegroom said to the bride: תהא לי לאנתו כדת משה וישראל כשתיכנסי לביתי, 'You shall become my wife according to the law of Moses and Israel *when you enter my house*' (Tos. Ket. 4:9; BM 104a; Freimann, 1964, p. 12).

A more sophisticated form of this conditional clause, known as *simpon* (סימפון) or 'codicil' was subsequently introduced in Palestine and remained standard practice there throughout the Amoraic period (J. Kid. 3:3; Freimann, 1964, p. 11). In Babylonia this was not done, but Takkanot (rabbinic decrees) were issued forbidding, under pain of severe punishment, betrothal without a prior engagement and parental consent (Kid. 12b; Freimann, 1964, pp. 12f).

A form of the Palestinian *simpon* was also used in pre-Expulsion Spain and, after 1492, in Palestine and Syria, usually to the effect that if the bridegroom did not claim the bride within one year, the betrothal would be retroactively voided (Freimann, 1964, pp. 34, 61, 112, 119). Of course all this was before the two stages, Kiddushin (betrothal) and Nissu'in (wedding) were combined into a single ceremony, which proved in the end the most effective solution (see Schauss, 1940, pp. 160f).

Conditional Divorce

Ultimately, therefore, the most commonly proposed remedy was not the conditional betrothal but the conditional divorce, גט על תנאי. An early example of this is a passage in the Talmud which asserts that King David's soldiers, before they went into battle, would write out גט כריתות, a bill of divorce, so that, if they did not return, their wives would be free to remarry (Ket. 9b).

The first known instance of modern times occurred in Algeria in 1812, when Rabbi Ben-Zion Alkalai, in order to overcome the problem of the recalcitrant husband, suggested that immediately before the betrothal benediction the bridegroom should make a deposition (צוויי) before two witnesses, authorising the Dayanim to have a Get written and signed whenever it is required, from the time of any civil divorce onwards (Freimann, 1964, p. 394).

A similar suggestion was made by Rabbi Jacob Meir (1856–1939), Sefardi Chief Rabbi of Palestine during the Mandate, with the addition that the witnesses to the Get should be appointed immediately after the marriage, and that the husband should remain responsible for his wife's maintenance until the Get had been transacted (ibid.).

In 1925 Rabbi Joseph Elijah Henkin (1880–?) of New York proposed a conference of Torah scholars in Jerusalem to consider various suggestions for the prevention of Agunah cases, including his own suggestion, which was, once again, that the bridegroom, at the time of the marriage, should give instructions for the execution of the Get (ibid., pp. 394f).

In 1930 Rabbi Judah Leib Epstein of Brooklyn made the novel suggestion that the bridegroom should authorise the bride to write a Get for herself if he should desert her, or fail to provide for her for three years, or divorce her civilly (ibid.).

In modern Britain, a form of גט על תנאי was proposed by Dayan Yehezkel Abramsky at a conference of Jewish Chaplains to the Forces during the Second World to protect the wives of serving men who might be killed in action in 'missing, presumed dead' circumstances. (This was reported to me by the late Rabbi Leslie I. Edgar, who was a Jewish Chaplain to the Forces at the time.)

Thus many suggestions have been made in the course of the ages to solve the Agunah problem, especially through the preventive measure of a conditional Get at the time of the marriage. But they have encountered strong opposition, chiefly because it is extraordinarily difficult to formulate the condition in a way that would not cause the Get to be מעושה, 'coerced' and therefore invalid. (See Bleich, 1977, pp. 150–176.)

To these remedial measures it should be added that attempts have also been made to *facilitate* the transaction of the Get. For instance, Rabbi Solomon Kluger of Brody (1783–1869), in a famous responsum, ruled that, since a Gentile could act as 'agent of transmission' (שליח להולכה), it was permissible so to designate the Post Office and hence to transact a Get by mail (see Freehof, 1955, pp. 136–40).

Pre-Nuptial Agreement

More recently the Agunah problem has come into renewed focus through the huge increase that has taken place in the incidence of marriage breakdown and divorce, and more particularly of cases in which there is a civil divorce without a Jewish one. That, in turn, can happen if the couple are not aware of the need for a Jewish divorce, or are reluctant to submit themselves to it, or, most commonly, if the husband, out of spite, refuses to co-operate or, out of greed, makes prior financial conditions which the wife considers unreasonable.

In Britain, through the initiative, first of Rabbi Berel Berkowits, then of Chief Rabbi Dr Jonathan Sacks, this situation led to the consideration, over a period of some twelve years, of a 'Pre-Nuptial Agreement' or PNA for short, which was finally adopted by the major Orthodox synagogal bodies in 1996.

Essentially, it is an undertaking by the bride and bridegroom, signed before the marriage, that, in the event of a matrimonial dispute, they will both attend the relevant Beit Din and comply with its instructions with respect to (a) mediation and (b) divorce. There is also a clause referring to arbitration by the Beit Din, but that was made optional in the United Synagogue.

The PNA, it could be said, is an attempt to restore a little of the power of law enforcement which the rabbinic courts lost with the Emancipation, by making Jewish marriage conditional on an undertaking to abide by its terms. How effective it will prove to be – depending on the willingness of Jewish couples to give, and abide by, such undertakings – remains to be seen.

The case for a form of pre-nuptial agreement, as a way of overcoming the problem of the recalcitrant husband, has also been strongly argued by Rabbi Shlomo Riskin, Chief Rabbi of Efrat, Israel, and founding rabbi of Lincoln Square Synagogue in New York (Riskin, 1989, pp. 139–142).

Communal Sanctions

The idea of 'communal sanctions', i.e., disciplinary measures against a husband who ought to give his wife a Get but refuses to do so, is not new. In former times rabbinic courts could even order corporal punishment in such a case. As the phrase goes, מכין אותו עד שיאמר רוצה אני, 'They flog him until he says: I am willing' (Yad, *Hilkhot Gerushin* 2:20). Such a procedure is not considered tantamount to coercion (!); consequently a Get written under these circumstances is deemed to be valid (ibid.).

Similarly, Israeli courts have been known to send a recalcitrant husband to prison, or to hold him liable for his wife's maintenance, until a Get has been transacted.

Such draconian measures are not available to Diaspora courts. However, in Britain, the Beit Din of the Federation of Synagogues has been known to issue a נידוי (a mild form of excommunication, renewable every thirty days) against a recalcitrant husband. Other measures that have been proposed include public announcements and the withholding of privileges (as distinct from rights) such as being called up to the Torah or elected to synagogue office.

Together with the PNA, these communal sanctions, and the publicity attending them, may do something to raise the level of 'Get consciousness' in the community and, to that extent, make it marginally more likely than hitherto that Jewish couples obtaining a civil divorce will seek to obtain, additionally, a Jewish divorce.

Enlisting the Civil Law

More effective than either the PNA or the communal sanctions might be the enlistment of the civil courts to exercise a power of law enforcement which rabbinic courts no longer possess. That was the purpose of the 'Jakobovits Amendment' to the Family Law Bill which was passed by the British Parliament in 1996. It will empower the civil courts in the United Kingdom to withhold or delay a civil divorce on the plea of either party that the other unreasonably refuses to co-operate in the matter of a religious divorce. How willing or reluctant the courts will be to exercise that power, remains to be seen.

Conservative Judaism

We have considered a number of attempts to deal with the Agunah and Mamzer problems *while upholding the authority of Rabbinic Law and keeping within its parameters.* In modern times that has been the approach of Orthodox Judaism. But Conservative Judaism, too, has sought to operate within these limitations. Thus the *Summary Index of the Committee on Jewish Law and Standards of the Rabbinical Assembly*, 1995 edition, lists seven ways of dealing with the Agunah problem, of which, it says, three 'are generally practised at the current time'.

1. A bet din may use the principle of כל דמקדש אדעתא דרבנן מקדש (that Jewish marriages are valid by virtue of Rabbinic law, Git. 33a) to annul a marriage in a case where a get cannot be obtained by any other means and the situation is considered appropriate. (Teshuvah by David Aronson, *Proceedings of the R.A.*, 1951, pp. 120–140).

2. A *takkanah* (the 'Lieberman clause') is added to the ketubah, in which the couple recognise the authority of the bet din to counsel them in the light of Jewish tradition, to summon either party at the request of the other, and to impose terms of compensation as it sees fit for failure to respond to its summons or to carry out its decision (*Proceedings of the R.A.*, 1954, pp. 64–68).

3. Marriages should be performed *al t'nai*, on the condition that if the husband does not give the wife a *get* within six months after a civil divorce, the *kiddushin* will have been null and void ... (*Proceedings of the R.A.*, 1968, pp. 229–241). In practice, rabbis will remarry a woman based on evidence that the *t'nai* has not been fulfilled. See also Klein, 1979, pp. 498f.

Progressive Judaism:
The Traditionalist Tendency

In the history of Progressive Judaism, three distinct though overlapping tendencies are discernible, and each has taken a different approach to the problems of divorce and remarriage, as they have to other controversial aspects of Jewish tradition.

The first, which might be called Traditionalist, differs little from the Conservative movement. It is represented in Britain and Israel by the Masorti movement, and is also broadly characteristic of the more conservative constituents of the Progressive movement, including the RSGB and most of the Progressive communities of Continental Europe and Israel.

Since it is the way of these movements to reform Judaism slowly, minimally and pragmatically, they have not tackled head-on the issues which are the subject of this chapter. Thus they have generally ignored in practice the problem of Mamzerut, but have rarely, if ever, said explicitly that they reject the concept.

Similarly, the RSGB has, since the establishment of its Beit Din in the aftermath of the Second World War, transacted the Get in its traditional, unilateral, Aramaic form, while dealing with the case of the recalcitrant husband by issuing its own certificate, which admittedly cannot claim traditional halachic validity, declaring the marriage to be dissolved (see Kershen and Romain, 1995, pp. 234, 238, 272f).

Progressive Judaism: The Radical Tendency

At the other extreme is the radical tendency, which goes back to Samuel Holdheim (1800–1860) and inspired, in a slightly less extreme form, the 'Classical Reform' that dominated Progressive Judaism in the United States from its beginnings in the nineteenth century until the 1930s. It also influenced, through its first rabbi, Israel I. Mattuck, the ULPS in Britain and some other constituents of the World Union for Progressive Judaism.

The Radical Tendency has always inclined towards antinomianism. Nevertheless, it has passed some resolutions of far-reaching halachic importance. One of these must be mentioned here because it goes to the root of the inequality of the sexes in Biblical and Rabbinic marriage law.

In 1869 the Philadelphia Conference declared: 'Polygamy contradicts the idea of marriage. The marriage of a married man to a second woman can, therefore, neither take place nor claim religious validity, just as little as the marriage of a married woman to another man, but like this it is null and void from the beginning' (Mielziner, 1901, p. 31; Sefton Temkin, 1971, p. 58).

On the specific subject of divorce, Samuel Holdheim (*Autonomie der Rabbinen*, 1843) argued that it should be regarded as a civil act only and that the Get was therefore superfluous.

The Philadelphia Conference essentially endorsed Holdheim's position (see Plaut, 1963, pp. 222f, and Temkin, 1971, pp. 84–87) and resolved: 'The dissolution of marriage is, on Mosaic and Rabbinical grounds, a civil act only, which never received religious consecration. It is to be recognised, therefore, as an act emanating altogether from the judicial authorities of the State. The so-called ritual Get is in all cases declared null and void. The dissolution of marriage, pronounced by a civil court, is also fully valid in the eyes of Judaism, if it can be ascertained from the judicial documents that both parties consented to the divorce; where, however, the court issues a decree against one or the other party by constraint, Judaism recognises the validity of the divorce then only, if the cause assigned is sufficient in conformity with the spirit of the Jewish religion. It is recommended, however, that the officiating rabbi, in rendering a decision, obtain the concurrence of competent colleagues.' (See Mielziner, 1901 p. 135. For a summary of the CCAR position and its history, see Jacob, 1983, pp. 511–14.)

Broadly speaking, the ULPS has always followed the policy of the 1869 Philadelphia Conference, and of the CCAR, in recognising a civil divorce as effectively dissolving a Jewish marriage. However, in the days when English divorce law was based on the concept of the matrimonial offence, the 'guilty' party of a civil divorce was required to satisfy the rabbi that he or she nevertheless had a responsible attitude to marriage (Rayner, 1960, p. 53).

In addition, a civilly but not Jewishly divorced *man* seeking remarriage within the ULPS has always been required, in appropriate cases, to give, or offer to give, his former wife an Orthodox Get, so that she may be free to remarry in an Orthodox synagogue, and that any future children of hers may not be subject to the disabilities of Mamzerut (Mattuck, 1950, pp. 6f.)

However, a civilly divorced *woman* whose former husband refuses to give her a Get, or makes unreasonable preconditions, has always been allowed to remarry in the ULPS without a Get, after the consequences of such remarriage have been explained to her.

Thus the general thrust of past ULPS policy has been threefold: (1) to recognise that a civilly dissolved marriage is no longer an existent marriage; (2) to protect individuals as far as possible from any disabilities in Orthodox Judaism; (3) nevertheless to grant remarriage to civilly-only divorced persons in cases where, on grounds of humaneness, it would be unreasonable to refuse.

Progressive Judaism:
The Intermediate Tendency

Broadly speaking, then, the Traditionalist Tendency has affirmed the Halachah and retained the Get; the Radical Tendency has negated the Halachah and abolished the Get.

But in addition to these, there has always been in Progressive Judaism an Intermediate Tendency. This may be said to go back to Abraham Geiger (1810–1874). In the later history of Progressive Judaism in Germany, it inspired rabbis like Cesar Seligmann and, through him, the 1912 *Richtlinien* (Guiding Principles) and the 1929 *Einheitsgebetbuch* (Union Prayerbook). In the United States the Intermediate Tendency produced the 1937 Columbus Platform, considerably modifying the radicalism of the 1885 Pittsburgh Platform.

More recently, in Britain (both RSGB and ULPS), the United States and some other countries, it has shown itself in a new desire to embrace the best of Tradition and Modernity – not one or the other but both. This can be seen most clearly in a new generation of prayerbooks, beginning with *Service of the Heart* (ULPS, 1967) that combine a notable return to tradition with innovative creativity.

What are the implications of this tendency for our subject? On the one hand, one would expect from it a clear affirmation of the principle of sex equality as well as an unequivocal repudiation of the law of the Mamzer, as a manifest case of misinterpretation of the Divine Will.

But one would not expect it to be satisfied with a mere rejection of the Get. After all, it makes perfectly good sense to say that a Jewishly inaugurated marriage should, when it has broken down irretrievably, be Jewishly terminated. That view has in fact been taken throughout Jewish history, and there is nothing wrong with it. It is only the antiquated, unilateral character of the traditional Get that is objectionable from a principled Progressive point of view.

Therefore, just as the attitude of the Intermediate Tendency towards the Halachah in general is one neither of uncritical acceptance nor of outright rejection, but of appropriate modification, so one would have expected this tendency long ago to have produced a modified Get, satisfying the principle of reciprocity.

Just such suggestions have in fact been made from time to time. Already at the Leipzig and Augsburg Synods of 1869 and 1871, Geiger and others submitted motions suggesting that the form of the Get should be revised, that it should be written in the vernacular, and that the wife should be allowed to remarry without it if the husband refused to give it. These matters were referred to a committee that was to report to the next Synod – which, however, never took place.

An interesting suggestion was made in Germany in 1910 by Rabbi Israel Goldschmidt. He proposed a reciprocal Get, in modified language, to be transacted in the context of a religious ceremony stressing both the sadness of the breakdown and the need for healing. 'The rabbi then should show that in this tragic moment there could be found a reconciling element which could silence the anger of the heart. Tragedy is a power which often is stronger than the human will. It must purify the heart and not poison it with hatred' (Plaut, 1965, p. 263).

In 1969 I wrote in the then quarterly journal of the ULPS: 'A respectable case can therefore be made for reintroducing the *get*, although in a modified form which would make it, formally and effectually, a reciprocal act' (*Pointer*, Autumn, 1969, p. 5).

In 1983 Rabbi Bernard H. Mehlman and Rabbi Rifat Sonsino published an article in the (American) *Journal of Reform Judaism* arguing for a modern Get and suggesting an appropriate Hebrew and English text ('A Reform *Get*: A Proposal', Summer 1983, pp. 31–36).

But nothing much came of any of these proposals, except that in 1988 the CCAR issued a new edition of its *Rabbi's Manual* which includes two important innovations. First, a 'Ritual of Release' (סדר פרידה) by which husband and wife, before a rabbi and in the presence of witnesses, declare their consent to the termination of their marriage (there is a modified version for when only one party is present). Secondly, a 'Document of Separation' (תעודת פרידה) which is a mutual release, in writing, 'from the sacred bonds that held us together'. 'The rabbi', says the Manual, 'will explain to the participants that this ceremony and the accompanying document do not constitute a halachic get' (Polish and Plaut, 1988, p. 97).

Finally, a Progressive Get

In 1996 the Rabbinic Conference of the ULPS accepted a proposal to introduce, on an optional basis, a truly Progressive version of the traditional Get, in Hebrew and English, to be known by its biblical name, ספר כריתות, translated as 'Document of Release', by which the parties release each other from their marriage vows and free each other to remarry. The considerations that persuaded the Conference to take this step may be summarised as follows:

1. Our marriages have both a civil and a religious aspect. In so far as they are civil, it is right that, when they have broken down irretrievably, they should be civilly terminated. But in so far as they are religious, it is, by the same token, appropriate that there should be a religious termination. This consideration is reinforced by the importance we attach to the vows of mutual love, respect and loyalty made in the marriage service, which point to the need for a formal release from them.
2. Divorce is often a traumatic experience, not unlike bereavement, and those involved in it may benefit from pastoral counselling or communal support. This may help to reassure them that they are still valued as individuals, and as members of their synagogue, fortify their self-respect, and make it more likely that they will remain associated with the community, and continue their children's religious education. Thus the availability of the proposed act of release would provide, for those who chose to take advantage of it, an occasion for a potentially beneficial contact with their rabbi and synagogue.
3. The proposed step would be a logical conclusion of a trend which, since the 1960s, has been manifest in the ULPS in other respects (e.g., in its liturgy), to move from a radical towards an intermediate position, and, in particular, from a negation of the Halachah towards a qualified affirmation and principled reconstruction of it. At the same time it may serve as an example to other Progressive movements and thus prove to be a step towards re-unifying the various branches of Progressive Judaism in an area in which their practices have hitherto diverged.

The ULPS Rabbinic Conference, in deciding to introduce its 'Document of Release', was clear that it was unlikely to be recognised by the authorities of Orthodox Judaism, and insistent that this fact and its implications must always be meticulously explained to applicants; also that, in cases where serious consequences might otherwise ensue, they should still be advised, as hitherto, to take the precaution of obtaining an Orthodox Get either in lieu of or in addition to the ULPS one.

Finally, the Conference decided that in cases where one party of the former marriage cannot be traced or persuaded to co-operate, it would take upon itself the power to declare the marriage dissolved, and issue an appropriate certificate, on request, to that effect.

The ULPS divorce certificate is in Hebrew and English, and in two parts, identically worded except in gender, since by one the husband releases the wife, and by the other the wife releases the husband, and is signed by both parties as well as two witnesses and the rabbi. The text incorporates both the Hosea verse (2:4) and the essential formula prescribed in Gittin 9:3, and thus satisfies the requirements of the Mishnah. Here is the translation of the key phrases:

> I hereby release you of my own free will from the marriage bonds which have hitherto united us, so that henceforth you are not my wife (husband) and I am not your husband (wife), and you are free to marry another man (woman). Accordingly I ask you to accept from me this document as a bill of separation and a certificate of divorce, according to the law of Moses and Israel.

The introduction of this document may be said to complete the process by which the fundamental inequality of men and women under biblical and talmudic marriage-and-divorce law has been progressively – in both senses of that word! – rectified.

Chapter 24

❖   ❖   ❖

THE LAND, THE LAW AND THE LIBERAL CONSCIENCE

For some years now the question has been hotly debated whether it is right that, for the sake of peace, the State of Israel should be prepared to relinquish some of the territories under its control. The assassination of Prime Minister Yitzchak Rabin on 4 November 1995, motivated by fanatical opposition to a peace process involving acceptance of that principle, brought the issue into sharp and tragic focus.

The issue is one not only of political but also of religious controversy. But the religious debate has been conducted mainly between Orthodox rabbis. There have been few contributions from exponents of Progressive Judaism. This absence of a Progressive voice is unfortunate. For it leaves the field to the Orthodox – apart from the secular, who are themselves divided on the issue – and obscures the fact that there is an alternative religious view.

The Orthodox Approach

From an Orthodox point of view, the Hebrew Bible, as interpreted in the Rabbinic Tradition, is divinely authoritative both in its totality and in every particular. Sometimes, admittedly, it is not immediately clear what it means; hence the qualification 'as interpreted'. And sometimes the interpreters themselves are not completely in agreement; hence the גדולי הדור (pre-eminent exponents of the Tradition in each generation) may incline towards one שיטה (school of thought) or another, or even offer their own חידוש (innovative interpretation). Thus there is *some* room for manœuvre, but not much; for all essentials were long ago definitively settled. Certainly there is never any question but that whatever Scripture says concerning God's promises and commandments, once its correct interpretation has been determined, is to be believed and obeyed.

Furthermore – and this is crucial to our inquiry – the Hebrew Bible, as correctly interpreted, is the *sole* authority for all questions of conduct, both in matters of ritual and in matters of ethics. Indeed, the difference between these two spheres is barely recognised. Admittedly, the Tradition speaks of מצוות שבין אדם למקום (duties to God) and מצוות שבין אדם לחברו (duties to fellow human beings); but little is made of the distinction. As there are right and wrong ways of treating employees, so there are right and wrong ways of waving a Lulav; and there is little hint of any awareness that in the two instances 'right' and 'wrong' are used in fundamentally different senses. In both cases, what is right is what the Halachah enjoins, what is wrong is what the Halachah forbids. Essentially, there is no ethic independent of the Halachah. (See, however, Spero, 1983, especially Chapter 6.)

The Progressive Approach

Progressive Judaism's understanding is very different. At least that is true of the liberal tendency within it. (Other, more conservative tendencies tend to fudge the issue.) According to this view, the Hebrew Bible is a literature spanning a thousand years which displays both unity and diversity, the latter being manifest in a broad spectrum of literary styles and religious perceptions. Those who wrote it were not only human and therefore fallible, but also products of the socio-cultural milieu of the ancient Near East in which they lived. Sometimes they nevertheless expressed ideas far ahead of their times; in these we may legitimately see both the impact of revelation or inspiration and the working out of the implications of monotheism. Sometimes their thinking was on a level with what one finds in other contemporary civilisations, and in no way remarkable, and in not a few instances it has been left behind by subsequent advances in Jewish or in human thought.

Furthermore, there is *development* discernible in the diversity. Admittedly, this is not always unidirectional, for there are ups and downs. But *on the whole* the monotheism becomes more categorical, the ethical consciousness more humane, and the conception of Israel's role in human history more universalistic; and when one encounters evidences of retrogression, it takes only a little discernment to recognise that that is what they are.

Therefore, too, the Bible as a whole is only a stage – albeit the first and greatest stage – in the historical development of Judaism. Rabbinic

Judaism shows many advances, of which the change from Temple sacrifice to Synagogue prayer is the most obvious; and there have been advances since the Talmud, such as the prohibition of polygamy.

Above all, the liberal approach to the Bible, and likewise to its Rabbinic interpretation, rests on the conviction that there are universal ethical principles by which particular teachings of the Tradition may be evaluated. These principles derive in large measure from the Tradition itself, but not in the simplistic sense that we accept them on its authority. Rather, we affirm them because, as beings endowed by God with a capacity for ethical cognition, we can see for ourselves that they are true. Where the Tradition speaks with different voices, it is the same ethical cognition that enables us to discern the higher from the lower. And occasionally we may be able to advance beyond the Tradition by extrapolating tendencies that are discernible but incomplete within it. The raising of the status of women to one of equality with men is an example of that.

Progressive Judaism, therefore, views the Tradition *historically* and – with all due reverence – *critically,* evaluating it by the criteria of an ethical conscience which, though largely nurtured by the Tradition, is nevertheless independent of it.

Scriptural Promises

The Hebrew Bible is replete with passages that affirm a unique bond between the Jewish people and a particular territory which is at first referred to as the land of Canaan and later by various other terms including ארץ ישראל, the Land of Israel. (The latter occurs only rarely in the Bible, e.g. Ezek. 40:2, but is the regular designation of the country in post-Biblical Jewish literature, from the Mishnah onwards.) In Roman times and subsequently it became known as Palestine. Each of these names prejudges issues that have yet to be discussed. We shall therefore call it simply 'the Land'.

Many of the passages in question are in the nature of divine promises to Abraham (Gen. 12:2, 13:15, 15:7, 18, 17:8), Isaac (Gen. 26:3), Jacob (Gen. 28:13, 35:12, 48:4), Moses (Exod. 3:8, 6:8, Num. 33:53, 34:2, Deut. 11:24) and Joshua (Josh. 1:3). Some of them go on to define the borders of the Land, a subject to which we shall return. Several include the phrase, 'To you do I give it, and to your seed, for ever', which is a legal formula known from other ancient Near Eastern texts.

Some of these promises occur in the specific context of the Covenant (Gen. 15:18, 17:7), suggesting the possibility that if the people fail to fulfil their Covenantal obligations, they may forfeit their title to the Land, or be exiled from it. And sometimes that implication is spelt out, e.g., 'You shall keep My statutes and My ordinances ... so that the land does not vomit you out, as it vomited out the nation that was before you' (Lev. 18:26ff; cf. Lev. 26:27–39, Jer. 18:7f). But for the most part, the divine promises appear to be unconditional. Accordingly, Orthodox Judaism draws from them the inference that, in theory, the Land 'belongs' to the Jewish people, and to no other people, in perpetuity.

A liberal view would acknowledge that that is what the writers of the Bible believed. But it would try to understand the belief in its historical context. One aspect of this is the notion, common in the ancient Near East, of territorial deities; another is the need to reconcile that notion with the monotheistic idea. The argument, we must imagine, ran as follows. On the one hand God is the Owner of all lands, for 'The earth is God's and all its fullness' (Ps. 24:1). On the other hand God is the Owner of *the* Land in a special sense, calling it 'My land' (Joel 4:2) and keeping it under constant surveillance (Deut. 11:12). The resolution of the paradox is that God, at an early time, parcelled out the earth to its various peoples, assigning the choicest land to the chosen people (Deut. 32:8). This idea should also be seen in the context of the ætiological motif – the desire to explain, often fancifully, how things came to be as they are – which features so prominently in the Bible.

Even though our ancestors believed what they did, it does not follow that they were right. Surely it would be theologically naïve to suppose that God 'gave' the Land to them in any straightforward sense. It is indeed entirely credible that their settlement in the Land for the purpose of creating in it a monotheistic society would have accorded with the Divine Will. But the *means* by which they are said to have appropriated it, involving genocidal war against its inhabitants, raises serious questions, to which we shall return.

As for the further assertion that the Land was given to the Jewish people *in perpetuity*, that raises still other difficulties. For the Biblical writers had no means of knowing what God's long-term geopolitical plans were, nor indeed could there have been such if human free will is a fact. Because of that fact, as we have seen, the Israelites might conceivably forfeit their moral title to the Land; and for the same reason there are, in the course of history, conquests and migrations which may materially alter the factors relevant to a just land distribution.

In addition, we have to reckon with the possibility that, while it was God's intention that the Jewish people should *grow up* in the Land, it was not God's intention that they should remain confined

within it for ever. This view can draw support from statements in the
classical sources of Judaism which see positive value in the Diaspora, for instance that 'God scattered Israel among the nations for
the sole purpose that proselytes should become numerous among
them' (Pes. 87b). It is also a view that has been strongly held by Progressive Jewish thinkers in the past, as in this prayer: 'Enlighten all
that call themselves by thy name with the knowledge that the sanc-
tuary of wood and stone which once crowned Zion's hill was but a
gate, through which Israel stepped out into the world to lead mankind nearer unto thee' (*Liberal Jewish Prayer Book*, Vol. II, 1937, p. 281,
based on David Einhorn's *Olat Tamid* of 1856). Today most Progressive Jews would wish to qualify that by stressing the positive value of
the rebirth of Israel in its ancient homeland, but without therefore
negating the Diaspora.

It would certainly be consistent with a liberal Jewish theology to
believe that it was God's will, not only that the Jewish people
should grow up in the Land, but that they should maintain their
love for it and, whenever conditions permit, live in it, cultivate it,
and establish in it the most flourishing possible Jewish communal
life. But to invoke alleged divine promises contained in ancient
Hebrew literature as a ground for claiming present ownership of
the Land, in disregard of all other considerations, is not an option
open to non-fundamentalists.

The 'Holiness' of the Land

In addition to divine promises of the Land, the Bible abounds in
praises of it. It is said to be 'a land flowing with milk and honey'
(Exod. 13:8); 'a good land, with streams and springs and fountains
issuing from plain and hill; a land of wheat and barley, of vines, figs
and pomegranates … a land where you may eat bread without scarc-
ity, where you will lack nothing' (Deut. 8:7ff); 'the most beautiful of
all lands' (Ezek. 20:6, 15); and so forth. These eulogies, which continue in the Rabbinic Aggadah and in subsequent Jewish literature,
not least in the poetry of Judah Halevi, are authentic expressions of a
love for the Land which Jews have felt throughout their history, and
which requires no apology.

More difficult is the concept of the 'holiness' of the Land (קדושת הארץ).
As a matter of fact, the term 'Holy Land' is more commonly used by
Christians than by Jews. One of its Hebrew equivalents, אדמת הקדש, is
found, in that sense, only once in the Bible (Zech. 2:16); another,
ארץ הקדש, is first found in medieval sources. Nevertheless, the

underlying idea is implied in the Bible and spelt out in Rabbinic literature. 'The Land of Israel', says the Mishnah, 'is the holiest of all lands' (Kelim 1:6). Admittedly, the term is there used in a technical legal sense, the issue being the provenance of agricultural produce for the purpose of various kinds of Temple offerings.

A leading Anglo-Jewish scholar, Hyam Maccoby, has written: 'The Land of Israel was indeed regarded as holy in various halachic ways, but this territorial holiness is not a mystical value in Judaism' (Maccoby, 1993). Nevertheless, the concept of holiness as a quality that in some supernatural way inheres in the Land does seem to be implied in the disqualification of other lands for cultic purposes. Likewise in a number of aggadic statements, for instance, that 'the very air of the Land of Israel makes wise' (BB 158a); that 'those who live in the Land of Israel are as if they had a God, whereas those who live outside the Land of Israel are as if they had no God' (Ket. 110b); that 'those who live in the Land of Israel live without sin' (Ket. 11a) ; and that, 'once the Land of Israel had been chosen, all other lands were excluded from divine revelation' (Mechilta, Pischa 1 to Exod. 12:1).

At any rate, in so far as such a 'mystical' concept is to be found in Jewish tradition, it must be repudiated from a liberal point of view. For it is clearly incompatible with the omnipresence of God, which is a necessary corollary of monotheism, and it obscures an essential distinction: between the holiness of God, which is primary, and the 'holiness' of things, persons, places and times *associated* with God, which is only a 'reflected' holiness, and therefore secondary. Of course the Land has many 'holy' associations for Progressives, as for all Jews, but they would deem it all the more important nevertheless to emphasise that 'the Eternal One is great beyond the borders of Israel' (Mal. 1:5).

The Borders of The Land

The question of the 'holiness' of the Land is closely related to that of its borders, for it is only within these that its 'holiness' is said to reside, and from that distinction a number of legal consequences follow for the so-called מצוות התלויות בארץ ('commandments dependent on the Land'). Most of these relate to the Temple, the monarchy and agriculture, and do not concern us here. But there are also one or two related Mitzvot, concerning settlement in the Land, which are very relevant to our inquiry and to which we shall return.

There is, however, no simple answer to the question of borders, for the fact is that they were variously conceived in different periods,

depending partly on the actual extent of Israel's territorial control at
the time, and partly on the writer's idealising imagination. Within
the Biblical period, it is customary to distinguish three stages, respectively associated with Abraham, Joshua and Ezra.

The divine promise to Abraham reads: 'To your descendants I
give this land, from the river of Egypt to the great river, the river
Euphrates, the land of the Kenites, the Kenizzites, the Kadmonites,
the Hittites, the Perizzites, the Rephaim, the Amorites, the Canaanites, the Girgashites, and the Jebusites' (Gen. 15:18–21). This, the
most extensive definition, is regarded as an idealistic one which will
be fully realised only in the messianic age. In that sense it is reiterated elsewhere; e.g., 'I will set your borders from the Red Sea to the
sea of the Philistines, and from the wilderness to the Euphrates'
(Exod. 23:31), and, 'Every place on which you set foot shall be yours;
your territory shall extend from the wilderness to the Lebanon and
from the River, the river Euphrates, to the Western sea' (Deut. 11:24;
cf. Josh. 1:4).

Considerably more modest in extent is the territory which the
generation of the Exodus are promised through Moses, and subsequently occupy – in large part though not entirely – under the leadership of Joshua. This is defined in great detail in Numbers (34:1–13)
and Joshua (12:1–6, 13:1–7), and similar references can be found in
Ezekiel (47:15–20). It is largely bounded by the Mediterranean in the
west and the Jordan in the east, but spreads some way towards Egypt
in the southwest and into Syria in the northeast. This area, in so far
as it was conquered under Joshua, is said to have acquired by virtue
of that fact a 'first sanctification' (קדושה ראשונה). According to many
authorities, however, this conferred on it only a *temporary* 'holiness',
for what is gained by conquest can be lost by conquest (Chag. 3b;
Yad, Hilchot Terumot 1:5; Bleich, 1983, pp. 171–75; Talmudic Encyclopædia, Hebrew edition, Vol. II, Jerusalem, 1979, pp. 113–16).

Even less extensive (perhaps stretching from Akko in the north to
Ashkelon in the south) was the area occupied by the Jewish exiles
who returned from Babylonia following the decree of Cyrus, King of
Persia, and in the days of Ezra. This area is said to have acquired a
'second sanctification' (קדושה שנייה). According to some authorities,
that, too, lapsed after the Dispersion; according to others, perhaps
because it resulted from a never-rescinded royal decree, it has remained in force ever since (Tos. Shevi'it 1:6; Sifrei Deut. 51 to Deut.
11:24; Talmudic Encyclopædia, pp. 116ff).

The foregoing is only a simplified summary. In fact, the question
of the borders of the Land is a great deal more complicated, both
from a halakhic and from a historical point of view. In the words of

a contemporary Israeli Orthodox rabbi: 'There is a great discrepancy between the actual borders of the Land of Canaan at the time of Abraham (Gen. 10:19), concerning which it is said: "to your seed have I given this land ..." and the Land promised by God to Abraham (Gen. 15:18–21). Both outlines differ from the boundary promised to Israel in the wilderness (Exod. 23:32) and the promise made prior to their entry into the Land (Deut. 1:7, 32:2–4). Moreover, all the Biblical borders differ from what was to be the ideal future boundary (Ezek. 47:13). Then, again, all the aforesaid borders were not identical with the Land actually divided up between the twelve Tribes by lot (Num. 34:2–12). Furthermore, the areas thus divided did not tally with the "inheritance" and "settlement" in the days of Joshua and the Judges (Josh. 12, 13, Jud. 3:4), which. again, differed from the "second inheritance" during the days of Ezra and Nehemia, King Yannai and Agrippas I' (Rav Yishai Yuval in Tomaschoff, 1978, pp. 122f).

However, we need not pursue these complications any further, for we shall argue that the precise nature of the various ancient borders has no relevance to the contemporary territorial question which concerns us.

Jewish Settlement

The Bible devotes much attention to the manner in which, by various stages, the Israelites entered the Land, settled in it, and gained possession of it. In the period of the Patriarchs the process is depicted as a largely peaceful one, involving migrations (Gen. 12:1–6), treaties (Gen. 21:22–34, 26:26–31) and purchases (Gen. 23:3–20, Gen. 33:19). By contrast, the occupation of the Land under Joshua involved violent conflict with its resident inhabitants. As related in the Bible, it was nevertheless carried out in response to divine exhortations. Here are some of the key passages:

> The Eternal One spoke to Moses in the plains of Moab by the Jordan near Jericho, saying, Speak to the children of Israel and say to them: When you cross over the Jordan into the land of Canaan, you shall drive out (והורשתם) all the inhabitants of the land from before you ... You shall take possession of the land, and settle in it (וישבתם בה), for I have given the land to you to possess (Num. 33:52f).

> When the Eternal One your God brings you into the land which you are about to enter and possess, and casts out many nations before you – the Hittites, the Girgashites, the Amorites, the Canaanites, the Perizzites, the Hivites, and the Jebusites, seven nations mightier and more numerous

than you – and when the Eternal One your God gives them over to you and you defeat them, then you shall utterly destroy them; you shall make no covenant with them and show them no mercy (ולא תחנם) (Deut. 7:1f).

For you are about to cross over the Jordan to go in to possess the land which the Eternal One your God is giving you; therefore take possession of it, and settle in it (וירשתם אותה וישבתם בה) (Deut. 11:31).

When the Eternal One your God has cut off from before you the nations which you are to penetrate and dispossess, you shall dispossess them and settle in their land (וירשת אותם וישבת בארצם) (Deut. 12:29).

These passages raise an obvious difficulty: how can they be reconciled with the belief in a universal, just and merciful God? Presumably we are dealing here with an *ex post facto* justification of past events. In reality, the Occupation was most probably effected, not by one major campaign, as recounted in the book of Joshua, but by a series of minor incursions, and it is therefore legitimate to wonder whether it could have been effected by peaceful means. But these are matters of academic speculation, and not of any contemporary relevance. So, at least, one might have thought.

However, because these passages contain a number of imperatives, the question arises from a halachic point of view whether they were addressed only to the generation of the wilderness and then lapsed, or whether they remained in force. In other words, is there a continuing obligation upon Jews to settle and live in the Land?

The prevailing but not unanimous answer of the Halachah is 'yes'. Rabbinic literature goes so far as to say that the Mitzvah of living in the Land is as weighty as all the other Mitzvot put together (Sifrei Deut. 80 to Deut. 11:31f; Tos. AZ 4[5]:3)! Of the Rishonim (earlier authorities) the outstanding exponent of the view that the Mitzvah remains in force was Nachmanides. 'Ramban understands all the passages of the Torah instructing the Jewish People and Joshua to conquer, take possession and settle the Land as being commands not addressed to that generation alone, but to all future generations' (Rav Avraham Elkana-Shapira in Tomaschoff, 1978, p. 166). Accordingly, he regarded it as a Biblical law (מדאורייתא), based on Num. 33:53 (see above), and criticised Maimonides for not including it in his compilation of the 613 commandments (Nachmanides' Torah commentary to Num. 33:53 and his addendum No. 4 to Maimonides' Sefer ha-Mitzvot, Mitzvot Aseh).

As to why Maimonides did not include the Mitzvah, there has been much speculation. According to the Talmudic Encyclopædia, he regarded it as having the force of only rabbinic (מדרבנן), not Biblical law (Vol. II, p. 223b). It should also be noted that Maimonides does include the Mitzvah in his Mishneh Torah, Hilchot Melachim 5:12. But Rabbi David Bleich writes: 'The simplest and most obvious reason for this omission is that Rambam does not view this injunction as constituting a mandatory obligation binding upon all generations. Rambam may well have deemed the commandment to have been binding only upon the generation of the wilderness to whom it was addressed and to those who were charged with the original conquest of the land of Canaan, but not intended as a binding commandment for all posterity. Alternatively, Rambam may have interpreted the verse as constituting sage counsel, as did Rashi, rather than a commandment. It thus follows that, in our time, according to Rambam, there is no divine imperative requiring a Jew to remove himself from the Diaspora and to establish residence in Israel' (Bleich, 1983, pp. 195f). But he goes on to concede that, 'in the absence of Rambam's position one would be hard put to excuse failure to settle in Israel' (ibid., p. 204).

Progressive Jews would be inclined to endorse the most liberal interpretation of Maimonides' opinion. There can be no question of an *obligation* on all Jews to settle in Israel. Of course Progressive Judaism recognises the unique opportunities and challenges which the State of Israel presents. Many Progressive Jews have indeed settled there, and Progressive Jewish organisations have endorsed the 1951 Jerusalem Programme of the World Zionist Organisation with its call for 'the ingathering of the Jewish people in its historic homeland Eretz Israel through *aliyah* from all countries', but with the explicit or implicit proviso that *aliyah* is to be only encouraged, not demanded, and on the understanding that Jewish life in the Diaspora also continues to have positive value.

The Rights of Non-Jews

We must now return to the negative side of the Bible's exhortations concerning the occupation of the Land, namely its call for the expulsion, if not annihilation, of its indigenous population. We have already touched briefly on the moral difficulties this raises. Here we should like, additionally, to draw attention to an excellent discussion of the topic by Rabbi W. Gunther Plaut in his *Torah Commentary* (Plaut, 1981, pp. 1381f), where he points out, *inter alia*, that the injunction to annihilate the Canaanites was, as a matter of historical fact, never carried out, and that the passages in question, attributed to the age of Moses, need to be understood in the light of a much later struggle against Canaanite idolatry.

The question we nevertheless need to raise is whether these anti-gentile injunctions play any role in post-Biblical Jewish law; and here again the answer is: to some extent, yes.

We may indeed take it from Bleich that 'there is, in our day, no obligation to wage war for conquest of *Eretz Yisrael* or for retention of sanctified territories, even according to the opinion of Ramban' (Bleich, 1983, p. 211). But the fact is that the modern State of Israel, as a result of a series of defensive wars, has gained control over extensive territories that include a large Palestinian-Arab population. Therefore questions about the status of these and other non-Jewish residents cannot be avoided, and have received attention from Orthodox rabbinic authorities according to their understanding of the Halachah.

The key verse here is Deuteronomy 7:2, quoted above, and especially the phrase לא תחנם, which is usually translated 'you shall show them no mercy'. However, already the Talmud took the verb as coming, not from the root חנן, 'to have mercy', but from the root חנה, 'to camp', interpreting it as a prohibition against the sale of real estate to non-Jews within the borders of the Land (AZ 20a; Yad, Hilchot Avodat Kochavim 10:3f; Sh.Ar., YD 151:8).

That, it may be thought, is restrictive enough, but there are one or two further restrictions. When Jews are in control of the Land, says Maimonides (Yad, Hilchot Avodat Kochavim 10:6), they may not permit non-Jews to live in it at all, except in so far as they undertake to observe the Seven Noachide Laws (which include the prohibition of idolatry), since it says, 'They shall not live in your land' (Exod. 23:33). Seeing that Christians and Muslims have since the Middle Ages been considered monotheists in Jewish law, that should present no problem; yet there is a rigorous view which would require non-Jews claiming such status to make a formal declaration of allegiance to the Noachide Laws before a rabbinical court (Rav Yehoshua Menachem Ehrenberg in Tomaschoff, 1978, p. 178; cf. Maimonides, Yad, Hilchot Melachim 8:10)!

Furthermore, since these prohibitions apply to all areas now under Israel's control that fall within the boundaries of the Land as halachically defined, they could be, and have been, used as an argument against the surrender of any of the territories in question on the ground that such surrender would cause real estate that 'belongs' to the Jewish people to fall into non-Jewish hands. Accordingly, an eminent Israeli Orthodox rabbi has stated that 'the precept of *lo techonnem* certainly applies and no part of Eretz Israel must on any account be handed over to non-Jews, whether individually or by the national authorities' (Tomaschoff, 1978, p. 168).

Territory and Peace

Such extreme views are held by much of the ultra-Orthodox leadership, both in Israel and in the Diaspora. Why that should be, is an interesting question. It is partly due, one presumes, to the rejection of history, reason, and any ethic independent of the Halachah, characteristic of that tendency. It also has something to do with its traditional negativism towards the whole culture of Enlightenment and liberalism. But it has been intensified by a strong feeling, often amounting to a fervent conviction, that recent events – the rebirth of a Jewish State after two thousand years, the War of Independence, the Six Day War, the Entebbe Raid, etc. – betoken nothing less than עקבי המשיח ('the footsteps of the Messiah') and אתחלתא דגאולה ('the beginning of redemption'). They are seen as a triumphant demonstration of God's power to fulfil ancient prophecies and thus as a validation of the fundamentalist reading of Scripture. To such an eschatological way of thinking, all things are possible, and ethical scruples may be suspended.

Those who share this mentality live in a dream-world which has its own logic but bears no relation to any solid reality, and become natural allies of secular forms of ultra-nationalist fanaticism, which are likewise disdainful of reason.

Thus Rav Avraham Elkana Kahana-Shapira writes: 'The very existence of a mitzvah to conquer Eretz Israel indicates that it is God's will that the whole of Eretz Israel should be in our possession' (Tomaschoff, 1978, p. 170). Similarly, Rav Yakov Ariel (Shtiglitz), interpreting R. Yehoshua of Kotna's view of מצות ישוב הארץ (the commandment to settle the Land), concludes: 'Any form of withdrawal from the regained territories constitutes a negation of the mitzvah and a hindrance to the process of Redemption' (ibid., p. 139).

But it should not be thought that *all* Orthodox rabbis, even of the 'old school', take such a hawkish view. For instance, the former Sefardi Chief Rabbi of Israel, Ovadiah Yosef, holds that the halachic arguments for the retention of all the conquered territories must give way before the following considerations: that peace is unattainable without territorial concession; that in the absence of peace, there will be more war and bloodshed; that פקוח נפש (saving human life) must be the overriding objective; and that it is for the political and military experts, not the rabbis, to judge what measures are best calculated to achieve that end (Zemer, 1993, pp. 161f, quoting *Torah she-b'al Peh*, ed. Yitzchak Raphael, Jerusalem, 1980, p. 14).

Similar views have been expressed by the former Chief Rabbi of the United Hebrew Congregations of the British Commonwealth,

Lord (Immanuel) Jakobovits, and by his successor, Rabbi Dr Jonathan Sacks. Hyam Maccoby summed up their position, which seems to be also his own, when he wrote that 'the requirements of peace come before considerations of territory in rabbinic thinking. The holiness of the Land does not preclude the right of a Jewish ruling body to come to terms with an enemy in the interests of overall peace, even when such terms involve the ceding of a portion of the land categorised as holy' (Maccoby, 1993).

This line of argument is very powerful in view of Judaism's immense emphasis on the ideal of peace (e.g., 'Seek peace, and pursue it', Psalm 34:15) as well as the halachic principle that פקוח נפש (saving life) takes priority over all other commandments except the prohibitions of idolatry, incest and murder (San. 74a).

Unfortunately, however, the argument is not unassailable. For it is possible to contend that since war, by its very nature, involves casualties, therefore the principle of פקוח נפש does not apply to it, and that, since any war which may be necessary to defend the conquered territories would be in the nature of מלחמת מצוה ('obligatory war'), the risk involved must be taken.

Thus Rav Shlomo Aviner quotes Rav Avraham Kook as follows: 'All activities designed to transfer ownership of parts of Eretz Israel from the hands of gentiles to those of Jews come within the definition of the Divine commandment to conquer the Land of Israel, outweighing all the commandments of the Torah. This is borne out by the fact that by definition the Torah obliges us to implement this precept even to the point of war, which naturally entails risking the loss of life' (Tomaschoff, 1978, p. 115). Similarly, Rav Yehoshua Menachem Ehrenberg writes: 'Since the Torah obliges us to conquer Eretz Israel with all the danger to life that this involves, how can we justify giving up territory that we have already conquered because of *pikkuah nefesh*?' (ibid., p. 176)· And Rav Avraham Elkana Kahana-Shapira makes it clear that according to his interpretation of Maimonides 'wars of conquest in the Holyland – at all times, fall into the category of *Milchamot Mitzvah*' (ibid., pp. 166f).

Summary of the Orthodox Position

The Orthodox position, as we have seen, is not monolithic. But there is fundamental agreement that the divine promises of the Hebrew Bible are to be taken at face value; that the Land, whatever may be its precise extent, is, within those limits, holy; that *de jure* it belongs to the Jewish people, and to no other, for ever; and that in the messianic age, the imminent approach of which we may or may not be witnessing in our time, it will be so *de facto*.

Thus the Jewish people's claim to the Land is grounded in the Divine Will as revealed in Scripture, a point commonly reinforced by reference to Rashi's comment on the first verse of Genesis, where he asks why the Bible begins with the creation of the world and, quoting Psalm 111:6, replies: 'So that, if the nations were to say to Israel, "You are robbers, because you conquered the seven nations of Canaan," they may be able to reply, "The whole earth belongs to God, who created it and gave it to whomever He thought fit; by His will He gave it to the seven nations, and by His will He took it from them and gave it to us".'

Beyond that basic principle, there is divergence, particularly on the rights of non-Jews in the Land and the question whether or not it is permissible to relinquish some portions of it for the sake of peace. Some authorities believe that, in furtherance of the Divine Plan, the non-Jewish population of the Land should be kept as low as possible, and their rights of residence subject to stringent conditions. Thus Professor Yehudah Elizur writes: 'This, then, is the message and iron rule of the Bible, that no people can ever strike roots in Eretz Israel, the Land awaiting the homecoming of its sons and daughters' (Tomaschoff, 1978, p. 96). And, interpreting Nachmanides, he continues: 'Israel and the Land of Israel belong to one another; when united, both flourish and are blessed. The converse is true when Land and people are separated, then misfortune takes hold of both, Israel turning into a wasteland and the Jews suffering persecution, exile and migration from one place to another' (ibid., p. 97).

Many Orthodox leaders would no doubt wish to distance themselves from such statements, and adopt a more positive attitude to the rights of non-Jews in the Land. Similarly, as we have seen, some take an extremely hawkish, others a much more dovish, view on the question of territorial concessions for the sake of peace. The latter, in addition to those already mentioned, include Rabbi Yehudah Amital, Professor Aviezer Ravitzky, Uriel Simon, David Kretchmer, and the late Professor Yeshayahu Leibowitz. It also needs to be acknowledged that Orthodox organisations such as *Oz v'Shalom* and *Netivei Shalom* have played an important role in supporting the 'Peace Now' movement.

What is nevertheless striking about Orthodox Jewish halachic literature on the subject – unless I am misled by insufficient acquaintance with it – is an astonishing lack of concern with, or emphasis upon, what seems to me so obviously the very nub of the problem: that the Land is the subject of conflicting claims by two peoples,

Jewish and Palestinian, and that this conflict needs to be considered
and settled in the light of universal-ethical principles.

In an otherwise ultra-Orthodox anthology, from which we have
already quoted several times, one dissentient contributor, Yisrael
Yaacov Yuval, writes: 'Action seen from a political-theological view-
point as constituting a decisive stage in a divinely ordained redemp-
tive process, appears to dispense with the need of applying moral
criteria to problems such as the subjugation of another people, the
refugees and Arab claims to this country … All types of nationalism
are characterized by this kind of particularist mystique, that ignores
the existence of generally valid rules of ethics … It is against this, so
startlingly simple theologico-political canvas, the natural outgrowth
of Messianism, where God demands acts of injustice towards one
party in order to benefit his chosen favourite, that we find an explanation for an aristocratic ethic, so devoid of humanity' (Tomaschoff,
1978, pp. 103f).

The Liberal Conscience

A liberal view would begin by denying the fundamentalist basis on
which the Orthodox view rests. It would say that the alleged divine
promises contained in Scripture are not objective statements of
God's Will but subjective perceptions of it which need to be understood in their historical context; that the fundamentalist reading of
them rests on a misunderstanding of what the Bible is; and that the
invocation of such texts to 'prove' Jewish ownership of the Land
three millennia later is altogether inadmissible.

Similarly, it would maintain that the concept of the 'holiness' of the
Land is only a matter of historical associations, not of supernatural reality, and has no relevance to the present debate. Likewise, it would contend that such issues as the borders of the Land, and the rights of
non-Jews within it, need to be determined by considerations quite other
than technical-legal interpretations of Biblical and Talmudic texts.

What these considerations are, has already been indicated: they
are universal-ethical considerations. That does not mean that they
are extraneous to Judaism. On the contrary, they are very much
rooted in Judaism, but in its general values rather than its legal
minutiae, and therefore in the teachings of the Prophets as well as
the Torah, and of the Aggadah as well as the Halakhah. Although
rooted in Judaism, these values also transcend it, because by their
universal nature they rightfully claim, as they have in large measure received, the assent of civilised humanity. They are: justice,

humaneness, compassion, democracy, the need for international law-and-order, and the imperative of peace.

Judged by these criteria, the Jewish claim to the Land is very strong, and needs no support from an antiquated theology. The millennia-old association of the Jewish people with the Land; their persistent love and longing for it; their unjust expulsions from it (even though many emigrated of their own free will); the fact that they have nevertheless always maintained a presence in it; their desperate need for a haven of refuge from persecution, especially before and after the Holocaust; the agricultural achievements of the *chalutzim* (pioneers) who began to resettle the Land towards the end of the nineteenth century; the even greater cultural, economic, political and military achievements of the State of Israel itself, including the absorption of a vast number of immigrants from Arab lands as well as Ethiopia and the former Soviet Union: all these constitute an extremely powerful claim which no fair-minded person would deny.

But not an exclusive claim! For the Land was not empty when the Zionist resettlement began. It had a large Arab population, which until after the Second World War still constituted a substantial majority. Many of these Arabs had lived in Palestine for generations, even centuries, and were deeply attached to its soil. Understandably, they resented the ever-increasing Jewish immigration and, still more, the displacement of hundreds of thousands of their people during the War of Independence. Therefore they have developed their own Palestinian nationalism, which is in many ways a mirror image of Jewish nationalism, and demands similarly to be heard by the international community. Thus the Palestinian-Arab claim to the Land, though different from the Jewish one, also has considerable weight.

That being the case, it has been totally obvious to liberal-minded people all along that, if there is to be any kind of justice, the two peoples, Jewish and Arab, must in one way or another *share* the Land. One way might have been the creation of a binational state, as advocated by the first President of the Hebrew University, Judah L. Magnes, who was a Progressive rabbi. But it was rejected by both sides, and left partition as the only remaining just option.

That has been the all but unanimous view of the international community for the past fifty years. It was the United Nations' partition resolution of 1947 which made possible the establishment of the State of Israel, and gave it legitimacy in international law. Moreover, the partition principle has been periodically reaffirmed by the United Nations, for instance by Resolution 242 of 1967 and Resolution 338 of 1973, as it was affirmed yet again by the Preamble of the Camp David Accords of 1979, all of which the State of Israel has endorsed.

The current Peace Process, which began in 1991/1992, honours the principle by calling for mutual recognition between Israel and the Palestinians and promising the latter autonomy in Gaza and parts of the West Bank. The solution it envisages may be far from perfect, and has yet to be fully worked out by negotiation, but it represents a large step towards a just solution of the conflict, or as just a solution as is now realistically attainable. As such, it should be welcomed and supported by all Jews both in Israel and in the Diaspora.

What is here argued is not a political but a religious view. It is predicated on the most basic principles of Judaism, as Progressive Jews understand it. First, that the God of Judaism is the universal God, who has created all human beings in the Divine Image, and cares for them with an impartial love, so that a prophet was able to say in God's name: 'Blessed be Egypt My people, and Assyria the work of My hands, and Israel My heritage' (Isa. 19:25). Secondly, that the God of Judaism is a moral God, so that justice and compassion are of the essence both of God's nature and of God's demands; for 'the Eternal One is righteous, and loves righteous deeds' (Psalm 11:7). Thirdly, that God's plan for the future of humanity is a time when the nations will 'beat their swords into ploughshares, and their spears into pruning-hooks' (Isa. 2:4), and live together in amity, concord and peace. Fourth, that God expects the Jewish people, not only to pursue its own self-interest, but to set a moral example, and so to be 'a light to the nations' (Isa. 49:6). Fifth, that this involves applying the principle of 'Love your neighbour' (Lev. 19:18) not only to interpersonal but also to international relations, so that we may not then deny to another people what we demand for ourselves.

It is these religious and moral principles which make it incumbent on Jews to seek a relationship of mutual respect, understanding, accommodation and reconciliation with the Palestinian people. The present Peace Process gives Israel a unique opportunity to do that, and so to demonstrate to a world which is crying out for just such a demonstration that it is possible to transcend nationalism, show magnanimity, achieve compromise, and transform enmity into friendship.

NOTES AND ACKNOWLEDGMENTS

❖   ❖   ❖

All of the chapters of this book are edited versions of lectures given or articles previously published as shown below. For permission to use them we wish to thank the relevant journals and organisations as indicated.

Progressive Judaism Published as 'A New Kind of Judaism' in *Manna,* No. 46, Winter 1995; based on the author's Claude Goldsmid Montefiore Lecture given at the Liberal Jewish Synagogue, 27 June 1990.

Progressive Judaism Fifty Years after the Holocaust Lecture, International Conference of the World Union for Progressive Judaism, Paris, 1 July 1975; published in *European Judaism,* Vol. 29, No. 2, Autumn 1996.

Halachah and Aggadah: Law and Lore in Judaism Lecture, Leo Baeck College Study Week, 30 June 1982.

The Need for a New Approach to Halachah Chairman's Inaugural Lecture, Council of Reform and Liberal Rabbis, 10 February 1970; published as 'Towards a Modern Halachah' in *Reform Judaism,* ed. Dow Marmur, RSGB, 1973.

Rethinking our Relationship with Halachah Lecture, Conference of European Rabbis, Amsterdam, 29 June 1970.

Towards a Progressive Halachah Lecture, International Rabbinic Kallah in association with the World Union for Progressive Judaism, Jerusalem, 27 February 1980.

Between Antinomianism and Conservatism Lecture, Founding Colloquium, Freehof Institute of Progressive Halakhah, 6 May 1990; published in *Dynamic Jewish Law,* Freehof Institute, 1991.

A Genuinely Progressive Halachah Lecture, Conference of the European Region of the World Union for Progressive Judaism, Geneva, 8 November 1996.

Praying with Kavvanah The Harold Reinhart Memorial Lecture, Westminster Synagogue, 23 January 1973; published in *A Rabbi's Journal,* No. 5, November 1979.

The Language of Prayer The David Goldstein Memorial Lecture, ULPS, 11 January 1993.

The Posture of Prayer Published as 'What We Stand For' in *Manna,* No. 41, Autumn 1993.

Women and Worship Published as 'Let Us Pray' in *Manna*, No. 44, Summer 1994.

On Seeing Halley's Comet Reply to an inquiry from a colleague in the United States, 29 December 1985.

Returning a Scroll to its Owner Reply to an inquiry from a colleague in France, 20 May 1996.

Recycling Old Prayerbooks Reply to an inquiry from a colleague in Britain, 19 November 1990.

Medical Confidentiality Lecture, Manor House Medical Ethics Society, 11 December 1994; published as 'When Secrets Must Not Be Kept' in *Manna*, No. 47, Spring 1995.

Organ Transplantation Published as 'Transplants – A Jewish Response Demands Priorities' in *Manna*, No. 21, Autumn 1988.

A Matter of Life and Death Lecture, Manor House Medical Ethics Society, 17 December 1989; published in *Manna*, No. 29, Autumn 1990.

Euthanasia Lecture, Manor House Medical Ethics Society, 16 December 1990.

Burial of Progressive Proselyte in Orthodox Cemetery Reply to an inquiry from a colleague in Switzerland, 7 May 1992.

Jewish Identity Based on a paper given at a discussion group led by Alan Montefiore at the Wiener Library, London, 10 December 1997

Conception and Contraception Published in *Pointer* (ULPS), Vol. IV, No. 1, Autumn 1968.

From Unilateralism to Reciprocity: A Short History of Jewish Divorce Paper read at a meeting of the Freehof Institute of Progressive Halakhah, Hochschule für Musik, Munich, 1 November 1997.

The Land, the Law and the Liberal Conscience Published in *Israel and Diaspora*, Freehof Institute of Progressive Halakhah, 1997; an abridged version appeared in *Manna*, No. 50, Winter 1996.

Note on Translations

As in the author's previous books in this series, *An Understanding of Judaism* and *A Jewish Understanding of the World*, all translations of Hebrew texts are his own, though based on, or influenced by, published translations where they exist, especially the *New Revised Standard Version* of the Bible and the Soncino translations of the Babylonian Talmud and Midrash Rabbah.

BIBLIOGRAPHY

❖   ❖   ❖

Abrahams, Israel, 1932 *Jewish Life in the Middle Ages.* Edward Goldston, London

Barth, Lewis M., ed., 1990 *Berit Mila in the Reform Context.* Berit Mila Board of Reform Judaism, USA

Bacher, Wilhelm, 1965 *Die exegetische Terminologie der jüdischen Traditionsliteratur.* Georg Olms, Hildesheim. First published 1899

Bayfield, Anthony M., 1993 *Sinai, Law and Responsible Autonomy.* RSGB, London

Berkovits, Eliezer, 1983 *Not in Heaven, the Nature and Function of Halakha.* Ktav, New York

Biale, Rachel, 1984 *Women and Jewish Law: An Exploration of Women's Issues in Halakhic Sources.* Schocken, New York

Bialik, Ch.N., 1951 כל כתבי ח.נ. ביאליק [Complete Works of Ch.N. Bialik]. Dvir, Tel-Aviv

Bleich, J. David, 1977 *Contemporary Halakhic Problems.* Ktav, New York

—— 1983 *Ditto, Vol. II.* Ditto

—— 1989 *Ditto, Vol. III.* Ditto

—— 1995 *Ditto, Vol. IV.* Ditto

BMA (British Medical Association), 1993 *Medical Ethics Today, Its Practice and Philosophy.* BMJ Publishing Group, London

Bok, Sissela, 1984 *Secrets, Concealment and Revelation.* OUP, Oxford and Melbourne

Borowitz, Eugene B., 1969 *Choosing a Sex Ethic, A Jewish Inquiry ....* Schocken, USA

—— 1988 *Reform Jewish Ethics and the Halakhah, An Experiment in Decision Making,* Behrman House, New Jersey

Chajes, Z.H., 1952 *The Student's Guide through the Talmud.* Trsl. Jacob Schachter. East and West, London

Chesser, Eustace, 1967 *Living with Suicide.* Hutchinson, London

Cowley, A., 1923 *Aramaic Papyri of the Fifth Century B.C.* Clarendon Press, Oxford

Doppelt, Frederic A., and David Polish, 1957 *A Guide for Reform Jews.* Bloch, New York

Eisenstein, J.D., 1970 אוצר דינים ומנהגים, *A Digest of Jewish Laws and Customs.* Tel-Aviv

Elon, Menachem, 1994 *Jewish Law, History, Sources, Principles.* 4 volumes, JPS, Philadelphia and Jerusalem

Epstein, Louis M., 1967 *Sex Laws and Customs in Judaism.* Ktav. First published 1948

Falk, Ze'ev W., 1966 *Jewish Matrimonial Law in the Middle Ages.* OUP

Feldman, David M., 1968 *Birth Control in Jewish Law.* New York University Press and University of London Press

Freehof, Solomon B., 1923 'Devotional Literature in the Vernacular' in *CCAR Yearbook XXXIII*

—— 1955 *The Responsa Literature.* JPS, Philadelphia

—— 1960 *Reform Responsa*. HUC Press, Cincinnati
—— 1961 'Reform Judaism and the Jewish Legal Tradition' (pamphlet). Association of Reform Rabbis of New York and Vicinity
—— 1963 (i) *Reform Jewish Practice and its Rabbinic Background*. UAHC, New York. First published 1944
—— 1963 (ii) *Recent Reform Responsa*. Ditto
—— 1969 *Current Reform Responsa*. Ditto
—— 1971 *Modern Reform Responsa*. Ditto
—— 1974 *Contemporary Reform Responsa*. Ditto
—— 1977 *Reform Responsa for our Time*. Ditto
—— 1980 *New Reform Responsa*. HUC Press, Cincinnati
Freimann, Abraham Chayim, 1964 סדר קדושין ונשואין ['The Order of Betrothal and Marriage']. Mossad Harav Kook, Jerusalem
Ginzberg, Louis, 1958 *Students, Scholars and Saints*. Meridian Books, New York. First published 1928
—— 1962 *On Jewish Law and Lore*. Meridian Books, New York. First published 1955
Goldberg, David J., and John D. Rayner, 1989 *The Jewish People, Their History and their Religion*. Penguin. First published 1987
Goldin, Hyman E., 1939 *Hamadrikh, The Rabbi's Guide,*. Hebrew Publishing Company, New York
Greenberg, Blu, 1981 *On Women and Judaism, A View from Tradition*. JPS, Philadelphia
Guttmann, Alexander, 1977 *The Struggle over Reform in Rabbinic Literature*. World Union for Progressive Judaism, Jerusalem and New York
Herring, Basil F., 1984 *Jewish Ethics and Halakhah for our Time, Sources and Commentary* . Ktav and Yeshivah University Press, New York
Hoffman, Lawrence A., 1979 *The Canonization of the Synagogue Service* University of Notre Dame Press, Notre Dame and London
Homolka, Walter, Walter Jacob and Esther Seidel, 1997 *Not by Birth Alone, Conversion to Judaism*. Cassell, London and Washington
Jacob, Walter, 1992 *Questions and Reform Jewish Answers, New American Reform Responsa*. CCAR, New York
—— ed., 1983 *American Reform Responsa, Collected Responsa of the Central Conference of Amertican Rabbis 1889–1983*. CCAR, New York
—— ed., 1987 *Contemporary American Reform Responsa*. CCAR, New York
—— ed., 1988 *Liberal Judaism and Halakhah*. Rodef ShalomCongregation, Pittsburgh
Jacob, Walter, and Moshe Zemer, eds., 1991 *Progressive Halakhah, Essence and Application*. Freehof Institute of Progressive Halakhah, Tel Aviv and Pittsburgh
—— 1993 *Rabbinic-Lay Relations in Jewish Law*. Ditto
—— 1994 *Conversion to Judaism, Essays and Responsa*. Ditto
—— 1995 (i) *The Fetus and Fertility in Jewish Law, Essays and Responsa*. Ditto
—— 1995 (ii) *Death and Euthanasia in Jewish Law, Essays and Responsa*. Ditto
—— 1997 *Israel and Diaspora in Jewish Law, Essays and Responsa*. Ditto
Jacobs, Louis, 1962 'Montefiore and Loewe on the Rabbis' (pamphlet), Liberal Jewish Synagogue, London
—— 1973 *What Judaism says about ...* Keter, Jerusalem
—— 1975 *Theology in the Responsa*. Littman Library, Routledge & Kegan Paul, Boston and London
—— 1981 *Teyku, The Unsolved Problem in the Babylonian Talmud*. Leo Baeck College, Cornwall Books, London and New York
—— 1984 *A Tree of Life*. Littman Library, OUP
Jacobson, Issachar, 1968 נתיב בינה [The Path of Understanding]. 2 vols, Sinai, Tel Aviv

Jakobovits, Immanuel, 1975 *Jewish Medical Ethics.* Bloch, New York. First published 1959

Kagan, Israel Meir ha-Kohen, 5734 [1973–1974] חפץ חיים ['The one who desires life', alluding to Psalm 34:13] Radin, Jerusalem. First published 1873

Kaufman, Michael, 1983 *The Woman in Jewish Law and Tradition.* Jason Aronson, Northvale, New Jersey, London

Kellner, Menachem Marc, 1978 ed., *Contemporary Jewish Ethics.* Sanhedrin Press, New York

Kershen, Anne and Jonathan Romain, 1995 *Tradition and Change, A History of Reform Judaism in Britain 1840–1995.* Vallentine Mitchell, London

Klein, Isaac, 1979 *A Guide to Jewish Religious Practice.* Jewish Theological Seminary, New York

Knobel, Peter S., 1983 ed., *Gates of the Seasons, A Guide to the Jewish Year.* CCAR, New York

Lauterbach, Jakob Z., 1927 'Birth Control' in *CCAR Yearbook,* Vol. XXXVII, USA
—— 1951 *Rabbinic Essays,* HUC Press

Levi, Eliezer, 1961 יסודות התפלה ['Origins of the Liturgy']. A. Zioni, Tel Aviv

Maccoby, Hyam, 1993 'Does halachah allow surrender of land?' in *Jewish Chronicle,* 22 October 1993

Maslin, Simeon J., 1982 ed., *Gates of Mitzvah, A Guide to the Jewish Life Cycle.* CCAR, New York

Mattuck, Israel I., 1950 *Marriage, Doctrine and Practice of Liberal Judaism.* Pamphlet, ULPS
—— 1953 *Jewish Ethics.* Hutchinson's University Library, London

Meyer, Michael A., 1988 *Response to Modernity, A History of the Reform Movement in Judaism.* Oxford University Press

Mielziner, Moses, 1901 *Jewish Law of Marriage and Divorce and its Relation to the Law of the State.* HUC Press, Cincinnati. First published 1884

Montefiore, C.G., and H. Loewe, 1938 *A Rabbinic Anthology.* Macmillan and Co., London

Novak, David, 1992 *Jewish Social Ethics.* OUP, New York and Oxford

Petuchowski, Jakob J., 1968 *Prayerbook Reform in Europe.* World Union for Progressive Judaism, New York
—— 1972 *Understanding Jewish Prayer.* Ktav, New York

Philipson, David, 1967 *The Reform Movement in Judaism.* Ktav, New York. First published 1907, revised 1930

Plaut, W. Gunther, 1972 *A Shabbat Manual.* CCAR and Ktav, New York

Plaut, W. Gunther, 1963 ed., *The Rise of Reform Judaism, A Sourcebook of its European Origins.* World Union for Progressive Judaism, New York
—— 1965 ed., *The Growth of Reform Judaism, American and European Sources until 1948.* Ditto
—— 1981 ed., *The Torah Commentary.* UAHC, New York

Plaut, W. Gunther, and Mark Washofsky, 1997 eds., *Teshuvot for the Nineties, Reform Judaism's Answers to Today's Dilemmas.* CCAR, New York

Polish, David, and W. Gunther Plaut, 1988 eds., *Rabbi's Manuel.* CCAR, New York

Rayner, John D., 1960 *The Practices of Liberal Judaism.* ULPS, London. First published 1958
—— 1975 *Guide to Jewish Marriage.* ULPS, London.

Rayner, John D., and Bernard Hooker, 1978 *Judaism for Today, An Ancient Faith with a Modern Message.* ULPS, London

Riemer, Jack, 1976 ed., *Jewish Reflections on Death.* Schocken, New York. First published 1974

Riskin, Shlomo, 1989 *Women and Jewish Divorce.* Ktav, Hoboken, New Jersey

Romain, Jonathan A., 1991 *Faith and Practice, A Guide to Reform Judaism Today.* RSGB, London

Rosner, Fred, 1991 *Modern Medicine and Jewish Ethics.* Ktav, Hoboken, New Jersey, and Yeshiva University

Rosner, Fred, and J. David Bleich, 1979 eds., *Jewish Bioethics.* Hebrew Publishing Company, New York, New York

Schauss, Hayyim, 1940 *The Lifetime of a Jew.* UAHC, Cincinnati

Shapiro, Mark Dov, 1991 *Gates of Shabbat, A Guide for Observing Shabbat.* CCAR, New York

Siddur Lev Chadash, 1995 ['New Heart Prayerbook'],*Services and Prayers for Weekdays and Sabbaths, Festivals and Various Occasions,* ULPS, London

Sperling, Abraham Isaac, 1957 ספר טעמי המנהגים ומקורי הדינים ['The Reasons of the Customs and the Sources of the Laws']. Eshkol, Jerusalem

Spero, Schubert, 1983 *Morality, Halakha and the Jewish Tradition* Ktav, New York

Spiro, Abram, 1959 'A Law on the Sharing of Information' in *American Academy for Jewish Research, Proceedings,* Vol. XXVIII. New York

Steinberg, Abraham, 5738 [1977–1978] ed., הלכות רופאים ורפואה ע׳פ שו׳ת ציץ אליעזר ['The Laws Concerning Physicians and Medicine according to the Responsa of Eliezer Judah Waldenberg']. Jerusalem

Stevens, Elliot L., 1982 ed., *Rabbinic Authority, Papers Presented before the Ninety-First Annual Conference of the CCAR.* CCAR, New York

Temkin, Sefton D., 1971 *The New World of Reform.* Leo Baeck College, London

Tigay, Jeffrey H., 1996 *The JPS Torah Commentary, Deuteronomy.* JPS, Philadelphia and Jerusalem

Tomaschoff, Avner, 1978 *Whose Homeland, Eretz Yisrael, Roots of the Jewish Claim.* World Zionist Organisation, Department of Torah Education and Culture in the Diaspora, Jerusalem

Trachtenberg, Joshua, 1961 *Jewish Magic and Superstition, A Study in Jewish Folklore.* Meridian Books, The World Publishing Company, Cleveland and New York, and JPS, Philadelphia

Vorspan, Albert, and Eugene J. Lipman, 1959 *Justice and Judaism, The Work of Social Action.* UAHC, New York. First published 1956

Wegner, Judith, 1988 *Chattel or Person? The Status of Women in the Mishnah.* OUP, New York and Oxford

Yaron, Reuven, 1961 *Introduction to the Law of the Aramaic Papyri.* Clarendon Press, Oxford

Zemer, Moshe, 1993 הלכה שפויה ['Sane Halachah']. Dvir, Tel Aviv

Progressive Judaism Today Series

The first two volumes in this series are collections of Liberal Jewish sermons by John D. Rayner, given mostly at the Liberal Jewish Synagogue in St John's Wood, London; together, they span the greater part of the second half of the twentieth century. Eloquent, reasoned, with flashes of humour, these sermons not only provide a major anthology of Jewish teachings, applied in a modern context to contemporary issues, but also demonstrate that the largely lost craft of homiletics still has at least one outstanding practitioner.

Volume one, **An Understanding of Judaism**, combines forthright radical thinking with spirituality, love of Jewish Tradition, and an abundance of carefully documented quotations from classical Jewish texts. It is divided into two parts, An Examination of the Scriptures, and Seasons of the Jewish Year, which explores the significance of Jewish Festivals.

In volume two, **A Jewish Understanding of the World,** Rayner seeks to understand contemporary history from a 'prophetic' point of view. His comments cover a wide range of topics, including Jewish Continuity, Progressive Judaism, Zionism, the State of Israel, world events, social issues, and Jewish-Christian relations.

To order:

UK and Europe
Plymbridge Distributors Ltd., Estover Road, Plymouth PL6 7PZ UK
Tel: (01752) 202301 • Fax: (01752) 202333

USA and Rest of World
Berghahn Books Inc., P.O. Box 605, Herndon, VA 20172
Tel: (800) 540-8663 • Fax: (703) 689-0660

Also from *Berghahn Books*

EUROPEAN JUDAISM

A Journal for the New Europe

For thirty years, *European Judaism* has provided a voice for the postwar Jewish world in Europe. It has reflected the different realities of each country and helped to rebuild Jewish consciousness after the Holocaust. *European Judaism* offers:

* STIMULATING DEBATES – exploring the responses of Judaism to contemporary political, social and philosophical challenges
* ARTICLES – reflecting the full range of contemporary Jewish life in Europe, and including documentation of the latest developments in Jewish-Muslim dialogue
* NEW INSIGHTS – derived from science, psychotherapy, and theology as they impact upon Jewish life and thought
* LITERARY EXCHANGE – a unique exploration of ideas from leading Jewish writers, poets, scholars and intellectuals with a variety of documentation, poetry and book reviews section
* BOOK REVIEWS – covering a wide range of international publications

Editors: **Jonathan Magonet**, Principal, Leo Baeck College, London and **Albert H. Friedlander**, Rabbi, Westminster Synagogue, London In association with the **Leo Baeck College** and the **Michael Goulston Education Foundation**.

ISBN 0014-3006 • 2 issues per year
Annual rates for 1998: £18/$27 (Individuals); £60/$90 (Institutions)

Method of Payment: ☐ Check, drawn on a US or British bank,
made payable to Berghahn Books   Amount: . . . .

☐ Mastercard   ☐ Visa   Credit card no.: . . . .

Exp.date: . . . . . . / . . . . . .   Amount: . . . .

Signature: . . . . Date: . . . .

Name: . . . .

Address: . . . .

. . . .

165 Taber Avenue, Providence, RI 02906
Tel: (401) 861-9330 • Fax: (401) 521-0046 • E-mail: BerghahnUS@juno.com

3, NewTec Place, Magdalen Road, Oxford OX4 1RE
Tel: (01865) 250011 • Fax: (01865) 250056 • E-mail: BerghahnUK@aol.com